D

i

THE FEDERAL TRUST

GUIDE TO THE EU INSTITUTIONS

editor
Rohan Bolton

assistant editor
Joanne Eastwood

THE FEDERAL TRUST
for education & research

This book is published by the Federal Trust whose aim is to enlighten public debate on issues arising from the interaction of national, European and global levels of government. It does this in the light of its statutes which state that it shall promote 'studies in the principles of international relations, international justice and supranational government.'

The Federal Trust conducts enquiries, promotes seminars and conferences and publishes reports and teaching materials. It is the UK member of the Trans-European Policy Studies Association (TEPSA), a grouping of fifteen think-tanks from member states of the European Union.

Up-to-date information about the Federal Trust can be found on the internet at www.fedtrust.co.uk

ISBN 1 903403 09 X

The Federal Trust is a Registered Charity No. 272241

7 Graphite Square, Vauxhall Walk,

London SE11 5EE

Company Limited by Guarantee No.1269848

Marketing and Distribution by Kogan Page Ltd

Printed in the European Union

Contents

other eu bodies

community agencies:

other institutions:

editors' preface

We have aimed in this directory to present concise details for individual countries of Western, Central and Eastern Europe, background on the functioning of the EU institutions, agencies and other European organisations, and an up-to-date listing of senior staff and contact points. Links to websites have also been included, to provide a convenient means of keeping up with new developments and appointments.

Despite the welcome increase in data produced by and about Europe and the European institutions, it is still not always easy to identify appropriate websites or locate relevant information. Here in one volume are the answers to many basic queries about Europe and the EU institutions without the necessity of surfing through a mass of possible websites. There are occasions when it is not convenient to consult the web for answers to simple questions; while researching the data for this book we found many examples of how time-consuming it can be to find even quite simple material. Some of the individual country information is hard to locate in English. We hope you will find it helpful to have all the facts in one place.

In almost half a century since the establishment of the EEC in 1957 there have rarely been more challenging times:

- with the prospect of up to thirteen new members joining the Union
- the debate on the future institutional arrangements for Europe, with the current European Convention on the Future of the EU discussing the modernisation of the Union's Treaty arrangements and the determination of Europe's future shape
- the establishment of monetary union
- and the efforts of the Prodi Commission to modernise the way in which the Commission manages the highest levels of the Commission's civil service.

This book is for all those who are following these important developments.

Rohan Bolton and Joanna Eastwood

March 2003

sources of eu information for the united kingdom

european union

The **Europa website** (http://europa.eu.int and http://europa.eu.int/geninfo/info-en.htm) is a starting point for up-to-date information on all aspects of EU institutions and policies. It contains 1.5 million documents and more than 50 databases open to the public (in most cases free of charge).

An online portal to EU legal texts called **EUR-Lex** (http://europa.eu.int/eur-lex) is also largely free of charge. It offers search functions for all types of documents - the Official Journal, the Treaties, legislation in preparation, legislation, case-law, parliamentary questions and documents of public interest.

Europe Direct (http://europa.eu.int/europedirect/en/index_en.html) provides information and advice on Community policies and activities or on specific matters such as the rights of European citizens and the opportunities for living, working and studying in other member states. Alternatively there is a freephone number that can be used within any of the 15 member states: 00800 6 7 8 9 10 11. Operators are available in all EU languages.

The Commission's website for information on **grants and loans** (http://europa.eu.int/comm/ secretariat_general/sgc/aides/index_en.htm) has an index by theme, acronyms and an overview of programmes sorted by Directorate-General.

united kingdom

The office of the European Commission's Representation in the UK no longer provides information directly to the public. They have decentralised their activities by developing and supporting a network of over 4000 contact points or **European Information Relays** in the UK. Their website (http:// www.cec.org.uk) provides links to these networks as well as other official and non-official sources of information about the EU in the UK.

The website of the **European Information Network** (http://www.europe.org.uk) brings together contact details for organisations and individuals in the UK and its regions that provide EU information and advice for the general public, the academic community and business.

sources of eu information

networks

The website http://europa.eu.int/geninfo/info-en.htm provides Europe-wide information and links to a number of networks serving different specialised information groups:

Public libraries or **European Public Information Centres** (EPICs) hold reference documents as well as a small stock of handout material for use by the general public.

European Information Centres (EICs) are usually based in chambers of commerce or in organisations which have links with the business community. They provide up-to-date information on the EU for small and medium-sized businesses.

European Documentation Centres (EDCs) promote and develop study in the field of European integration and provide access to information on the EU to university students and the academic community in their region.

European Resource Centres (ERCs) for schools and colleges provide teachers and pupils with information on Europe and support the development of the European dimension in the curriculum. These are also listed in the website http://www.britishcouncil.org/education/resource/europe/index.htm

The **European Information Association** (Tel: 0161 228 3691; Website: http://www.eia.org.uk) is a body of information specialists whose aim is to develop, co-ordinate and improve access to EU information. Members pay an annual subscription and receive a number of benefits, including copies of the monthly newsletter EIA Update and quarterly journal European Information as well as discounts on publications and electronic products produced by other publishers. Regular EIA events and training courses give members the opportunity to develop ideas and skills in EU information, exchange experience and make contacts.

Official publications of the EU are available in the UK from The Stationery Office (Tel: 0870 600 5522; Fax: 0870 600 5533; Website: http://www.tso.co.uk). Their website http://www.accesstoeurope.com offers online access to all official publications, legislative activities and policies of the Union. There is also a section on new and forthcoming titles.

The library of the **European Parliament's UK Information Office** (http://www.europarl.org.uk/office/LibraryMain.htm; Fax for inquiries: 0207 227 4301) provides information on the work of the Parliament, its committees and MEPs.

idea – the electronic directory of the european institutions

home page:
http://europa.eu.int/idea/en/index.htm

main list of EU institutions:
http://europa.eu.int/idea/bin/dispinst.pl?lang=en

This database contains organisation charts listing senior staff of all the different EU institutions, including the European Commission, European Parliament, Council of Ministers, Court of Justice, the Economic and Social Committee, the Committee of the Regions, the European Investment Bank, European Investment Fund and the Ombudsman as well as the decentralised Community agencies.

Searches are possible by person's name or by organisational entity.

Annexes II and III of the **Commission** section contain details of the 'Representations in the EU member states' and the 'External delegations, representations and offices' in non-member countries (which includes the applicant member states).

Two useful categories are to be found in the **Council** section of IDEA: Coreper representations are to be found under the heading 'Permanent Representatives Committee' while details of the applicant member states' delegations in Brussels can be found under the heading 'Association Councils.'

chronology

April 1949 North Atlantic Treaty signed (NATO)

May 1949 Council of Europe established

May 1950 Schuman Declaration opens process leading to European Coal and Steel Community (ECSC)

April 1951 ECSC Treaty signed by Belgium, France, Germany, Italy, Luxembourg and the Netherlands (The Six)

May 1952 The Six sign European Defence Community Treaty (EDC)

August 1954 French Assembly declines EDC

October 1954 The Six and UK establish Western European Union (WEU)

June 1955 Messina Conference launches European Economic Community (EEC) and Euratom negotiation

March 1957 The Six sign Treaty of Rome (EEC) and Euratom Treaty

August 1961 UK, Ireland and Denmark apply to join EEC, ECSC and Euratom

January 1963 General de Gaulle breaks off accession negotiations

May 1967 UK, Ireland, Denmark and Norway reapply, but remain blocked by General de Gaulle

June 1970 Accession negotiations with 4 applicants begin

January 1972 Accession Treaties signed (but Norway subsequently rejects membership in referendum)

January 1973 UK, Ireland, Denmark join European Community (EEC, ECSC and Euratom)

December 1974 Beginning of regular Heads of Government meetings (European Council)

June 1975 Greece applies to join EC

June 1975 UK vote in favour of continued membership in the EC

March/July 1977 Portugal and Spain apply to join EC

June 1979 First direct elections to European Parliament (five year term)

January 1981 Greece joins European Community

January 1986 Spain and Portugal join European Community

February 1986 Single European Act signed (in force July 1987)

July 1989 Austria applies to join EC

November 1989 Fall of Berlin Wall

July 1990 Cyprus and Malta apply to join EC

October 1990 Unification of Germany

July 1991 Sweden applies to join EC

February 1992 Treaty of Maastricht signed (in force November 1993)

March 1992 Finland applies to join EC

chronology

May 1992 Switzerland applies to join EC

November 1992 Norway applies to join EC

December 1992 Switzerland shelves application following rejection of EEA agreement by referendum

December 1992 Negotiations begin with Austria, Norway, Sweden and Finland

March 1994 Committee of the Regions holds first session

March/April 1994 Hungary and Poland apply to join EU

November 1994 Norway rejects accession treaty in referendum

January 1995 Austria, Sweden and Finland join EU

June 1997 Treaty of Amsterdam agreed (in force May 1999)

March 1998 Accession negotiations start with Cyprus, Czech Republic, Estonia, Hungary, Poland and Slovenia

June 1998 European Central Bank established

December 1998 Euro conversion rates fixed in eleven participating national currencies: Austria, Belgium, Finland, France, Germany, Ireland, Italy, Luxembourg, Netherlands, Portugal and Spain

January 2000 Accession negotiations start with Bulgaria, Latvia, Lithuania, Malta, Romania and Slovakia

May 2000 Greece joins Euro, making 12 participating states

December 2000 Treaty of Nice agreed, lifting institutional obstacles to further enlargement

December 2001 Declaration of Laeken on the Future of Europe

January 2002 Introduction of Euro notes and coins replacing 12 currencies

2002 Conclusion of accession negotiations with 10 candidate countries

2003/2004 Intergovernmental Conference to revise Treaties in light of Future of Europe Convention

June 2004 Sixth Election to European Parliament involving candidate countries

January 2005 Appointment of new Commission including Cyprus, Czech Republic, Estonia, Hungary, Latvia, Lithuania, Malta, Poland, Slovakia and Slovenia

country data

Republic of Austria

Geography

Area: 83,857 sq. km. (32,377 sq. miles)
Capital: Vienna (pop. 1.6 million)
Borders: Czech Republic 362 km, Germany 784 km, Hungary 366 km, Italy 430 km, Liechtenstein 35 km, Slovakia 91 km, Slovenia 330 km, Switzerland 164 km, Coastline 0 km
Natural resources: iron ore, petroleum, timber, magnesite, lead, coal, lignite, copper, hydropower

People

Population (July 2002): 8,169,929
Age structure: 0-14 years 17%, 15-64 years 68%, 65 years and over 15%
Population growth rate (2002): 0.23%
Life expectancy (2002): male 74.85 years, female 81.31 years
Infant mortality rate (2002): 4.39/1,000
Ethnic groups: German 88%, Croatian, Slovene, Hungarian, Czech, Slovak, Roma
Religions: Roman Catholic 78%, Protestant 5%, Muslim and other 17%
Language: German
Literacy: 98%
Work force (2002): 4.3 million - Services 67%, Industry and crafts 29%, Agriculture and forestry 4%
Unemployment rate (2002): 4.8%

Government

Heads of Government: Chancellor Wolfgang Schuessel (since February 2000), Vice Chancellor Herbert Haupt (since February 2003)
Elections: National Council - last held November 2002 (next to be held Autumn 2006)
Coalition Parties: Christian Democrats (OVP) and Freedom Party (FPO). Coalition is fragile

Economy

GDP (2001): $189.7 billion
GDP purchasing power parity (2002): $226 billion
GDP real growth rate (2002): 0.6%
Per capita income p.p.p. (2002): $27,700
Population below poverty line: NA
Inflation rate (consumer prices 2002): 1.8%
Exports (2002): EU 63% (Germany 35%, Italy 9%, France 5%), Switzerland 5%, Hungary 5%, US 5%
Imports (2002): EU 70% (Germany 42%, Italy 8%, France 5%), US 5%, Switzerland 5%, Hungary 4%

Contacts

EU Commission office, Vienna:
Head of Representation: Karl DOUTLICK
Phone: (43-1) 51 61 80, Fax: (43-1) 5 13 42 25
http://europa.eu.int/austria

Kingdom of Belgium

Geography
Area: 30,528 sq. km. (11,800 sq. miles)
Capital: Brussels (metropolitan pop. 950,000)
Borders: France 620 km, Germany 167 km, Luxembourg 148 km, Netherlands 450 km, Coastline 66 km
Natural resources: coal, natural gas
Most Western European capitals are within 1,000 km of Brussels, seat of the EU and NATO

People
Population (July 2002): 10,274,595
Age structure: 0-14 years 17%, 15-64 years 66%, 65 years and over 17%
Population growth rate (2002): 0.15%
Life expectancy (2002): male 74.8 years, female 81.62 years
Infant mortality rate (2002): 4.64/1,000
Ethnic groups: Fleming 58%, Walloon 31%, mixed or other 11%
Religions: Roman Catholic 75%, Protestant or other 25%
Languages: Dutch 60%, French 40% (legally bilingual), German
Literacy: 98%
Work force (2001): 4.341 million - Services 73%, Industry 25%, Agriculture 2%
Unemployment rate (1999): 9%

Government
Head of Government: Prime Minister Guy Verhofstadt (since July 1999)
Elections: Senate and Chamber of Deputies - last held June 1999 (next to be held in 2003)
Coalition Parties: Flemish Liberal Party (VLD) with Liberals, Socialists and Greens. First coalition in 40 years without the Christian Democrats

Economy
GDP (2001): $256.1 billion
GDP purchasing power parity (2001): $254 billion
GDP real growth rate (2002): 0.6%
Per capita income p.p.p. (2002): $29,000
Population below poverty line: 4%
Inflation rate (consumer prices 2002): 1.7%
Exports (2001): EU 75% (Germany 18%, France 17%, Netherlands 12%, UK 10%)
Imports (2001): EU 69% (Netherlands 18%, Germany 17%, France 14%, UK 8%), US 7%

Contacts
EU Commission office, Brussels:
Head of Representation: Guy VANDEBON
Phone: (32-2) 2 95 38 44, Fax: (32-2) 29 50 66
http://europa.eu.int/comm/represent/be

Kingdom of Denmark

Geography, excluding Greenland and the Faeroe Islands
Area: 43,094 sq. km. (16,640 sq. miles)
Capital: Copenhagen (pop. 1.3 million)
Borders: Germany 68 km, Coastline 7,314 km
Natural resources: petroleum, natural gas, fish, salt, limestone, stone, gravel, sand

People
Population (July 2002): 5,368,854
Age structure (2002): 0-14 years 19%, 15-64 years 66%, 65 years and over 15%
Population growth rate (2002): 0.29%
Life expectancy (2002): male 74.3 years, female 79.67 years
Infant mortality rate (2002): 4.97/1,000
Ethnic groups: Scandinavian, Inuit, Faroese, German, Turkish, Iranian, Somali
Religions: Evangelical Lutheran 95%, other Protestant and Roman Catholic 3%, Muslim 2%
Languages: Danish, Faroese, Greenlandic (Inuit dialect), some German
Literacy: 100%
Work force (2002): 2.9 million - Services 79%, Industry 17%, Agriculture 4%
Unemployment rate (2002): 5.1%

Government
Head of Government: Prime Minister Anders Fogh Rasmussen (since November 2001)
Elections: last held November 2001 (next to be held November 2005)
Coalition Parties: The Liberal Party and the Conservative People's Party. Right-of-centre

Economy
GDP (2001): $161 billion
GDP purchasing power parity (2002): $155.5 billion
GDP real growth rate (2002): 1.3%
Per capita income p.p.p. (2002): $29,000
Population below poverty line: NA
Inflation rate (consumer prices 2002): 2.3%
Exports (2001): EU 65% (Germany 20%, Sweden 12%, UK 10%, France 5%, Netherlands 5%), US 7%, Norway 6%
Imports (2001): EU 70% (Germany 22%, Sweden 12%, UK 8%, Netherlands 7%, France 6%), US 4%

Contacts
EU Commission office, Copenhagen:
Phone: (45-33) 14 41 40, Fax: (45-33) 11 12 03
Email: eu@europa-kommissionen.dk
http://www.europa-kommissionen.dk/repraesetationem

25

Republic of Finland

Geography
Area: 337,113 sq. km. (130,160 sq. miles)
Capital: Helsinki (pop. 520,000)
Borders: Norway 729 km, Sweden 586 km, Russia 1,313 km, Coastline 1,126 km (excludes islands and coastal indentations)
Natural resources: timber, copper, zinc, iron ore, silver

People
Population (July 2002): 5,183,545
Age structure (2002): 0-14 years 18%, 15-64 years 67%, 65 years and over 15%
Population growth rate (2002): 0.14%
Life expectancy (2002): male 77.75 years, female 81.52 years
Infant mortality rate (2002): 3.76/1,000
Ethnic groups: Finn 93%, Swede 6%, Sami, Roma, Tatar
Religions: Evangelical Lutheran 89%, Russian Orthodox 1%, unaffiliated 9%
Languages: Finnish 93%, Swedish 6% (legally bilingual), Sami, Russian
Literacy: 100%
Work force (2000): 2.6 million - Public services 32%, Industry 22%, Commerce 14%, Finance, insurance, and business services 10%, Agriculture and forestry 8%, Transport and communications 8%, Construction 6%
Unemployment rate (2002): 8.5%

Government
Heads of Government: Prime Minister Paavo Lipponen (since April 1995), Deputy Prime Minister Ville Itala (since August 2001)
Elections: last held February 2000 (next to be held February 2006)
Coalition Parties: Social Democratic (SDP), National Coalition (KOK), Leftist Alliance, Swedish People's (SFP), Green League. Moderate left-of-centre

Economy
GDP (2001): $118.3 billion
GDP purchasing power parity (2002): $136.2 billion
GDP real growth rate (2002): 1.1%
Per capita income p.p.p. (2002): $26,200
Population below poverty line: NA
Inflation rate (consumer prices 2002): 1.9%
Exports (2001): EU 56% (Germany 12%, UK 10%, Sweden 8%, France 5%), US 10%, Russia 6%
Imports (2001): EU 60% (Germany 15%, Sweden 10%, UK 6%, France 5%), Russia 10%, US 7%

Contact

EU Commission office, Helsinki:
Head of Representation: Timo MÄKELÄ
Phone: (358-9) 6 22 65 44, Fax: (358-9) 65 67 28
http://www.eukomissio.fi

French Republic

Geography

Area: 551,670 sq. km. (220,668 sq. miles)
Capital: Paris
Borders: Andorra 57 km, Belgium 620 km, Germany 451 km, Italy 488 km, Luxembourg 73 km, Monaco 4 km, Spain 623 km, Switzerland 573 km, Coastline 3,427 km
Natural resources: coal, iron ore, bauxite, zinc, potash, fish, timber

People

Population (July 2002): 59,329,691
Age structure: 0-14 years 19%, 15-64 years 65%, 65 years and over 16%
Population growth rate (2002): 0.35%
Life expectancy at birth (2002): male 75.17 years, female 83.14 years
Infant mortality rate (2002): 4.41/1,000
Ethnic groups: Celtic and Latin with Teutonic, Slavic, North African, Indochinese, Basque
Religions: Roman Catholic 83-88%, Muslim 5-10%, Protestant 2%, Jewish 1%
Language: French
Literacy: 99%
Work force (2001): 26.6 million - Services 71%, Industry 25%, Agriculture 4%
Unemployment rate (1999): 11%

Government

Head of Government: Prime Minister Jean-Pierre Raffarin (since May 2002)
Elections: Senate - last held September 2001 (next to be held September 2004); National Assembly - last held June 2002 (next to be held June 2007)
Coalition Parties: Union for a Popular Movement (UMP), a coalition of right-of-centre parties including the Rally for the Republic (RPR)

Economy

GDP (2002): $1.661 trillion
GDP purchasing power parity (2002): $1.54 trillion
GDP real growth rate (2002): 1.1%
Per capita income p.p.p. (2002 including overseas departments): $25,700
Population below poverty line: NA
Inflation rate (consumer prices 2002): 1.8%
Exports (2001): EU 61% (Germany 15%, UK 10%, Italy 9%, Spain 9%), US 9%
Imports (2001): EU 59% (Germany 17%, Italy 9%, Benelux 7%, UK 8%), US 9%

Contacts

EU Commission office, Paris:
Acting Head of Representation: Marie Sixtine BOUYGUES-CARLANDER
Phone: (33-1) 40 63 38 00, Fax: (33-1) 45 56 94 17/18/19
http://europa.eu.int/france

Federal Republic of Germany

Geography
Area: 357,000 sq. km. (137,821 sq. miles)
Capital: Berlin (pop. 3.5 million)
Borders: Austria 784 km, Belgium 167 km, Czech Republic 646 km, Denmark 68 km, France 451 km, Luxembourg 138 km, Netherlands 577 km, Poland 456 km, Switzerland 334 km, Coastline 2,389 km
Natural resources: iron ore, coal, potash, timber, lignite, uranium, copper, natural gas, salt, nickel, arable land

People
Population (July 2002): 83,251,851
Age structure: 0-14 years 15%, 15-64 years 68%, 65 years and over 17%
Population growth rate (2002): 0.26%
Life expectancy (2002): male 77.78 years, female 81.09 years
Infant mortality rate: 4.65/1,000
Ethnic groups: German, Danish, Sorbian (Slavic), 7.3 million foreign residents
Religions: Protestant 34%, Roman Catholic 34%, Muslim 4%, unaffiliated or other 28%
Language: German
Literacy: 99%
Work force (2002): 41.9 million - Industry 34%, Services 64%, Agriculture 3%
Unemployment rate (2002): 9.8%

Government
Head of Government: Chancellor Gerhard Schröder (since 27 October 1998)
Elections: Federal Assembly - last held September 2002 (next to be held September 2006)
Coalition Parties: SPD, Alliance 90/The Greens. Left-of-centre

Economy
GDP (2001): $1.8713 trillion
GDP purchasing power parity (2002): $1.864 trillion
GDP real growth rate (2002): 0.4%
Per capita income p.p.p. (2002): $26,600
Population below poverty line: NA
Inflation rate (consumer prices 2002): 1.3%
Exports (2001): EU 56% (France 11%, UK 11%, Netherlands 6%, Belgium 5%, Spain 5%, Austria 5%), US 11%, Switzerland 4%
Imports (2001): EU 54% (France 9%, Netherlands 8%, Italy 7%, UK 7%, Belgium 5%, Austria 4%), US 8%, Japan 4%

Contacts
EU Commission Office, Berlin:
Head of Representation: Axel R. BUNZ
Phone: (49-30) 22 80 20 00, Fax: (49-30) 22 80 22 22
http://www.eu-kommission.de

Hellenic Republic (Greece)

Geography
Area: 131,957 sq. km. (51,146 sq. miles)
Capital: Athens (pop. Gtr. Athens 3.1 million)
Borders: Albania 282 km, Bulgaria 494 km, Turkey 206 km, The Former Yugoslav Republic of Macedonia 228 km, Coastline 13,676 km
Natural resources: bauxite, lignite, magnesite, petroleum, marble, hydropower

People
Population (July 2002): 10,645,343
Age structure: 0-14 years 15%, 15-64 years 67%, 65 years and over 18%
Population growth rate (2002): 0.2%
Life expectancy (2002): male 78.74 years, female 81.84 years
Infant mortality rate (2002): 6.25/1,000
Ethnic groups: Greek 98%, other 2%
Religions: Greek Orthodox 98% (official), Muslim 1%, other 1%
Languages: Greek 99% (official), English, French
Literacy: 97%
Work force (1999): 4.32 million - Services 59%, Industry 21%, Agriculture 20%
Unemployment rate (2002): 10.3%

Government
Head of Government: Prime Minister Konstandinos Simitis (since January 1996)
Elections: last held April 2000 (next to be held April 2004)
Party in Government: Pan Hellenic Socialist Movement (PASOK). Centre-left, free-market reformist

Economy
GDP (2001): $114 billion
GDP purchasing power parity (2002): $201.1 billion
GDP real growth rate (2002): 3.5%
Per capita income p.p.p. (2002): $19,000
Population below poverty line: NA
Inflation rate (consumer prices 2002): 3.6%
Exports (1999): EU 52% (Germany 16%, Italy 14%, UK 6%), US 6%
Imports (1999): EU 66% (Italy 16%, Germany 15%, France 9%, Netherlands 6%)

Contacts
EU Commission office, Athens:
Head of Representation: Georgios MARKOPOULIOTAS
Phone: (30-1) 7 27 21 00, Fax: (30-1) 7 24 46 20
http://europa.eu.int/hellas

Ireland

Geography
Area: 70,282 sq. km. (27,136 sq. miles)
Capital: Dublin (pop. 1.1 million)
Borders: UK 360 km, Coastline 1,448 km
Natural resources: zinc, lead, natural gas, barite, copper, gypsum, limestone, dolomite, peat, silver

People
Population (July 2002): 3,883,159
Age structure: 0-14 years 21%, 15-64 years 67%, 65 years and over 11%
Population growth rate (2002): 1.07%
Life expectancy (2002): male 77.17 years, female 80.12 years
Infant mortality rate (2002): 5.43/1,000
Ethnic groups: Celtic, English
Religions: Roman Catholic 92% (official religion, close ties to state), Church of Ireland 3%, other 6%
Languages: English, Irish (Gaelic)
Literacy: 98%
Work force (2001): 1.8 million - Services 64%, Industry 28%, Agriculture 8%
Unemployment rate (2002): 4.7%

Government
Head of Government: Prime Minister Bertie Ahern (since June 1997)
Elections: Senate - last held July 2002 (next to be held July 2007); House of Representatives - last held July 2002 (next to be held July 2007)
Coalition Parties: Fianna Fail and the Progressive Democrats. Moderately populist

Economy
GDP (2001): $103.4 billion
GDP purchasing power parity (2002): $111.3 billion
GDP real growth rate (2002): 3.9%
Per capita income p.p.p. (2002): $28,500
Population below poverty line: 10%
Inflation rate (consumer prices 2002): 4.6%
Exports (2000): EU 63% (UK 20%, Germany 11%, France 8%, Netherlands 6%, Belgium 5%), US 17%
Imports (2000): EU 61% (UK 33%, Germany 6%, France 5%, Netherlands 4%), US 16%, Japan 4%

Contacts

EU Commission office, Dublin:
Head of Representation: Peter DOYLE
Phone: (353-1) 6 62 51 13, Fax: (353-1) 6 62 51 18
http://www.euireland.ie

Italian Republic

Geography

Area: 301,225 sq. km. (116,303 sq. miles)

Capital: Rome (pop. 2.7 million)

Borders: Austria 430 km, France 488 km, Holy See (Vatican City) 3 km, San Marino 39 km, Slovenia 232 km, Switzerland 740 km, Coastline 7,600 km

Natural resources: mercury, potash, marble, sulphur, dwindling natural gas and crude oil reserves, fish, coal, arable land

People

Population (July 2002): 57,715,625

Age structure: 0-14 years 14%, 15-64 years 67%, 65 years and over 19%

Population growth rate (2002): 0.05%

Life expectancy (2002): male 76.08 years, female 82.63 years

Infant mortality rate (2002): 5.76/1,000

Ethnic groups: Italian, German-, French-, Slovene-, Albanian-, Greek-Italian

Religion: Roman Catholic (majority), Protestant, Jewish, Muslim

Language: Italian (official), German, French, Slovene

Literacy: 98%

Work force (2001): 23.6 million - Services 63%, Industry 32%, Agriculture 5%

Unemployment rate (2002): 9.2%

Government

Head of Government: Silvio Berlusconi (since June 2001)

Elections: Senate and Chamber of Deputies - last held May 2001 (next to be held May 2006)

Coalition Parties (Freedom House coalition): Forza Italia, National Alliance, Northern League, Democratic Christian Centre, United Christian Democrats. Right-of-centre

Economy

GDP (2001): $1.1 trillion

GDP purchasing power parity (2002): $1.438 trillion

GDP real growth rate (2002): 0.4%

Per capita income p.p.p. (2002): $25,000

Population below poverty line: NA

Inflation rate (consumer prices 2002): 2.4%

Exports (2001): EU 54% (Germany 15%, France 12%, UK 7%, Spain 6%), US 10%

Imports (2001): EU 57% (Germany 18%, France 11%, Netherlands 6%, UK 5%), US 5%

Contacts

EU Commission office, Rome:

Heads of Representation: Lucio BATTISTOTTI, Fabrizio GRILLENZONI

Phone: (39-6) 69 99 91, Fax: (39-6) 6 79 16 58

http://www.comeur.it

Grand Duchy of Luxembourg

Geography
Area: 2,586 sq. km. (1,034 sq. miles)
Capital: Luxembourg (pop. 76,000)
Borders: Belgium 148 km, France 73 km, Germany 138 km, Coastline 0 km
Natural resources: iron ore (no longer exploited), arable land

People
Population (July 2002): 448,569
Age structure: 0-14 years 19%, 15-64 years 67%, 65 years and over 14%
Population growth rate (2002): 1.25%
Life expectancy (2002): male 77.48 years, female 80.97 years
Infant mortality rate (2002): 4.71/1000
Ethnic groups: Celtic (with French and German), Portuguese, Italian, Slav (Montenegran, Albanian, Kosovan)
Religions: Roman Catholic (majority), Protestant, Jewish
Languages: Luxembourgish, French, German, English widely spoken
Literacy: 100%
Work force (2000): 236,000 - Services 90%, Industry 8%, Agriculture 2%
Unemployment rate (2002): 4.1%

Government
Head of Government: Prime Minister Jean-Claude Juncker (since January 1995); Vice Prime Minister Lydie Polfer (since August 1999)
Elections: last held June 1999 (next to be held June 2004)
Coalition Parties: Christian Social People's Party (CSV), Democratic Party (DP). Right-of-centre

Economy
GDP (2001): $23.2 billion
GDP purchasing power parity (2002): $20 billion
GDP real growth rate (2002): 2.3%
Per capita income p.p.p. (2002): $44,000
Population below poverty line: NA
Inflation rate (2002): 1.6%
Exports (2001): EU 85% (Germany 25%, France 20%, Belgium 12%), US 4%
Imports (2001): EU 87% (Belgium 34%, Germany 25%, France 13%), US 6%

Contact

EU Commission office, Luxembourg:

Head of Representation: Alphonse THEIS

Phone: (352-4) 30 13 29 25, Fax: (352-4) 4 30 13 44 33

http://europa.eu.int/luxembourg

Kingdom of the Netherlands

Geography

Area: 41,526 sq. km. (16,485 sq. miles)
Capital: Amsterdam (pop. 72,000)
Borders: Belgium 450 km, Germany 577 km, Coastline 451 km
Natural resources: natural gas, petroleum, arable land

People

Population (July 2002): 16,067,754
Age structure: 0-14 years 18%, 15-64 years 68%, 65 years and over 14%
Population growth rate (2002): 0.53%
Life expectancy (2002): male 75.7 years, female 81.59 years
Infant mortality rate (2002): 4.31/1,000
Ethnic groups: Dutch, Moroccan, Turkish, Antillean, Surinamese, Indonesian
Religions: Unaffiliated 40%, Roman Catholic 31%, Protestant 21%, Muslim 4%, other 4%
Language: Dutch
Literacy: 99%
Work force (2000): 7.2 million - Services 73%, Industry 23%, agriculture 4%
Unemployment rate (2002): 3%

Government

Heads of Government: Prime Minister Jan Peter Balkenende (since July 2002), Vice Prime Ministers
Johan Remkes and Roelf de Boer (since 2002)
Elections: First Chamber - last held May 1999 (next to be held May 2003); Second Chamber - last held
January 2003 (next to be held January 2007)
Coalition Parties: Christian Democrat Appeal (CDA) in negotiation with Labour (PvdA) to form coalition
at time of going to press

Economy

GDP (2001): $375 billion
GDP purchasing power parity (2002): $434 billion
GDP real growth rate (2002): 0.3%
Per capita income p.p.p. (2002): $26,900
Population below poverty line: NA
Inflation rate (consumer prices 2002): 3.4%
Exports (2001): EU 78% (Germany 26%, Benelux 12%, UK 11%, France 10%, Italy 6%)
Imports (2001): EU 55% (Germany 18%, Benelux 9%, UK 9%, France 6%), US 10%

Contacts

EU Commission Office, The Hague:
Head of Representation: Henk BEEREBOOM
Phone: (31-70) 3 13 53 00, Fax: (31-70) 3 64 66 19
http://www.eu.nl

Portuguese Republic

Geography
Area: 92,391 sq. km. (35,670 miles)
Capital: Lisbon (pop. 680,000)
Borders: Spain 1,214 km, Coastline 1,793 km
Natural resources: fish, forests (cork), tungsten, iron ore, uranium, marble, arable land, hydropower

People
Population (July 2002): 10,084,245
Age structure: 0-14 years 17%, 15-64 years 67%, 65 years and over 16%
Population growth rate (2002): 0.18%
Life expectancy (2002): male 72.65 years, female 79.87 years
Infant mortality rate (2002): 5.84/1,000
Ethnic groups: Mediterranean, black African minority
Religions: Roman Catholic 94%, Protestant
Language: Portuguese
Literacy: 87.4%
Work force (2000): 4.75 million - Services 60%, Industry 30%, Agriculture 10%
Unemployment rate (2002): 4.7%

Government
Head of Government: Prime Minister José Manuel Durão Barroso (since April 2002)
Elections: last held March 2002 (next to be held in 2006)
Coalition parties: Social Democratic Party (PSD), Popular Party (PP). Right-of-centre

Economy
GDP (2001): $131.5 billion
GDP purchasing power parity (2002): $182 billion
GDP real growth rate (2002): 0.8%
Per capita income p.p.p. (2002): $18,000
Population below poverty line: NA
Inflation rate (consumer prices 2002): 3.7%
Exports (2001): EU 80% (Germany 19%, Spain 17%, France 13%, UK 10%, Benelux 5%), US 6%
Imports (2001): EU 74% (Spain 27%, Germany 14%, France 10%, Italy 7%, UK 5%), US 4%, Japan 2%

Contact

EU Commission office, Lisbon:

Head of Representation: Ricardo CHARTERS D'AZEVEDO

Phone: (351-21) 3 50 98 00, Fax: (351-21) 3 50 98 01/02

http://euroinfo.ce.pt

Kingdom of Spain

Geography
Area: 504,750 sq. km. (194,884 sq. miles)
Capital: Madrid (pop. 2.9 million)
Borders: Andorra 64 km, France 623 km, Gibraltar 1 km, Portugal 1,214 km, Morocco (Ceuta) 6 km, Morocco (Melilla) 10 km, Coastline 4,964 km
Natural resources: coal, lignite, iron ore, uranium, mercury, pyrites, fluorspar, gypsum, zinc, lead, tungsten, copper, kaolin, potash, hydropower, arable land

People
Population (July 2002): 40,077,100
Age structure: 0-14 years 15%, 15-64 years 68%, 65 years and over 17%
Population growth rate (2002): 0.09%
Life expectancy at birth (2002): male 75.63 years, female 82.76 years
Infant mortality rate (2002): 4.85/1,000
Ethnic groups: Basque, Catalan, Galician, other Mediterranean-Nordic composite
Religion: Roman Catholic 94%, other 6%
Languages: Castilian Spanish 74% (official), Catalan 17%, Galician 7%, Basque 2%
Literacy: 97%
Work force (2001): 16.2 million - Services 64%, Agriculture 7%, Manufacture, mining and construction 9.8%
Unemployment rate (2002): 11.3%

Government
Heads of Government: President José María Aznar Lopez (since May 1996); First Vice President Mariano Rajoy, Second Vice President Rodrigo Rato Figaredo (since May 1996)
Elections: Senate and Congress of Deputies - last held March 2000 (next to be held March 2004)
Party in Government: People's Party (PP). Reformist, centre

Economy
GDP (2000): $558.2 billion
GDP purchasing power parity (2002): $828 billion
GDP real growth rate (2002): 2%
Per capita income p.p.p. (2002): $20,700
Population below poverty line: NA
Inflation rate (consumer prices 2002): 3%
Exports (2001): EU 71% (France 20%, Germany 12%, Portugal 10%, Italy 9%, UK 9%), Latin America 6%, US 4%
Imports (2001): EU 64% (France 17%, Germany 16%, Italy 9%, UK 7%, Benelux 7%), OPEC 7%, US 5%, Latin America 4%, Japan 3%

Contacts
EU Commission Office, Madrid:
Head of Representation: Miguel MOLTÓ-CALVO
Phone: (34-91) 4 23 80 00, Fax: (34-91) 5 76 03 87
http://europa.eu.int/spain

Kingdom of Sweden

Geography
Area: 449,964 sq. km. (173,731 sq. miles)
Capital: Stockholm (700,000)
Borders: Finland 586 km, Norway 1,619 km , Coastline 3,218 km
Natural resources: zinc, iron ore, lead, copper, silver, timber, uranium, hydropower

People
Population (July 2002): 8,876,744
Age structure: 0-14 years 18%, 15-64 years 65%, 65 years and over 17%
Population growth rate (2002): 0.02%
Life expectancy (2002): male 77.19 years, female 82.64 years
Infant mortality rate (2002): 3.44/1,000
Ethnic groups: Swede, Finnish, Sami, Yugoslav, Danish, Norwegian, Greek, Turkish
Religions: Lutheran 87%, Roman Catholic, Orthodox, Baptist, Muslim, Jewish, Buddhist
Languages: Swedish, Finnish, Sami
Literacy: 99%
Work force (2000): 4.4 million - Services 74%, Industry 24%, Agriculture 2%
Unemployment rate (2002): 4%

Government
Head of government: Prime Minister Göran Persson (since March 1996)
Elections: last held September 2002 (next to be held September 2006)
Party in Government: Social Democratic Labour Party (SDP). Minority government

Economy
GDP (2001): $250 billion
GDP purchasing power parity (2002): $227.4 billion
GDP real growth rate: 1.8%
Per capita income p.p.p. (2002): $25,400
Population below poverty line: NA
Inflation rate (2002): 2.2%
Inflation rate (consumer prices 2002): 2.2%
Exports (2001): EU 55% (Germany 11%, UK 9%, Denmark 6%, Finland 6%), US 11%, Norway 9%
Imports (2001): EU 66% (Germany 18%, UK 9%, Denmark 8%, Netherlands 7%, France 7%), Norway 9%, US 7%

Contact
EU Commission office, Stockholm:
Head of Representation: Hans Johan ALLDEN
Phone: (46-8) 56 24 44 11, Fax: (46-8) 56 24 44 12
http://www.eukomm.se

United Kingdom of Great Britain and Northern Ireland

Geography
Area: 244,820 sq. km. (94,525 sq. miles)
Capital: London (metropolitan pop. 7.1 million)
Borders: Ireland 360 km, Coastline 12,429 km
Natural resources: coal, petroleum, natural gas, tin, limestone, iron ore, salt, clay, chalk, gypsum, lead, silica, arable land

People
Population (July 2002): 59,778,002
Age structure: 0-14 years 19%, 15-64 years 66%, 65 years and over 16%
Population growth rate (2002): 0.2%
Life expectancy (2002): male 75.29 years, female 80.84 years
Infant mortality rate (2002): 5.45/1,000
Ethnic groups: English 82%, Scottish 10%, Irish 2%, Welsh 2%, Ulster 2%, West Indian, Indian, Pakistani
Religions: Church of England (Anglican), Roman Catholic, Muslim, Church of Scotland (Presbyterian), Methodist, Sikh, Hindu, Jewish
Languages: English, Welsh, Irish Gaelic, Scottish Gaelic
Literacy: 99%
Work force (2001): 29 million - Services 75%, Manufacturing 16%, Construction 7%, Agriculture and fishing 2%, Energy and water 1%
Unemployment rate (2002): 5.2%

Government
Head of Government: Prime Minister Tony Blair (since May 1997)
Elections: House of Commons - last held June 2001 (next to be held May 2006)
Party in Government: New Labour. Left-of-centre

Economy
GDP (2001): $1.4 trillion
GDP purchasing power parity (2002): $1.52 trillion
GDP real growth rate (2002): 1.6%
Per capita income p.p.p. (2002): $25,300
Population below poverty line: 17%
Inflation rate (consumer prices 2002): 2.1%
Exports (2001): EU 52% (Germany 13%, France 10%, Netherlands 8%, Ireland 7%), US 15%
Imports (2001): EU 52% (Germany 13%, France 9%, Netherlands 7%, Italy 5%, Benelux 5%), US 13%

Contacts
EU Commission office, London:
Head of Representation: Jim DOUGAL
Phone: (44-20) 79 73 19 92, Fax: (44-20) 79 73 19 00 (reception) / 79 73 19 10 (policy and coordination)
http://www.cec.org.uk

37

Republic of Bulgaria

Geography
Area: 110,994 sq. km (42,906 sq. miles)
Capital: Sofia (pop. 1.2 million)
Borders: Greece 494 km, Former Yugoslav Republic of Macedonia 148 km, Romania 608 km, Serbia 318 km, Turkey 240 km, Coastline 354 km
Natural resources: bauxite, copper, lead, zinc, coal, timber, arable land

People
Population (July 2002): 7,621,337
Age structure: 0-14 years 15%, 15-64 years 69%, 65 years and over 17%
Population growth rate (2002): -1.11%
Life expectancy (2002): male 67.98 years, female 75.22 years
Infant mortality rate (2002): 14.18/1,000
Ethnic groups: Bulgarian 84%, Turk 10%, Roma 5%, Macedonian, Armenian, Tatar, Circassian
Religions: Bulgarian Orthodox 84%, Muslim 13%, Roman Catholic 2%, Jewish, Protestant, Gregorian-Armenian
Languages: Bulgarian, secondary languages resemble ethnic breakdown
Literacy: 98%
Work force (2000): 3.3 million - Services 43%, Industry 31%, Agriculture 26%
Unemployment rate (2002): 18%

Government
Head of Government: Prime Minister Simeon Saxe-Coburg-Gotha (since July 2001)
Elections: National Assembly - last held June 2001 (next to be held June 2005)
Coalition Parties: National Movement Simeon II, Turk Movement for Rights and Freedoms (MRF). Right-of-centre, reformist

Economy
GDP (2001): $12.7 billion
GDP purchasing power parity (2002): $50.6 billion
GDP real growth rate (2002): 3.4%
Per capita income p.p.p. (2002): $6,600
Population below poverty line: NA
Inflation rate (consumer prices 2002): 5.9%
Exports (2001): Italy 14%, Turkey 10%, Germany 9%, Greece 8%, Serbia and Montenegro 8%
Imports (2001): Russia 20%, Germany 15%, Italy 10%, France 6%

Contacts

Mission of Bulgaria to the EU, Brussels
Ambassador: Stanislav DASKALOV
Tel (32-2) 3 74 84 68/(32-2) 3 75 22 34, Fax (32-2) 3 74 91 88
E-mail: info@missionbg.be

Delegation to the EU-Bulgaria Joint Parliamentary Committee:
Chairman: Gil-Robles Gil-Delgado; Vice Chairmen: Guy-Quint, Sartori
Members: Averoff, Baltas, Celli, Fatuzzo, Kessler, Koulourianos, Nistico

Republic of Cyprus

Geography
Area: 9,251 sq. km. (3,572 sq. miles)
Capital: Nicosia (pop. 190,000)
Borders: Coastline 648 km
Natural resources: copper, pyrites, asbestos, gypsum, timber, salt, marble, clay earth pigment

People
Population (July 2002): 767,314
Age structure: 0-14 years 22%, 15-64 years 67%, 65 years and over 11%
Population growth rate (2002): 0.57%
Life expectancy (2002): male 74.77 years, female 79.5 years
Infant mortality rate (2002): 7.71/1,000
Ethnic groups: Greek 78%, Turkish 18%
Religions: Greek Orthodox 78%, Muslim 18%, Maronite, Armenian Apostolic
Languages: Greek, Turkish, English
Literacy: 97%
Work force (2000): Greek Cypriot 291,000 - Services 73%, Industry 22%, Agriculture 5%; Turkish Cypriot
86,300 - Services 56%, Industry 23%, Agriculture 21%
Unemployment rate (1999): Greek Cypriot area 3.3%, Turkish Cypriot area 6%

Government
Heads of Government: President Tassos Papadopoulos (since March 2003); Vice President (guaranteed
Turkish Cypriot), position unfilled since 1964
Elections: President - last held February 2003 (next to be held February 2008); Greek Cypriot House of
Representatives - last held May 2001 (next to be held May 2006); Turkish Cypriot House of
Representatives - last held December 1998 (next to be held December 2003)
Coalition Parties: Main party communist (AKEL). Coalition left-wing

Economy
GDP (2000): $8.8 billion
GDP purchasing power parity (2001): Greek Cypriot area $9.1 billion, Turkish Cypriot area $1.1 billion
GDP real growth rate (2001): Greek Cypriot area 2.6%, Turkish Cypriot area 0.8%
Per capita income p.p.p. (2001): Greek Cypriot area $15,000, Turkish Cypriot area $7000
Population below poverty line: NA
Inflation rate (consumer prices 2001): Greek Cypriot area 1.9%, Turkish Cypriot area 53.2%
Exports: Greek Cypriot area (2000) - EU 36% (UK 17%, Greece 8%), Russia 8%, Syria 7%, Lebanon 5%,
US 2%; Turkish Cypriot area (1999) - Turkey 51%, UK 31%, other EU 16.5%
Imports: Greek Cypriot area (2000) - EU 52% (UK 11%, Italy 9%, Greece 9%, Germany 7%), US 10%;
Turkish Cypriot area (1999) - Turkey 59%, UK 13%, other EU 13%

Contacts
Mission of Cyprus to the EU, Brussels:
Ambassador: Theophilos THEOPHILOU
Tel: (32-2) 7 35 35 10, Fax: (32-2) 7 35 45 52
E-mail: cyprus.embassy@skynet.be

Delegation to the EU-Cyprus Joint Parliamentary Committee:
Chairman: Rothe; Vice Chairmen: Alyssandrakis, Marinos
Members: Davies, Elles, Frassoni, Garaud, Grosch, Grossetête, Honeyball, Musumeci, de Roo, Tsatsos,
Villiers

Czech Republic

Geography
Area: 78,864 sq. km. (204,258 sq. miles)
Capital: Prague (pop. 1.2 million)
Borders: Austria 362 km, Germany 646 km, Poland 658 km, Slovakia 215 km, Coastline 0 km
Natural resources: hard coal, soft coal, kaolin, timber, clay, graphite

People
Population (July 2002): 10,256,760
Age structure: 0-14 years 16%, 15-64 years 70%, 65 years and over 14%
Population growth rate (2002): -0.07%
Life expectancy at birth (2002): male 71.46 years, female 78.65 years
Infant mortality rate (2002): 5.46/1,000
Ethnic groups: Czech 81%, Moravian 13%, Slovak 3%, Polish, German, Silesian, Roma, Hungarian
Religions: Roman Catholic 39%, Protestant 5%, Orthodox 3%, other 13%, unaffiliated 40%
Languages: Czech
Literacy: 99.9%
Work force (1999): 5.203 million - Services 60%, Industry 35%, Agriculture 5%
Unemployment rate (2002): 9%

Government
Heads of Government: Prime Minister Vladimir Spidla (since July 2002); Deputy Prime Ministers
Stanislav Gross, Cyril Svoboda, Pavel Rychetsky, Petr Mares (since July 2002)
Elections: Senate - last held November 2002 (next to be held November 2004); Chamber of Deputies -
last held June 2002 (next to be held June 2006)
Coalition Parties: Social Democrats (CSSD), Christian Democrats (KDU-CSL), Freedom Union

Economy
GDP (2001): $56.4 billion
GDP purchasing power parity (2002): $155.9 billion
GDP real growth rate (2002): 2.6%
Per capita income p.p.p. (2002): $15,300
Population below poverty line: NA
Inflation rate (consumer prices 2002): 2.2%
Exports (2001): Germany 35%, Slovakia 7%, UK 6%, Austria 5%, Poland 5%
Imports (2001): Germany 33%, Slovakia 6%, Russia 6%, Italy 6%, Austria 5%

Contacts

Mission of the Czech Republic to the EU, Brussels:
Ambassador: Libor SECKA
Tel: (32-2) 2 13 01 11, Fax: (32-2) 5 13 71 54
E-mail: eu.brussels@embassy.mzv.cz

Delegation to the EU-Czech Republic Joint Parliamentary Committee:
Chairman: Stenzel; Vice Chairmen: Modrow, Posselt
Members: Arvidsson, Berger, Knolle, Moreira Da Silva, Olsson, Posselt, Schmid, Sornosa Martínez,
Whitehead, Wyn

Republic of Estonia

Geography
Area: 45,227 sq. km. (17483 sq. miles)
Capital: Tallinn (pop. 470,000)
Borders: Latvia 339 km, Russia 294 km, Coastline 3,794 km
Natural resources: shale oil (kukersite), peat, phosphorite, amber, cambrian blue clay, limestone, sand, dolomite, arable land

People
Population (July 2002): 1,415,681
Age structure: 0-14 years 16%, 15-64 years 69%, 65 years and over 15%
Population growth rate (2002): -0.52%
Life expectancy (2002): male 64.03 years, female 76.31 years
Infant mortality rate: 12.32/1,000
Ethnic groups: Estonian 65%, Russian 28%, Ukrainian 3%, Belarusian 2%, Finnish 1%
Religions: Evangelical Lutheran, Russian Orthodox, Estonian Orthodox, Baptist, Methodist, Seventh-Day Adventist, Roman Catholic, Pentecostal, Word of Life, Jewish
Languages: Estonian (official), Russian, Ukrainian, Finnish
Literacy: 100%
Work force (2001): 608,600 - Services 69%, Industry 20%, Agriculture 11%
Unemployment rate (2001): 12.4%

Government
Head of Government: Prime Minister Siim Kallas (since 28 January 2002)
Elections: last held March 2003 (next to be held March 2007)
Coalition Parties: Coalition negotiations underway at time of going to press. Major parties: Centre Party (populist, left-of-centre), Res Publica (new, reformist), Reform (free market liberals)

Economy
GDP (2001): $5.3
GDP purchasing power parity (2002): $15.2 billion
GDP real growth rate (2002): 4.4%
Per capita income p.p.p. (2002): $10,900
Population below poverty line: NA
Inflation rate (consumer prices 2002): 3.7%
Exports (2001): Finland 34%, Sweden 14%, Latvia 7%, Germany 7%, UK 4%
Imports (2001): Finland 18%, Germany 11%, Russia 8%, Sweden 9%, China 9%

Contacts
Mission of Estonia to the EU, Brussels:
Ambassador: Priit KOLBRE
Tel: (32-2) 2 27 39 10, Fax: (32-2) 2 27 39 25
E-mail: mailto@eu.estemb.be, Priit.Kolbre@eu.estemb.be

Delegation to the EU-Estonia Joint Parliamentary Committee:
Chairman: Beazley; Vice Chairmen: Iivari, Vermeer
Members: Fraisse, Laschett, Karlsson, Raymond, Paisley, Piecyk, Stenmarck, Suominen, Wuori

Republic of Hungary

Geography
Area: 93,030 sq. km. (35,910 sq. miles)
Capital: Budapest (pop. 2.0 million)
Borders: Austria 366 km, Croatia 329 km, Romania 443 km, Serbia 151 km, Slovakia 515 km, Slovenia 102 km, Ukraine 103 km, Coastline 0 km
Natural resources: bauxite, coal, natural gas, arable land

People
Population (July 2002): 10,075,034
Age structure: 0-14 years 16%, 15-64 years 69%, 65 years 15%
Population growth rate (2002): -0.3%
Life expectancy (2002): male 67.55 years, female 76.55 years
Infant mortality rate (2002): 8.77/1,000
Ethnic Groups: Hungarian 90%, Roma 4%, German 3%, Serb 2%, Slovak, Romanian
Religions: Roman Catholic 68%, Calvinist 20%, Lutheran 5%, atheist and other 8%
Languages: Hungarian 98%, other 2%
Literacy: 99%
Work force (1997): 4.2 million - Services 65%, Industry 27%, Agriculture 8%
Unemployment rate (2002): 5.8%

Government
Head of Government: Prime Minister Peter Medgyessy (since May 2002)
Elections: last held April 2002 (next to be held April 2006)
Coalition parties: Socialists and Free Democrats. Left-of-centre

Economy
GDP (2001): $58.14 billion
GDP purchasing power parity (2002): $134.7 billion
GDP real growth rate (2002): 3.2%
Per capita income p.p.p. (2002): $13,300
Population below poverty line: 9%
Inflation rate (consumer prices 2002): 5.3%
Exports (2001): Germany 35%, Austria 9%, Italy 6%, US 6%
Imports (2001): Germany 26%, Austria 8%, Italy 8%, Russia 7%

Contacts

Mission of Hungary to the EU, Brussels:
Ambassador: Endre JUHASZ
Tel: (32-2) 3 79 09 00, Fax: (32-2) 3 72 07 84
E-mail: Nktitkarsag@humisbeu.be

Delegation to the EU-Hungary Joint Parliamentary Committee:
Chairman: Papayannakis; Vice Chairmen: Malmstrom, Mastella
Members: Echerrer, Friedrick, Karas, ó Neachtain, Raschhofer, Scarbonchi, Scheele, Stihler, Vatanen

Republic of Latvia

Geography
Area: 64,100 sq. km. (25,640 sq. miles)
Capital: Riga (pop. 870,000)
Borders: Belarus 141 km, Estonia 339 km, Lithuania 453 km, Russia 217 km, Coastline 531 km
Natural resources: amber, peat, limestone, dolomite, arable land, hydropower

People
Population (July 2002): 2,366,515
Age structure: 0-14 years 16%, 15-64 years 69%, 65 years and over 16%
Population growth rate (2002): -0.77%
Life expectancy (2002): male 63.13 years, female 75.17 years
Infant mortality rate (2002): 14.96/1,000
Ethnic groups: Latvian 58%, Russian 30%, Belarusian 4%, Ukrainian 3%, Polish 3%, Lithuanian 2%,
other 2%
Religions: Lutheran, Roman Catholic, Russian Orthodox
Languages: Latvian (official), Lithuanian, Russian
Literacy: 99.8%
Work force (2001): 1.4 million - Services 60%, Industry 25%, Agriculture 5%
Unemployment rate (2001): 7.6%

Government
Head of Government: Prime Minister Einars Repse (since November 2002)
Elections: last held October 2002 (next to be held October 2006)
Coalition Parties: New Era, First Party, Green Party, Farmer's Union, Fatherland and Freedom

Economy
GDP (2001): $7.8 billion
GDP purchasing power parity (2002): $20 billion
GDP real growth rate (2002): 4.5%
Per capita income p.p.p. (2002): $8,300
Population below poverty line: NA
Inflation rate (consumer prices 2002): 2%
Exports (2001): Germany 17%, UK 16%, Russia 6%, Sweden 10%, Lithuania 8%
Imports (2001): Germany 17%, Russia 9%, Finland 8%, Sweden 7%, Lithuania 8%

Contacts
Mission of Latvia to the EU, Brussels:
Ambassador: Andris PIEBALGS
Tel: (32-2) 2 82 03 60, Fax: (32-2) 2 82 03 69
E-mail: missioneu@mfa.lv

Delegation to the EU-Latvia Joint Parliamentary Committee:
Chairman: Gomolka; Vice Chairmen: Thorning-Schmidt, Walter
Members: von Boetticher, Borghezio, Daul, Korhola, Matikainen-Kallstrom, Miller, Montfort

Republic of Lithuania

Geography
Area: 65,200 sq. km. (26,080 sq. miles)
Capital: Vilnius (pop. 590,000)
Borders: Belarus 502 km, Latvia 453 km, Poland 91 km, Russia (Kaliningrad) 227 km, Coastline 99 km
Natural resources: peat, arable land

People
Population (July 2002): 3,601,138
Age structure: 0-14 years 18%, 15-64 years 68%, 65 years and over 14%
Population growth rate (2002): -0.25%
Life expectancy (2002): male 63.54 years, female 75.6 years
Infant mortality rate (2002): 14.34/1,000
Ethnic groups: Lithuanian 81%, Russian 9%, Polish 7%, Belarusian 2%, other 2%
Religions: Roman Catholic (majority), Lutheran, Russian Orthodox, Protestant, Evangelical Christian
Baptist, Muslim, Jewish
Languages: Lithuanian (official), Polish, Russian
Literacy: 98%
Work force (2001): 1.5 million - Services 50%, Industry 30%, Agriculture 20%
Unemployment rate (2001): 12.5%

Government
Head of Government: Prime Minister Algirdas Mykolas Brazauskas (since July 2001)
Elections: last held October 2000 (next to be held October 2004)
Coalition Parties: Social Democratic Party, Social Liberal Party. Left wing, some ministers remain from
the previous coalition that fell in July 2001

Economy
GDP (2001): $12.8 billion
GDP purchasing power parity (2002): $29.2 billion
GDP real growth rate (2002): 4.5%
Population below poverty line: NA
Inflation rate (consumer prices 2002): 0.8%
Exports (2001): UK 14%, Germany 13%, Latvia 13%, Russia 11%, Poland 6%
Imports (2001): Russia 25%, Germany 17%, Poland 5%, Italy 4%, France 4%

Contacts

Mission of Lithuania to the EU, Brussels:

Ambassador: Oskaras JUSYS

Tel: (32-2) 7 71 01 40, Fax: (32-2) 7 71 45 97

E-mail: office@lt-mission-eu.be

Delegation to the EU-Lithuania Joint Parliamentary Committee:
Chairman: Adam; Vice Chairmen: Gahler, Sjöstedt
Members: Evans, Grönfeldt Bergman, Herrez García, Jensen, Lang, Myller, Thomas-Mauro

Republic of Malta

Geography
Area: 320 Sq Km (124 Sq Miles)
Capital: Valletta (pop. 9,200)
Borders: Coastline 140 km
Natural Resources: limestone, salt, arable land

People
Population (July 2002): 397,499
Age structure: 0-14 years 20%, 15-64 years 68%, 65 years and over 13%
Population growth rate (2002): 0.73%
Life expectancy (2002): male 75.78 years, female 80.96 years
Infant mortality rate (2002): 5.72/1,000
Ethnic groups: Maltese
Religions: Roman Catholic 98%
Languages: Maltese (official), English (official), Italian
Literacy: 88.8%
Work force (2002): 160,000 - Services 71%, Industry 24%, Agriculture 5%
Unemployment rate (2002): 7%

Government
Head of Government: Prime Minister Eddie Fenech Adami (since September 1998); Deputy Prime
Minister Lawrence Gonzi (since May 1999)
Elections: House of Representatives - last held September 1998 (next to be held September 2003)
Party in Government: Nationalist Party. Christian democratic, europhile

Economy
GDP (2000): $3.6 billion
GDP purchasing power parity (2002): $7 billion
GDP real growth rate (2002): 2.2%
Per capita income p.p.p. (2002): $17,000
Population below poverty line: NA
Inflation rate (consumer prices 2002): 2.4%
Exports (2001): US 20%, Germany 14%, France 10%, UK 9%, Italy 3%
Imports (2001): Italy 20%, France 15%, US 12%, UK 10%, Germany 9%

Contacts
Mission of Malta to the EU, Brussels:
Ambassador: Victor CAMILLERI
Tel: (32-2) 3 43 01 95, Fax: (32-2) 3 43 01 06
E-mail: victor.camilleri@magnet.mt

Delegation to the EU-Malta Joint Parliamentary Committee:
Chairman: Cocilovo; Vice Chairmen: Dover, Watts
Members: Farage, Hyland, Izquierdo Rojo, Lambert, Lavarra, Turmes, Weiler, Wuermeling, Zabelle,
Zimmerling

Republic of Poland

Geography
Area: 312,683 sq. km. (120,725 sq. miles)
Capital: Warsaw (pop. 1.6 million)
Borders: Belarus 605 km, Czech Republic 658 km, Germany 456 km, Lithuania 91 km, Russia (Kaliningrad) 206 km, Slovakia 444 km, Ukraine 428 km, Coastline 491 km
Natural resources: coal, sulphur, copper, natural gas, silver, lead, salt, arable land

People
Population (July 2002): 38,625,478
Age structure: 0-14 years 18%, 15-64 years 70%, 65 years and over 13%
Population growth rate (2002): -0.02%
Life expectancy (2002): male 69.52 years, female 78.05 years
Infant mortality rate (2002): 9.17/1,000
Ethnic groups: Polish 98%, German, Ukrainian, Belarusian
Religions: Roman Catholic 95%, Eastern Orthodox, Protestant
Languages: Polish
Literacy: 98%
Work force (2000): 17.6 million - Services 50%, Agriculture 28%, Industry 22%
Unemployment rate (2002): 17%

Government
Head of Government: Prime Minister Leszek Miller (since October 2001)
Elections: National Assembly - last held September 2001 (next to be held September 2005); Senate - last held September 2001 (next to be held September 2005)
Coalition Parties: Democratic Left (SLD), Union of Labour (UP). Left wing, governing minority

Economy
GDP (2001): $174.6 billion
GDP purchasing power parity (2002): $368.1 billion
GDP real growth rate (2002): 1.2%
Per capita income p.p.p. (2002): $9,500
Population below poverty line: 18%
Inflation rate (consumer prices 2002): 2.5%
Exports (2001): Germany 34%, Italy 5%, France 5%, UK 5%
Imports (2001): Germany 24%, Russia 9%, Italy 8%, France 7%

Contacts

Mission of Poland to the EU, Brussels:

Ambassador: Marek GRELA

Tel: (32-2) 7 77 72 00, Fax: (32-2) 7 77 72 97

E-mail: 101642.2616@compuserve.com

Delegation to the EU-Poland Joint Parliamentary Committee:
Chairman: Bourlanges; Vice Chairmen: Frahm, Lund
Members: Caudron, Hieronymi, Kindermann, McMillan-Scott, Mulder, O'Toole, Sörensen, van Velzen, Wachtmeister

Romania

Geography
Area: 237,499 sq. km. (91,699 sq. miles)
Capital: Bucharest (pop. 2.4 million)
Borders: Bulgaria 608 km, Hungary 443 km, Moldova 450 km, Serbia 476 km, Ukraine (north) 362 km, Ukraine (east) 169 km, Coastline 225 km
Natural resources: petroleum, timber, natural gas, coal, salt, iron ore, arable land

People
Population (July 2002): 22,317,730
Age structure: 0-14 years 17%, 15-64 years 69%, 65 years and over 14%
Population growth rate (2002): -0.21%
Life expectancy (2002): male 66.62 years, female 74.39 years
Infant mortality rate (2002): 18.88/1,000
Ethnic groups: Romanian 90%, Hungarian 7%, Roma, Ukrainian, German, Russian, Turkish
Religions: Eastern Orthodox 87%, Protestant 7%, Catholic 6%, Muslim
Languages: Romanian (official), Hungarian, German
Literacy: 97%
Work force (1999): 9.9 million - Agriculture 40%, Services 35%, Industry 25%
Unemployment rate (2001): 9.1%

Government
Head of Government: Prime Minister Adrian Nastase (since December 2000)
Elections: Senate and Chamber of Deputies - last held November 2000 (next to be held in Autumn 2004)
Party in Government: Social Democratic Party (PSD). Left-of-centre, reformist

Economy
GDP (2001): $39.7 million
GDP purchasing power parity (2001): $152.7 million
GDP real growth rate (2001): 4.8%
Per capita income p.p.p. (2001): $6,800
Population below poverty line: 45%
Inflation rate (consumer prices 2002): 34.5%
Exports (2000): Italy 22%, Germany 16%, France 7%, Turkey 6%
Imports (2000): Italy 19%, Germany 15%, Russia 9%, France 6%

Contacts
Mission of Romania to the EU, Brussels:
Ambassador: Lazar COMANESCU
Tel: (32-2) 3 44 41 45, Fax: (32-2) 3 44 24 79
E-mail: rommis@pophost.eunet.be

Delegation to the EU-Romania Joint Parliamentary Committee:
Chairman: Mennitti; Vice Chairmen: Esclopé, Souladakis
Members: Gobbo, Grosch, Konrad, Leinen, MacCormick, Naranjo Escobar, Prets, Theato, Virrankoski

Slovak Republic

Geography
Area: 49,035 sq. km. (18,955 sq. miles)
Capital: Bratislava (pop. 450,000)
Borders: Austria 91 km, Czech Republic 215 km, Hungary 515 km, Poland 444 km, Ukraine 90 km,
Coastline 0 km
Natural resources: brown coal, lignite, mercury, iron, copper, lead, zinc

People
Population (July 2002): 5,422,366
Age structure: 0-14 years 18%, 15-64 years 70%, 65 years and over 12%
Population growth rate (2002): 0.14%
Life expectancy at birth (2002): male 70.19 years, female 78.41 years
Infant mortality rate (2002): 8.76/1,000
Ethnic groups: Slovak 86%, Hungarian 11%, Roma 2%, Czech, Moravian, Ruthenian, Silesian, Ukrainian,
German, Polish
Religions: Roman Catholic 60%, Protestant 8%, Orthodox 4%, Jewish, unaffiliated 10%
Languages: Slovak (official), Hungarian
Literacy: 99%
Work force (1999): 3.32 million - Services 46%, Industry 29%, Agriculture 9%, Construction 8%,
Transport and communication 8%
Unemployment rate (2002): 17.2%

Government
Head of Government: Prime Minister Mikulás Dzurinda (since October 1998)
Elections: National Council - last held September 2002 (next to be held September 2006)
Coalition Parties: Slovak Democratic Coalition, Party of the Democratic Left (SDL), Hungarian Coalition
Party (SMK), Party of Civic Understanding (SOP). Left-of-centre

Economy
GDP (2001): $20.5 billion
GDP purchasing power parity (2002): $66 billion
GDP real growth rate (2002): 4%
Per capita income p.p.p. (2002): $12,200
Population below poverty line: NA
Inflation rate (consumer prices 2002): 3.3%
Exports (2001): EU 60% (Germany 27%, Italy 9%, Austria 8%), Czech Republic 17%
Imports (2001): EU 50% (Germany 25%, Italy 6%), Czech Republic 15%, Russia 15%

Contacts
Mission of Slovakia to the EU, Brussels:
Ambassador: Juraj MIGAS
Tel: (32-2) 7 43 68 11, Fax: (32-2) 7 43 68 88
E-mail: pmsreu@pophost.eunet.be

Delegation to the EU-Slovak Republic Joint Parliamentary Committee:
President: Martin; Vice Chairmen: Blokland, Müller
Members: Boderato, Flemming, Jonckheer, Glante, Meijer, Murphy, Nobilia, Schmidt, Tannock

Republic of Slovenia

Geography
Area: 20,273 sq. km. (7,906 sq. miles)
Capital: Ljubljana (pop. 330,000)
Borders: Austria 330 km, Croatia 670 km, Italy 232 km, Hungary 102 km, Coastline 47 km
Natural resources: lignite coal, lead, zinc, mercury, uranium, silver, timber, hydropower

People
Population (July 2002): 1,932,917
Age structure: 0-14 years 16%, 15-64 years 70%, 65 years and over 15%
Population growth rate (2002): 0.14%
Life expectancy at birth (2002): male 71.42 years, female 79.37 years
Infant mortality rate (2002): 4.47/1,000
Ethnic groups: Slovene 88%, Croat, Serb, Bosnian, Hungarian
Religions: Roman Catholic 71%, Lutheran 1%, Muslim 1%, other 23%, unaffiliated 4%
Languages: Slovenian 91%, Serbo-Croatian 6%, Hungarian, Italian, German
Literacy: 99%
Work force (2001): 857,400 - Sector data unavailable
Unemployment rate (2002): 11%

Government
Head of Government: Prime Minister Janez Drnovsek (since December 2002)
Elections: National Assembly - last held October 2000 (next to be held October 2004)
Coalition Parties: Liberal Democrats (LDS), Social Democrats (ZLSD), Pensioners' Party (DeSUS),
Slovene People's Party (SLS and SKD). Centre-left, consensual

Economy
GDP (2001): $18.8 billion
GDP purchasing power parity (2002): $36 billion
GDP real growth rate (2002): 3%
Per capita income p.p.p. (2002): US$18,000
Population below poverty line: NA
Inflation rate (consumer prices 2002): 7.4%
Exports (2001): Germany 26%, Italy 12%, Croatia 9%, France 7%, Austria 7%
Imports (2001): Germany 20%, Italy 18%, France 11%, Austria 9%, Croatia 4%

Contacts
Mission of Slovenia to the EU, Brussels:
Ambassador: Ciril STOKELJ
Tel: (32-2) 5 12 44 66, Fax: (32-2) 5 12 09 97
E-mail: mission.bruxelles@mzz-dkp.sigov.si

Delegation to the EU-Slovenia Joint Parliamentary Committee:
Chairman: Ebner; Vice Chairmen: Costa, Ettl
Members: Carraro, Cesaro, Goepel, Krarup, Markov, Müller, Provan, van Brempt

Republic of Turkey

Geography
Area: 780,580 sq. km. (487,863 sq. miles)
Capital: Ankara (pop. 2.9 million)
Borders: Armenia 268 km, Azerbaijan 9 km, Bulgaria 240 km, Georgia 252 km, Greece 206 km, Iran 331 km, Syria 822 km, Coastline 7,200 km
Natural resources: antimony, coal, chromium, mercury, copper, borate, sulphur, iron ore, arable land, hydropower

People
Population (July 2002): 67,308,928
Age structure: 0-14 years 28%, 15-64 years 65%, 65 years and over 6%
Population growth rate (2002): 1.2%
Life expectancy at birth: male 69.15 years, female 74.01 years
Infant mortality rate (2002): 45.77/1,000
Ethnic groups: Turkish 80%, Kurdish 20%
Religions: Muslim 99.8% (mostly Sunni), Christian, Jewish
Languages: Turkish
Literacy: 85%
Work force (2001): 23.8 million - Agriculture 40%, Services 38%, Industry 22% (about 1.2 million Turks work abroad)
Unemployment rate (2002): 10.8%; Underemployment rate (2002): 6.1%

Government
Head of Government: Prime Minister Recep Tayyip Erdogan (since March 2003)
Elections: National Assembly - last held November 2002 (next to be held in 2007)
Party in Government: Justice and Development Party (AKP). Right, conservative

Economy
GDP (2001): $147.6 billion
GDP purchasing power parity (2002): $468 billion
GDP real growth rate (2002): 4.2%
Per capita income p.p.p. (2002): $7,000
Population below poverty line: NA
Inflation rate (consumer prices 2002): 45.2%
Exports (2001): Germany 17%, US 10%, Italy 8%, UK 7%, France 6%, Russia 3%
Imports (2001): Germany 13%, Italy 8%, US 8%, Russia 8%, France 6%, UK 5%

Contacts

Permanent Mission of Turkey to the EU:
Ambassador: Oguz Mustafa DAMIRALP
Phone: (32-2) 5 13 28 36, Fax: (32-2) 5 11 04 50
E-mail: turkdelegeu@euronet.be

Delegation to the EU-Turkey Joint Parliamentary Committee
Chairman: Joost; Vice Chairmen: Dprez, Duff
Members: Carnero Gonzalez, Ceyhun, Katiforis, Marini, Sacconi, Sommer, Uca, van Orden, Zacharakis

european parliament

introduction

The European Parliament is the EU institution that exercises democratic control over the running of the European Union. It consists of 626 MEPs elected from each of the 15 Member States, by direct universal suffrage. The European Parliament is the only Community institution that meets and deliberates in public. Its debates, opinions and resolutions are published in the *Official Journal of the European Union.*

contact details

E-mail format: initialsurname@europarl.eu.int
http://www.europarl.eu.int/home/default_en.htm

London office
2 Queen Anne's Gate, London SW1H 9AA
Tel: 0207 227 4300
General fax: 0207 227 4302
Library Fax: 0207 227 4301
E-mail: eplondon@europarl.eu.int
www.europarl.org.uk/index.htm

Director Dermot Scott
Press Officer Simon Duffin
Public Affairs Officer post vacant
Librarian Avis Furness

Scottish office
The Tun, 4 Jackson's Entry, Holyrood Road
Edinburgh EH8 8PJ
Tel: 0131 557 7866
Fax: 0131 557 4977
E-mail: epedinburgh@europarl.eu.int
Head post vacant

brussels

Rue Wiertz, B-1047 Brussels
Tel: +32 22 84 21 11
Fax: +32 22 84 90 75/77

luxembourg

Plateau du Kirchberg, B.P. 1601, L-2929 Luxembourg
Tel: +352 4 30 01
Fax: +352 4 30 02 94 94/93/92

strasbourg

Allée du Printemps, B.P. 1024/F, F-67070 Strasbourg
Cedex
Tel: +33 3 88 17 40 01
Fax: +33 3 88 25 65 01

uk political group offices

(also located at Queen Anne's Gate)

	Tel	Fax
British Conservatives	0207 222 1720	0207 222 5999
EP Labour Party	0207 222 1719	0207 233 1365
Liberal Democrats		0207 227 4319
Green Party	0207 227 4323	0207 233 4008
UK Independence Party		0207 227 4320

composition and election

Before 1979 representatives were selected from the membership of national parliaments and delegated by them. The first direct elections were held in June 1979 and have been held every five years since then. The UK retained its 'first-past-the-post' system for the European elections until 1994 and only joined the other states in the June 1999 elections in using proportional representation. Some Member States, for example in Italy, the UK and Belgium, use a PR system based on regions, and others such as France, Spain, Austria, Denmark and Luxembourg hold their European elections on the basis of national lists. Germany uses a mixed system.

The number of members elected for each country depends broadly on population:

Austria	21	Italy	87
Belgium	25	Luxembourg	6
Denmark	16	Netherlands	31
Finland	16	Portugal	25
France	87	Spain	64
Germany	99	Sweden	22
Greece	25	United Kingdom	87
Ireland	15	**TOTAL**	**626**

Looking ahead to the enlargement of the Union, the Treaty of Nice limits the number of MEPs to a maximum of 732 and allocates seats between Member States and candidate countries. The Treaty of Nice, signed by the member governments in Nice on 26th February 2001 entered into force once ratified by all the Member States on 1st February 2003.

The candidate countries will not of course be represented in the EP until they become members of the Union.

political groups

http://www.europarl.eu.int/groups/default.htm

In the Chamber, Members sit in political groups, not in national delegations. Parliament currently has eight political groups, plus some 'non-attached' or Independent Members. These political groups include members from over one hundred national political parties.

The following list shows the political groups that have been formed for the 1999-2004 session (TOTAL EP members 626):

EP Group members	UK membership	Total group
European People's Party and European Democrats (EPP/ED)	British Conservatives + 1 Ulster Unionist	232
Party of European Socialists (PES)	The British Labour Party + 1 SDLP	179
European Liberal Democratic and Reformist Group (ELDR)	The British Liberal Democrats	53
Greens/European Free Alliance (Greens/EFA)	The British Greens, the Scottish National Party and Plaid Cymru	45
European United Left/Nordic Green Left (EUL/NGL)	No UK members	44
Union for Europe of the Nations (UEN)	No UK members	22
Europe of Democracies and Diversities (EDD)	UK Independence Party	18
Independents (IND)	3 UK MEPs	33

working procedures

MEPs meet in plenary sitting for one week a month in Strasbourg. The parliamentary committees generally meet for two weeks a month in Brussels, for ease of contact with the Commission and Council. The fourth week is set aside for meetings of the political groups. Parliament also holds additional plenary sittings in Brussels. The secretariat is located in Luxembourg.

organisation

The **President** represents Parliament on official occasions and in international relations, presides over its plenary sittings and chairs meetings of the Bureau and the Conference of Presidents.

The **Bureau** is the regulatory body that is responsible for Parliament's budget and for administrative, organisational and staff matters. In addition to the President and fourteen Vice-Presidents, it includes five **quaestors** who deal in a consultative capacity with administrative and financial matters relating to Members and their statute.

The members of the Bureau are elected for a term of two and a half years (01/2002 - 05/2004):

President
 Pat COX (Ireland)

Vice-Presidents
 David MARTIN (UK)
 Giorgos DIMITRAKOPOULOS (Greece)
 Charlotte CEDERSCHIÖLD (Sweden)
 Renzo IMBENI (Italy)
 Alejo VIDAL-QUADRAS ROCA (Spain)
 Guido PODESTÀ (Italy)
 Ingo FRIEDRICH (Germany)
 Catherine LALUMIÈRE (France)
 Joan COLOM I NAVAL (Spain)
 José PACHECO PEREIRA (Portugal)

Vice-Presidents contd
 James PROVAN (UK)
 Gerhard SCHMID (Germany)
 Gérard ONESTA (France)
 Alonso José PUERTA (Spain)

Quaestors
 Mary BANOTTI (Ireland)
 Godelieve QUISTHOUDT-ROWOHL (Germany)
 Jacques POOS (Luxembourg)
 Miet SMET (Belgium)
 Richard BALFE (UK)

The **Conference of Presidents** comprises the President of Parliament and the political group chairs and is the political governing body of Parliament. It draws up the agenda for plenary sessions, fixes the timetable for the work of parliamentary bodies and establishes the terms of reference and size of parliamentary committees and delegations.

committees and delegations

committees

http://www.europarl.eu.int/committees/home_en.htm

In order to prepare the work of Parliament's plenary sessions, Members participate in 17 standing committees:

Agriculture and Rural Development (AGRI)

Budgets (BUDG)

Budgetary Control (CONT)

Citizens' Freedoms and Rights, Justice and Home Affairs (LIBE)

Constitutional Affairs (AFCO)

Culture, Youth, Education, the Media and Sport (CULT)

Development and Co-operation (DEVE)

Economic and Monetary Affairs (ECON)

Employment and Social Affairs (EMPL)

Environment, Public Health and Consumer Policy (ENVI)

Fisheries (PECH)

Foreign Affairs, Human Rights, Common Security and Defence Policy (AFET)

Industry, External Trade, Research and Energy (ITRE)

Legal Affairs and the Internal Market (JURI)

Petitions (PETI)

Regional Policy, Transport and Tourism (REGI OR RETT)

Women's Rights and Equal Opportunities (FEMM)

In addition to these standing committees, Parliament can also set up **subcommittees, temporary committees** that deal with specific problems, or **committees of inquiry** to investigate 'alleged contraventions of Community law or instances of maladministration'.

One temporary committee was established during the course of 2002:

Temporary Committee on foot and mouth disease, which held its constituent meeting in February and reported its findings to Parliament at the end in December 2002.

european parliament

delegations

http://www.europarl.eu.int/delegations/default_en.htm

Joint parliamentary committees maintain relations with the parliaments of states linked to the European Union by association agreements. *Interparliamentary delegations* maintain relations with the parliaments of many other countries and with international organisations.

1. Europe

a. Joint Parliamentary Committees
Bulgaria
Cyprus
Czech Republic
EEA (European Economic Area)
Estonia
Hungary
Latvia
Lithuania
Malta
Poland
Romania
Slovak Republic
Slovenia
Turkey

b. Parliamentary Co-operation Committees
Russia
Armenia, Azerbaijan and Georgia
Ukraine, Belarus and Moldova

c. Interparliamentary Delegations
South-East Europe
Switzerland, Iceland and Norway

2. Non Europe

a. Parliamentary Co-operation Committee
Kazakhstan, Kyrgyzstan, Uzbekistan, Tajikistan, Turkmenistan and Mongolia

b. Interparliamentary delegations
ASEAN, South-East Asia and the Republic of Korea
Australia and New Zealand
Canada
Central America and Mexico
China, People's Republic of
Israel
Japan
Maghreb countries and the Arab Maghreb Union
Mashreq countries and the Gulf States
Palestinian Legislative Council
South Africa
South America and Mercosur
South Asia and SAARC
United States

3. Other
Delegation for relations with the NATO Parliamentary Assembly

The ACP-EU Joint Parliamentary Assembly has joint responsibility for overseeing the implementation of the Lomé Convention with 77 African, Caribbean and Pacific states.

The EP Delegation to the European Convention represents the European Parliament in discussions on the future direction of the EU. The delegation was established on 29th January 2003. It has established a website at http://www.europarl.eu.int/europe2004/index_en.htm

powers of the ep

The European Parliament has steadily acquired greater influence and power through a series of treaties. These treaties, particularly the 1992 Maastricht Treaty and the 1997 Amsterdam Treaty, have transformed the European Parliament from a purely consultative assembly into a legislative parliament, exercising powers similar to those of the national parliaments. The Treaty of Nice enhances Parliament's role as co-legislator and extends the co-decision procedure to an additional seven areas including judicial co-operation in civil matters, a statute for European political parties, and measures for visas, asylum and immigration.

Like all parliaments, the European Parliament has three fundamental powers:

- legislative power
- budgetary powers
- the power to supervise the executive

legislative power

• Since the Treaty of Amsterdam entered into force, the standard legislative procedure is co-decision, which puts the European Parliament and the Council on an equal footing and leads to the adoption of joint Council and European Parliament acts.

• Through the co-decision procedure, a much larger number of Parliament's amendments find their way into Community laws; and no text subject to co-decision can now be adopted without the formal agreement of the European Parliament and the Council. Co-decision is now one of Parliament's most important powers.

• Although co-decision is the standard procedure, there are important areas, such as tax matters or the annual farm price review, in which Parliament simply gives an opinion.

budgetary powers

• The European Parliament is, with the Council of Ministers, the budgetary authority of the Community. The budget does not come into force until the President of the European Parliament has signed it. Where Parliament and the Council fail to agree on the amount of expenditure after two readings of the draft budget, between May and December, Parliament has the right to reject the budget as a whole and the procedure has to begin again.

• Parliament has the last word on spending on the regions (European Regional Development Fund), the fight against unemployment, particularly among young people and women (European Social Fund), cultural and educational programmes. It uses its powers to increase the funds for humanitarian aid and refugee programmes.

• When it comes to spending on agriculture, Parliament can propose modifications but the Council has the final say.

• Having adopted the budget, Parliament also monitors the proper use of public funds through its Committee on Budgetary Control. This Committee can call on the Court of Auditors to carry out special enquiries, and it can advise Parliament to refuse to accept the annual accounts if it is not satisfied.

power of democratic supervision

• Parliament exercises democratic supervision over all Community activities. This power, which was originally applied to the activities of the Commission only, has been extended to the Council of Ministers, the European Council and the political co-operation bodies which are accountable to Parliament.

• The European Parliament plays a crucial role in the process of appointing the Commission. After approving the nomination for Commission President, Parliament holds hearings with the nominee Commissioners and then appoints the Commission by a vote of confidence.

• Parliament also has the right to censure the Commission - a powerful political weapon since the adoption of a motion of censure would force the Commission to resign. To date, no motion of censure has been adopted by the European Parliament. However, in March 1999, following a report on the Commission's management by a Committee of Independent Experts mandated by Parliament, the Commission opted to resign rather than face formal censure by Parliament.

• On a daily basis, Parliament exercises its supervisory powers by examining a large number of monthly or annual reports, which the Commission is obliged to submit to it (for example, its annual General Report and the monthly reports on the implementation of the budget).

• In addition, MEPs can put written or oral questions to the Commission. During plenary sessions, 'Question Time' provides a forum for a series of questions and answers on topical matters between MEPs and members of the Commission. Individual Members and the political groups put more than 5000 questions every year.

common foreign and security policy (CFSP)

The great importance which Parliament attaches to the CFSP is reflected in its debates, particularly those which take place in the Committee on Foreign Affairs, Human Rights, Common Security and Defence Policy. The Council Presidency consults the European Parliament on the main aspects of the common foreign and security policy and ensures that Parliament's views are taken into consideration. Parliament is regularly informed by the Presidency and the Commission of developments in the Union's foreign and security policy. The European Parliament can put questions to the Council or make recommendations to it. It holds an annual debate on progress in implementing the CFSP.

european parliament

justice and home affairs

Parliament is particularly concerned with the implementation of policies on matters of common interest such as asylum and immigration, the fight against drug abuse, fraud and international crime. Parliament is regularly consulted and informed on the co-operation between the justice and home affairs authorities of the Member States. It can ask questions of the Council or make recommendations to it. Parliament also holds a debate each year on the progress made in these fields.

european central bank

Parliament has been given an important role in relation to the European Central Bank (ECB). The ECB's operational independence is counterbalanced by its accountability to the European Parliament. Parliament's rules of procedure clearly define its role in the appointment of the ECB's President, Vice-President and the other members of the executive board. After committee hearings, the nominees have to be approved by Parliament before they can be appointed by the Council. The ECB President is required to present an annual report to the plenary sitting of Parliament. In addition, the ECB President and other members of the executive board appear before Parliament's Committee on Economic and Monetary Affairs at regular intervals.

protection of human rights

Parliament's assent is now needed for decisions on the accession of new Member States, association agreements with non-member countries and the conclusion of international agreements. This means that Parliament now has the right to ratify and the power to reject international agreements. Out of its concern to protect human rights, Parliament uses this power to require non-member countries to improve their human rights records.

right of petition

European citizens can, individually or in a group, exercise their right of petition and submit to the European Parliament their requests or grievances on matters within the European Union's jurisdiction.

MEPs

AUSTRIA

BERGER, Maria
Committee on Legal Affairs and the Internal Market;
Delegation to the EU-Czech Republic Joint Parliamentary Committee;

BÖSCH, Herbert
Committee on Budgetary Control;
Vice-Chairman Committee on Petitions;
Delegation to the EU-Ukraine and the EU-Moldova Parliamentary Cooperation Committees and Delegation for relations with Belarus;

ECHERER, Mercedes
Committee on Culture, Youth, Education, the Media and Sport;
Delegation to the EU-Hungary Joint Parliamentary Committee;

ETTL, Harald
Committee on Employment and Social Affairs;
Vice-Chairman Delegation to the EU-Slovenia Joint Parliamentary Committee;

FLEMMING, Marialiese
Committee on the Environment, Public Health and Consumer Policy;
Delegation to the EU-Slovak Republic Joint Parliamentary Committee;

HAGER, Gerhard
Committee on Constitutional Affairs;
Committee on Petitions;

ILGENFRITZ, Wolfgang
Committee on Budgets;
Delegation for relations with Switzerland, Iceland and Norway;

KARAS, Othmar
Committee on Economic and Monetary Affairs;
Delegation to the EU-Hungary Joint Parliamentary Committee;

KRONBERGER, Hans
Committee on the Environment, Public Health and Consumer Policy;
Delegation to the EU-Russia Parliamentary Co-operation Committee;

MARTIN, Hans-Peter
Committee on Constitutional Affairs;
Chairman Delegation to the EU-Slovak Republic Joint Parliamentary Committee;

PIRKER, Hubert
Committee on Citizens' Freedoms and Rights, Justice and Home Affairs;
Delegation for relations with the member states of ASEAN, South-East Asia and the Republic of Korea;

PRETS, Christa
Committee on Culture, Youth, Education, the Media and Sport;
Committee on Women's Rights and Equal Opportunities;
Delegation to the EU-Romania Joint Parliamentary Committee;

RACK, Reinhard
Committee on Regional Policy, Transport and Tourism;
ACP-EU Joint Parliamentary Assembly;

RASCHHOFER, Daniela
Committee on Industry, External Trade, Research and Energy;
Delegation to the EU-Hungary Joint Parliamentary Committee;

RÜBIG, Paul
Committee on Industry, External Trade, Research and Energy;
Vice-Chairman Delegation for relations with Switzerland, Iceland and Norway;

SCHEELE, Karin
Committee on the Environment, Public Health and Consumer Policy;
ACP-EU Joint Parliamentary Assembly;

SCHIERHUBER, Agnes
Committee on Agriculture and Rural Development;
Delegation for relations with Canada;

SICHROVSKY, Peter
Committee on Culture, Youth, Education, the Media and Sport;
Delegations to the EU-Kazakhstan, EU-Kyrgyzstan and EU-Uzbekistan Parliamentary Cooperation Committees and for relations with Tadjikistan, Turkmenistan and Mongolia;

STENZEL, Ursula
Committee on Foreign Affairs, Human Rights, Common Security and Defence Policy;
Chairman Delegation to the EU-Czech Republic Joint Parliamentary Committee;

SWOBODA, Hannes
Committee on Foreign Affairs, Human Rights, Common Security and Defence Policy;
Vice-Chairman Delegation for relations with South-East Europe;
Delegation for relations with the Palestinian Legislative Council;

VOGGENHUBER, Johannes
Committee on Constitutional Affairs;

BELGIUM

BEYSEN, Ward
Committee on Legal Affairs and the Internal Market;
Delegation for relations with the NATO Parliamentary
Assembly;

DE CLERCQ, Willy
Committee on Industry, External Trade, Research and Energy;
Chairman Delegation for relations with Canada;

DEHOUSSE, Jean-Maurice
Committee on Constitutional Affairs;
Delegation for relations with Japan;

DE KEYSER, Véronique
Committee on Foreign Affairs, Human Rights, Common
Security and Defence Policy;
Delegation for relations with the countries of Central America
and Mexico;

DEPREZ, Gérard
Committee on Citizens' Freedoms and Rights, Justice and
Home Affairs;
Vice-Chairman Delegation to the EU-Turkey Joint
Parliamentary Committee;

DHAENE, Jan
Committee on Regional Policy, Transport and Tourism;
Vice-Chairman Delegation for relations with Israel;

DILLEN, Karel
Committee on Foreign Affairs, Human Rights, Common
Security and Defence Policy;
Delegation to the European Economic Area Joint
Parliamentary Committee (EEA);

DUCARME, Daniel
Committee on Employment and Social Affairs;

FRASSONI, Monica
Co-president Group of the Greens/European Free Alliance;
Committee on Constitutional Affairs;
Delegation for relations with the countries of South America
and Mercosur;

GROSCH, Mathieu
Committee on Regional Policy, Transport and Tourism;
Delegation to the EU-Romania Joint Parliamentary Committee;

HANSENNE, Michel
Committee on Industry, External Trade, Research and Energy;
Delegation for relations with Japan;

JONCKHEER, Pierre
Committee on Citizens' Freedoms and Rights, Justice and
Home Affairs;
Delegation to the EU-Slovak Republic Joint Parliamentary
Committee;

LANNOYE, Paul
Committee on Development and Co-operation;
ACP-EU Joint Parliamentary Assembly;

MAES, Nelly
Committee on Regional Policy, Transport and Tourism;
ACP-EU Joint Parliamentary Assembly;

RIES, Frédérique
Committee on the Environment, Public Health and Consumer
Policy;
Delegation for relations with Israel;

SMET, Miet
Quaestor of the EP;
Committee on Employment and Social Affairs;
Committee on Women's Rights and Equal Opportunities;
Chairman Delegation for relations with South Africa;

SÖRENSEN, Patsy
Committee on Citizens' Freedoms and Rights, Justice and
Home Affairs;
Committee on Women's Rights and Equal Opportunities;
Delegation to the EU-Poland Joint Parliamentary Committee;

STAES, Bart
Committee on Budgetary Control;
Chairman Delegation to the EU-Russia Parliamentary
Cooperation Committee;
Delegations to the EU-Kazakhstan, EU-Kyrgyzstan and EU-
Uzbekistan Parliamentary Cooperation Committees and for
relations with Tadjikistan, Turkmenistan and Mongolia;

STERCKX, Dirk
Committee on Regional Policy, Transport and Tourism;
Delegation for relations with the United States;

THYSSEN, Marianne
Committee on Legal Affairs and the Internal Market;
Delegation for relations with Canada;

VAN BREMPT, Kathleen
Committee on the Environment, Public Health and Consumer
Policy;
Delegation to the EU-Slovenia Joint Parliamentary Committee;

VAN HECKE, Johan
Committee on Budgets;
ACP-EU Joint Parliamentary Assembly;

VANHECKE, Frank
Committee on Citizens' Freedoms and Rights, Justice and
Home Affairs;
Delegation to the EU-Russia Parliamentary Cooperation
Committee;

VAN LANCKER, Anne
Committee on Employment and Social Affairs;
Delegation for relations with the Member States of ASEAN, south-east Asia and the Republic of Korea;

ZRIHEN, Olga
Vice-Chairman Committee on Women's Rights and Equal Opportunities;
Committee on Industry, External Trade, Research and Energy;

DENMARK

ANDERSEN, Bent

ANDREASEN, Ole
Committee on Foreign Affairs, Human Rights, Common Security and Defence Policy;
Delegation for relations with South Africa;

BLAK, Freddy
Vice-Chairman Committee on Budgetary Control;
Delegation for relations with Canada;

BONDE, Jens-Peter
Chairman Group for a Europe of Democracies and Diversities;
Committee on Constitutional Affairs;
Delegation for relations with Switzerland, Iceland and Norway;

BUSK, Niels
Committee on Agriculture and Rural Development;
Committee on Fisheries;
Vice-President ACP-EU Joint Parliamentary Assembly;

CAMRE, Mogens
Committee on Budgetary Control;
Delegation for relations with the Maghreb countries and the Arab Maghreb Union;

DYBKJAER, Lone
Committee on Constitutional Affairs;
Committee on Women's Rights and Equal Opportunities;
ACP-EU Joint Parliamentary Assembly;

FRAHM, Pernille
Committee on the Environment, Public Health and Consumer Policy;
Vice-Chairman Delegation to the EU-Poland Joint Parliamentary Committee;

JENSEN, Anne Elisabet
Vice-Chairman Committee on Budgets;
Delegation to the EU-Lithuania Joint Parliamentary Committee;

KRARUP, Ole
Committee on Citizens' Freedoms and Rights, Justice and Home Affairs;
Delegation to the EU-Slovenia Joint Parliamentary Committee;

LUND, Torben
Committee on the Environment, Public Health and Consumer Policy;
Vice-Chairman Delegation to the EU-Poland Joint Parliamentary Committee;

RIIS-JØRGENSEN, Karin
Committee on Economic and Monetary Affairs;
Delegation for relations with the countries of South America and Mercosur;

ROVSING, Christian
Committee on Industry, External Trade, Research and Energy;
Delegation for relations with Japan;

SANDBÆK, Ulla
Committee on Development and Co-operation;
Delegation for relations with the Palestinian Legislative Council;
ACP-EU Joint Parliamentary Assembly;

SØRENSEN, Ole
Committee on Budgetary Control;
Delegation for relations with Japan;

THORNING-SCHMIDT, Helle
Committee on Employment and Social Affairs;
Vice-Chairman Delegation to the EU-Latvia Joint Parliamentary Committee;

FINLAND

IIVARI, Ulpu
Committee on Culture, Youth, Education the Media and Sport;
Vice-Chairman, Delegation to the EU-Estonia Joint Parliamentary Committee;

KAUPPI, Piia-Noora
Committee on Economic and Monetary Affairs;
Delegation for relations with the United States;

KORHOLA, Eija-Riita
Committee on the Environment, Public Health and Consumer Policy;
Delegation to the EU-Latvia Joint Parliamentary Committee;

MATIKAINEN-KALLSTRÖM, Marjo
Committee on Industry, External Trade, Research and Energy;
Vice-Chairman Delegation to the European Economic Area (EEA) Joint Parliamentary Committee;
Delegation to the EU-Latvia Joint Parliamentary Committee;

MYLLER, Riita
Committee on the Environment, Public Health and Consumer Policy;
Delegation to the EU-Lithuania Joint Parliamentary Committee;

PAASLINNA, Reino
Committee on Industry, External Trade, Research and Energy;
Vice-Chairman Delegation to the EU-Russia Parliamentary Co-operation Committee;

PESÄLÄ, Mikko
Committee on Agriculture and Rural Development;
Delegation for relations with Australia and New Zealand;

POHJAMO, Samuli
Committee on Regional Policy, Transport and Tourism;
Delegation to the EU-Ukraine and the EU-Moldova Parliamentary Cooperation Committees and Delegation for relations with Belarus;

SEPPÄNEN, Esko
Committee on Industry, External Trade, Research and Energy;
Delegation to the European Economic Area Joint Parliamentary Committee (EEA);
Delegation to the EU-Russia Parliamentary Co-operation Committee;

SUOMINEN, Ilkka
Committee on Foreign Affairs, Human Rights, Common Security and Defence Policy;
Delegation to the EU-Estonia Joint Parliamentary Committee;

THORS, Astrid
Vice-Chairman Committee on Petitions;
Committee on the Environment, Public Health and Consumer Policy;
Chairman Delegation to the EU-Latvia Joint Parliamentary Committee;

VÄYRYNEN, Paavo
Committee on Foreign Affairs, Human Rights, Common Security and Defence Policy;
Delegation to the EU-Russia Parliamentary Co-operation Committee;

VATANEN, Ari
Committee on Regional Policy, Transport and Tourism;
Delegation to the EU-Hungary Joint Parliamentary Committee
Delegations to the EU-Kazakhstan, EU-Kyrgyzstan and EU-Uzbekistan Parliamentary Cooperation Committees and for relations with Tadjikistan, Turkmenistan and Mongolia;

VIRRANKOSKI, Kyösti
Committee on Budgets;
Delegation to the EU-Romania Joint Parliamentary Committee;

WUORI, Matti
Committee on Foreign Affairs, Human Rights, Common Security and Defence Policy;
Delegation for relations with Switzerland, Iceland and Norway;

FRANCE

ABITBOL, William
Vice-Chairman Committee on Constitutional Affairs;
Delegation for relations with the countries of south-east Europe;

AINARDI, Sylviane
Committee on Employment and Social Affairs;
Committee on Regional Policy, Transport and Tourism;
Delegation for relations with South Africa;

AUROI, Danielle
Committee on Agriculture and Rural Development;
Delegation for relations with the Mashreq countries and the Gulf;

BEBEAR, Jean-Pierre
Committee on Development and Cooperation;

BERÈS, Pervenche
Committee on Economic and Monetary Affairs;

BERNIÉ, Jean-Louis
Committee on the Environment, Public Health and Consumer Policy;
Delegation for relations with China;

BERTHU, Georges
Committee on Constitutional Affairs;
Delegation for relations with Canada;

BORDES, Armonia
Committee on Economic and Monetary Affairs;
Committee on Women's Rights and Equal Opportunities;
Delegations to the EU-Kazakhstan, EU-Kyrgyzstan and EU-Uzbekistan Parliamentary Cooperation Committees and for relations with Tadjikistan, Turkmenistan and Mongolia;

BOUDJENAH, Yasmine
Committee on Development and Co-operation;
Delegation for relations with the Maghreb countries and the Arab Maghreb Union;

BOUMEDIENNE-THIERY, Alima
Committee on Citizens' Freedoms and Rights, Justice and Home Affairs;
Vice-Chairman, Delegation for relations with the Palestinian Legislative Council;

BOURLANGES, Jean-Louis
Committee on Constitutional Affairs;
Chairman Delegation to the EU-Poland Joint Parliamentary Committee;

BUTEL, Yves
Co-president Group for a Europe of Democracies and Diversities;
Committee on Industry, External Trade, Research and Energy;
Delegation to the EU-Ukraine and the EU-Moldova Parliamentary Cooperation Committees and Delegation for relations with Belarus;

CARLOTTI, Marie-Arlette
Committee on Development and Co-operation;
Delegation to the EU-Ukraine and the EU-Moldova Parliamentary Cooperation Committees and Delegation for relations with Belarus;
Vice-President ACP-EU Joint Parliamentary Assembly;

CAUDRON, Gérard
Committee on Industry, External Trade, Research and Energy;
Delegation to the EU-Poland Joint Parliamentary Committee;

CAULLERY, Isabelle
Committee on Development and Co-operation;
Vice-Chairman Delegation to the EU-Ukraine and the EU-Moldova Parliamentary Cooperation Committees and Delegation for relations with Belarus;

CAUQUIL, Chantal
Committee on Budgets;

COHN-BENDIT, Daniel
Committee on Culture, Youth, Education, the Media and Sport;
Delegation for relations with the NATO Parliamentary Assembly;

CORNILLET, Thierry
Committee on Citizens' Freedoms and Rights, Justice and Home Affairs;
Vice-President ACP-EU Joint Parliamentary Assembly;
Delegation for relations with Australia and New Zealand;

COÛTEAUX, Paul
Committee on Foreign Affairs, Human Rights, Common Security and Defence Policy;
ACP-EU Joint Parliamentary Assembly;

DARRAS, Danielle
Committee on Regional Policy, Transport and Tourism;

DARY, Michel
Committee on Legal Affairs and the Internal Market;
Delegation for relations with the Maghreb countries and the Arab Maghreb Union;
Chairman Delegation for relations with the Mashreq countries and the Gulf;

DAUL, Joseph
Chairman Committee on Agriculture and Rural Development;
Delegation to the EU-Latvia Joint Parliamentary Committee;

DECOURRIÈRE, Francis
Committee on Culture, Youth, Education, the Media and Sport;
Vice-Chairman Delegation for relations with Canada;

DE SARNEZ, Marielle
Committee on Culture, Youth, Education, the Media and Sport;
Committee on Women's Rights and Equal Opportunities;
Delegation for relations with the Maghreb countries and the Arab Maghreb Union;

DESCAMPS, Marie-Hélène
Committee on Petitions;

DÉSIR, Harlem
Committee on Industry, External Trade, Research and Energy;
Vice-Chairman Delegation for relations with the United States;
ACP-EU Joint Parliamentary Assembly;

DE VEYRAC, Christine
Committee on Regional Policy, Transport and Tourism;

DUHAMEL, Olivier
Committee on Constitutional Affairs;

ESCLOPÉ, Alain
Committee on Regional Policy, Transport and Tourism;
Vice-Chairman Delegation to the EU-Romania Joint Parliamentary Committee;

FERREIRA, Anne
Committee on the Environment, Public Health and Consumer Policy;
Delegation for relations with South Africa;

FLAUTRE, Hélène
Committee on Employment and Social Affairs;
Delegation for relations with the Maghreb countries and the Arab Maghreb Union;

FOURTOU, Janelly
Committee on Legal Affairs and the Internal Market;
Committee on Petitions;
Delegation for relations with the countries of Central America and Mexico;

FRAISSE, Geneviève
Committee on Culture, Youth, Education, the Media and Sport;
Committee on Women's Rights and Equal Opportunities;
Delegation to the EU-Estonia Joint Parliamentary Committee;

FRUTEAU, Jean-Claude
Committee on Agriculture and Rural Development;
ACP-EU Joint Parliamentary Assembly;
Delegation for relations with the countries of South Asia and the South Asia Association for Regional Co-operation (SAARC);

GARAUD, Marie-Françoise
Committee on Legal Affairs and the Internal Market;
Delegation to the EU-Cyprus Joint Parliamentary Committee;

GAROT, George
Committee on Agriculture and Rural Development;

DE GAULLE, Charles
Committee on Economic and Monetary Affairs;

GILLIG, Marie-Hélène
Vice-Chairman Committee on Employment and Social Affairs;
Delegation for relations with the countries of South America
and Mercosur;

GOLLNISCH, Bruno
Committee on Regional Policy, Transport and Tourism;
Delegation for relations with Japan;

GROSSETÊTE, Françoise
Committee on the Environment, Public Health and Consumer
Policy;
Delegation to the EU-Cyprus Joint Parliamentary Committee;

GUY-QUINT, Catherine
Committee on Budgets;
Vice-Chairman Delegation to the EU-Bulgaria Joint
Parliamentary Committee;

HAZAN, Adeline
Committee on Citizens' Freedoms and Rights, Justice and
Home Affairs;

HERMANGE, Marie-Thérèse
Vice-Chairman Committee on Employment and Social Affairs;
Delegation for relations with the Mashreq countries and the
Gulf;

HERZOG, Philippe
Vice-Chairman Committee on Economic and Monetary Affairs;
Delegation for relations with the United States;

HORTEFEUX, Brice
Committee on Economic and Monetary Affairs;
Delegation for relations with the countries of South Asia and
the South Asia Association for Regional co-operation (SAARC);

ISLER BÉGUIN, Marie Anne
Committee on the Environment, Public Health and Consumer
Policy;
ACP-EU Joint Parliamentary Assembly;
Delegation to the EU-Armenia, EU-Azerbaijan and EU-Georgia
Parliamentary Cooperation Committees;

JEAN-PIERRE, Thierry
Committee on Budgets;
Delegation to the EU-Russia Parliamentary Co-operation
Committee;

KRIVINE, Alain
Committee on Legal Affairs and the Internal Market;
Delegation for relations with the member states of ASEAN,
South-East Asia and the Republic of Korea;

KUNTZ, Florence
Committee on Culture, Youth, Education, the Media and Sport;
Delegation for relations with the Maghreb countries and the
Arab Maghreb Union;

LAGUILLER, Arlette
Committee on Employment and Social Affairs;

LALUMIÈRE, Catherine
Vice-President of the EP;
Committee on Foreign Affairs, Human Rights, Common
Security and Defence Policy;
Delegation for relations with the NATO Parliamentary
Assembly;
Delegation to the EU-Russia Parliamentary Co-operation
Committee;

LAMASSOURE, Alain
Committee on Foreign Affairs, Human Rights, Common
Security and Defence Policy;
Delegation for relations with countries of South-East Europe;

LANG, Carl
Committee on Employment and Social Affairs;
Delegation for relations with the Member States of ASEAN,
south-east Asia and the Republic of Korea;

DE LA PERRIÈRE, Thierry
Committee on Culture, Youth, Education, the Media and Sport;
Delegation to the EU-Armenia, EU-Azerbaijan and EU-Georgia
Parliamentary Cooperation Committees;

LE PEN, Jean-Marie
Committee on Regional Policy, Transport and Tourism;
Committee on Petitions;
Delegation for relations with South Africa;

LIPIETZ, Alain
Committee on Economic and Monetary Affairs;
Delegation for relations with the countries of South America
and Mercosur;

MARCHIANI, Jean-Charles
Committee on Foreign Affairs, Human Rights, Common
Security and Defence Policy;
Delegation for relations with the Maghreb countries and the
Arab Maghreb Union;

MARTIN, Hughes
Vice-Chairman Committee on Fisheries;
Committee on Foreign Affairs, Human Rights, Common
Security and Defence Policy;
Delegation for relations with the Maghreb countries and the
Arab Maghreb Union;

MARTINEZ, Jean-Claude
Committee on Agriculture and Rural Development;
Delegation for relations with the countries of South America and Mercosur;

MATHIEU, Véronique
Committee on Agriculture and Rural Development;
Committee on Petitions;

MONTFORT, Elizabeth
Committee on Industry, External Trade, Research and Energy;
Delegation to the EU-Latvia Joint Parliamentary Committee;

MORILLON, Philippe
Committee on Foreign Affairs, Human Rights, Common Security and Defence Policy;
Chairman Delegation for relations with the NATO Parliamentary Assembly;
ACP-EU Joint Parliamentary Assembly;

NAÏR, Sami
Committee on Foreign Affairs, Human Rights, Common Security and Defence Policy;
Delegation for relations with the Mashreq countries and the Gulf;

NORDMANN, Jean-Thomas
Committee on Foreign Affairs, Human Rights, Common Security and Defence Policy;
Delegation to the EU-Bulgaria Joint Parliamentary Committee;

ONESTA, Gérard
Vice-President of the EP;
Committee on Constitutional Affairs;
Delegation for relations with Australia and New Zealand;

PASQUA, Charles
Chairman Union for Europe of the Nations Group;
Committee on Employment and Social Affairs;
Delegation to the EU-Russia Parliamentary Co-operation Committee;

PATRIE, Beatrice
Committee on the Environment, Public Health and Consumer Policy;
Delegation to the EU-Ukraine and the EU-Moldova Parliamentary Cooperation Committees and Delegation for relations with Belarus;

PIÉTRASANTA, Yves
Vice-Chairman Committee on Industry, External Trade, Research and Energy;
Delegation for relations with the Mashreq countries and the Gulf;

POIGNANT, Bernard
Committee on Regional Policy, Transport and Tourism;
Committee on Fisheries;
Delegation for relations with South-East Europe;

RAYMOND, Michel
Committee on Budgets;
Delegation to the EU-Estonia Joint Parliamentary Committee;

ROCARD, Michel
Chairman Committee on Culture, Youth, Education, the Media and Sport;
Delegation for relations with the United States;

ROD, Didier
Committee on Development and Co-operation;
ACP-EU Joint Parliamentary Assembly;

ROURE, Martine
Committee on Citizens' Freedoms and Rights, Justice and Home Affairs;
Delegation for relations with China;

SAINT-JOSSE, Jean
Committee on Employment and Social Affairs;

SAVARY, Gilles
Vice-Chairman Committee on Regional Policy, Transport and Tourism;
Delegations to the EU-Kazakhstan, EU-Kyrgyzstan and EU-Uzbekistan Parliamentary Cooperation Committees and for relations with Tadjikistan, Turkmenistan and Mongolia;

SCARBONCHI, Michel Ange Mathieu
Committee on Budgetary Control;
Delegations to the EU-Hungary Joint Parliamentary Committee;

SCHAFFNER, Anne-Marie
Committee on Legal Affairs and the Internal Market;
Delegations to the EU-Kazakhstan, EU-Kyrgyzstan and EU-Uzbekistan Parliamentary Cooperation Committees and for relations with Tadjikistan, Turkmenistan and Mongolia;

SOUCHET, Dominique
Committee on Agriculture and Rural Development;
Committee on Fisheries;
ACP-EU Joint Parliamentary Assembly;

SUDRE, Margie
Committee on Regional Policy, Transport and Tourism;
Vice-Chairman Delegation for relations with the Mashreq countries and the Gulf;
ACP-EU Joint Parliamentary Assembly;

SYLLA, Fodé
Committee on Citizens' Freedoms and Rights, Justice and Home Affairs;
Vice-President ACP-EU Joint Parliamentary Assembly;

THOMAS-MAURO, Nicole
Committee on the Environment, Public Health and Consumer Policy;
Committee on Women's Rights and Equal Opportunities;
Delegation to the EU-Lithuania Joint Parliamentary Committee;

VACHETTA, Roseline
Committee on Industry, External Trade, Research and Energy;
Delegation for relations with the Palestinian Legislative Council;

VARAUT, Alexandre
Committee on Legal Affairs and the Internal Market;
Delegation for relations with Japan;

DE VEYRINAS, Françoise

VLASTO, Dominique
Committee on Industry, External Trade, Research and Energy;
Delegation for relations with the Maghreb countries and the Arab Maghreb Union;

WURTZ, Francis
Chairman Confederal Group of the European United Left/Nordic Green Left;
Committee on Budgets;
ACP-EU Joint Parliamentary Assembly;

ZIMERAY, François
Committee on Legal Affairs and the Internal Market;
Delegation for relations with Israel;

GERMANY

BEREND, Rolf
Committee on Regional Policy, Transport and Tourism;
ACP-EU Joint Parliamentary Assembly;

BÖGE, Reimer
Vice-Chairman Committee on Budgets;

VON BÖTTICHER, Christian
Committee on Citizens' Freedoms and Rights, Justice and Home Affairs;
Committee on Petitions;
Delegation for relations with Japan;
Delegation to the EU-Latvia Joint Parliamentary Committee;

BREYER, Hiltrud
Committee on the Environment, Public Health and Consumer Policy;
Delegation for relations with the member states of ASEAN, South-East Asia and the Republic of Korea;

BRIE, André
Committee on Foreign Affairs, Human Rights, Common Security and Defence Policy;
Delegation for relations with Israel;

BROK, Elmar
Chairman Committee on Foreign Affairs, Human Rights, Common Security and Defence Policy;
Delegation for relations with the United States;

BULLMANN, Hans Udo
Committee on Economic and Monetary Affairs;
ACP-EU Joint Parliamentary Assembly;

CEYHUN, Ozan
Committee on Citizens' Freedoms and Rights, Justice and Home Affairs;
Vice-Chairman Delegation to the EU-Turkey Joint Parliamentary Committee;

DUIN, Garrelt
Committee on Regional Policy, Transport and Tourism;
Delegation for relations with Switzerland, Iceland and Norway;

FERBER, Markus
Committee on Budgets;
Delegation to the European Economic Area (EEA) Joint Parliamentary Committee;

FIEBIGER, Christel
Committee on Agriculture and Rural Development;
Delegation to the EU-Ukraine and the EU-Moldova Parliamentary Cooperation Committees and Delegation for relations with Belarus;

FLORENZ, Karl-Heinz
Committee on the Environment, Public Health and Consumer Policy;
Delegation for relations with the countries of South America and Mercosur;

FRIEDRICH, Ingo
Vice-President of the EP;
Committee on Economic and Monetary Affairs;
Delegation to the EU-Hungary Joint Parliamentary Committee;

GAHLER, Michael
Committee on Foreign Affairs, Human Rights, Common Security and Defence Policy;
Vice-Chairman Delegation to the EU-Lithuania Joint Parliamentary Committee;

GEBHARDT, Evelyne
Committee on Legal Affairs and the Internal Market;
Delegation for relations with China;

GLANTE, Norbert
Committee on Industry, External Trade, Research and Energy;
Delegation to the EU-Slovak Republic Joint Parliamentary Committee;

GLASE, Anne-Karin
Committee on Employment and Social Affairs;
ACP-EU Joint Parliamentary Assembly;

GOEPEL, Lutz
Committee on Agriculture and Rural Development;
Delegation to the EU-Slovenia Joint Parliamentary Committee;

GOMOLKA, Alfred
Committee on Foreign Affairs, Human Rights, Common
Security and Defence Policy;
Chairman Delegation to the EU-Latvia Joint Parliamentary
Committee;

GÖRLACH, Willi
Committee on Agriculture and Rural Development;
Chairman Delegation for relations with Israel;
Vice-Chairman Delegation for relations with Canada;

GRAEFE ZU BARINGDORF, Friedrich-Wilhelm
Vice-Chairman Committee on Agriculture and Rural
Development;
Delegation for relations with South Africa;

GRÖNER, Lissy
Committee on Culture, Youth, Education, the Media and Sport;
Committee on Women's Rights and Equal Opportunities;
Delegation to the EU-Russia Parliamentary Cooperation
Committee;

HÄNSCH, Klaus
Committee on Foreign Affairs, Human Rights, Common
Security and Defence Policy;

HAUG, Jutta
Committee on Budgets;
ACP-EU Joint Parliamentary Assembly;

HIERONYMI, Ruth
Committee on Culture, Youth, Education, the Media and Sport;
Delegation to the EU-Poland Joint Parliamentary Committee;

HOFF, Magdalene
Committee on Foreign Affairs, Human Rights, Common
Security and Defence Policy;
Delegation for relations with the United States;

JARZEMBOWSKI, Georg
Committee on Regional Policy, Transport and Tourism;
Vice-Chairman Delegation for relations with Japan;

JEGGLE, Elisabeth
Committee on Agriculture and Rural Development;
Delegations to the EU-Kazakhstan, EU-Kyrgyzstan and EU-
Uzbekistan Parliamentary Cooperation Committees and for
relations with Tadjikistan, Turkmenistan and Mongolia;

JÖNS, Karin
Committee on Employment and Social Affairs;
Delegation for relations with countries of South-East Europe;

JUNKER, Karin
Committee on Development and Co-operation;
Vice-President ACP-EU Joint Parliamentary Assembly;

KAUFMANN, Sylvia-Yvonne
Committee on Constitutional Affairs;
Delegation for relations with Japan;

KEPPELHOFF-WIECHERT, Hedwig
Committee on Agriculture and Rural Development;
ACP-EU Joint Parliamentary Assembly;

KESSLER, Margot
Committee on Citizens' Freedoms and Rights, Justice and
Home Affairs;
Committee on Petitions;
Delegation to the EU-Bulgaria Joint Parliamentary Committee;

KINDERMANN, Heinz
Committee on Agriculture and Rural Development;
Committee on Fisheries;
Delegation to the EU-Poland Joint Parliamentary Committee;

KLAMT, Eva
Committee on Citizens' Freedoms and Rights, Justice and
Home Affairs;
Delegation for relations with Australia and New Zealand;

KLASS, Christa
Committee on the Environment, Public Health and Consumer
Policy;
Committee on Women's Rights and Equal Opportunities;
Delegation for relations with China;

KNOLLE, Karsten
Committee on Development and Co-operation;
Delegation to the EU-Czech Republic Joint Parliamentary

KOCH, Dieter-Lebrecht
Committee on Regional Policy, Transport and Tourism;
Delegation for relations with the Palestinian Legislative
Council;

KONRAD, Christoph Werner
Committee on Economic and Monetary Affairs;
Delegation to the EU-Romania Joint Parliamentary Committee;

KREHL, Constanze
Committee on Budgets;
Delegation for relations with Japan;

KREISSL-DÖRFLER, Wolfgang
Committee on Development and Co-operation;
Delegation for relations with the countries of Central America
and Mexico;

KUCKELHORN, Wilfried
Committee on Budgets;
Delegation for relations with Japan;

KUHNE, Helmut
Committee on Budgetary Control;
Delegation for relations with the NATO Parliamentary Assembly;

LANGE, Bernd
Committee on the Environment, Public Health and Consumer Policy;
Delegation for relations with South Africa;

LANGEN, Werner
Committee on Industry, External Trade, Research and Energy;
Delegation for relations with the countries of South America and Mercosur;
Delegation to the EU-Russia Parliamentary Cooperation Committee;

LANGENHAGEN, Brigitte
Committee on Budgetary Control;
Vice-Chairman Committee on Fisheries;
Delegation for relations with China;

LASCHET, Armin
Committee on Foreign Affairs, Human Rights, Common Security and Defence Policy;
Delegation to the EU-Estonia Joint Parliamentary Committee;

LECHNER, Kurt
Committee on Legal Affairs and the Internal Market;
Delegation to the EU-Ukraine and the EU-Moldova Parliamentary Cooperation Committees and Delegation for relations with Belarus;

LEHNE, Klaus-Heiner
Committee on Legal Affairs and the Internal Market;
Delegation for relations with the Maghreb countries and the Arab Maghreb Union;

LEINEN, Jo
Vice-Chairman Committee on Constitutional Affairs;
Delegation to the EU-Romania Joint Parliamentary Committee;

LIESE, Peter
Committee on the Environment, Public Health and Consumer Policy;
Vice-Chairman Delegation for relations with the countries of Central America and Mexico;

LINKOHR, Rolf
Committee on Industry, External Trade, Research and Energy;
Chairman Delegation for relations with the countries of South America and Mercosur;

MANN, Erika
Committee on Industry, External Trade, Research and Energy;
Chairman Delegation to the European Economic Area Joint Parliamentary Committee (EEA);

MANN, Thomas
Committee on Employment and Social Affairs;
Committee on Women's Rights and Equal Opportunities;
Vice-Chairman Delegation for relations with the countries of South Asia and the South Asia Association for Regional Co-operation (SAARC);

MARKOV, Helmuth
Vice-Chairman Committee on Regional Policy, Transport and Tourism;
Delegation to the EU-Slovenia Joint Parliamentary Committee;
Delegation to the EU-Russia Parliamentary Cooperation Committee;

MAYER, Hans-Peter
Committee on Economic and Monetary Affairs;
Delegation for relations with countries of South-East Europe;

MAYER, Xaver
Committee on Agriculture and Rural Development;
Delegation for relations with Switzerland, Iceland and Norway;

MENRAD, Winfried
Vice-Chairman Committee on Employment and Social Affairs;
Delegation for relations with Israel;

MODROW, Hans
Committee on Development and Co-operation;
Chairman Delegation to the EU-Czech Republic Joint Parliamentary Committee;

MOMBAUR, Peter
Vice-Chairman Committee on Industry, External Trade, Research and Energy;
Delegation for relations with the countries of South Asia and the South Asia Association for Regional Cooperation (SAARC);

MÜLLER, Emilia Franziska
Committee on the Environment, Public Health and Consumer Policy;
Committee on Women's Rights and Equal Opportunities;
Vice-Chairman Delegation to the EU-Slovak Republic Joint Parliamentary Committee;

MÜLLER, Rosemarie
Committee on the Environment, Public Health and Consumer Policy;
Delegation to the EU-Slovenia Joint Parliamentary Committee;

NASSAUER, Hartmut
Committee on Citizens' Freedoms and Rights, Justice and Home Affairs;
Chairman Delegation for relations with the member states of ASEAN, South-East Asia and the Republic of Korea;

NIEBLER, Angelika Victoria
Committee on Industry, External Trade, Research and Energy;
Delegation for relations with South Africa;

PACK, Doris
Committee on Culture, Youth, Education, the Media and Sport;
Chairman Delegation for relations with countries of South-East Europe;

PIECYK, Wilhelm
Committee on Regional Policy, Transport and Tourism;
Delegation to the EU-Estonia Joint Parliamentary Committee;

POETTERING, Hans-Gert
Chairman Group of the European People's Party (Christian Democrats) and European Democrats;
Delegation for relations with the Member States of ASEAN, south-east Asia and the Republic of Korea;

POSSELT, Bernd
Committee on Citizens' Freedoms and Rights, Justice and Home Affairs;
Vice-Chairman Delegation to the EU-Czech Republic Joint Parliamentary Committee;

QUISTHOUDT-ROWOHL, Godelieve
Quaestor of the EP;
Committee on Industry, External Trade, Research and Energy;
Delegation for relations with the United States;

RADWAN, Alexander
Committee on Economic and Monetary Affairs;
Delegation for relations with the Mashreq countries and the Gulf;

RANDZIO-PLATH, Christa
Chairman Committee on Economic and Monetary Affairs;
Delegation for relations with the member states of ASEAN, South-East Asia and the Republic of Korea;

RAPKAY, Bernhard
Committee on Economic and Monetary Affairs;
Delegation for relations with the countries of South Asia and the South Asia Association for Regional Cooperation (SAARC);

ROTH-BEHRENDT, Dagmar
Committee on the Environment, Public Health and Consumer Policy;
Vice-Chairman Delegation for relations with Australia and New Zealand;

ROTHE, Mechtild
Committee on Industry, External Trade, Research and Energy;
Chairman Delegation to the EU-Cyprus Joint Parliamentary Committee;

ROTHLEY, Willi
Vice-Chairman Committee on Legal Affairs and the Internal Market;

RÜHLE, Heide
Committee on Citizens' Freedoms and Rights, Justice and Home Affairs;
Delegation for relations with countires of South-East Europe;

SAKELLARIOU, Jannis
Committee on Foreign Affairs, Human Rights, Common Security and Defence Policy;
Delegation for relations with the Mashreq countries and the Gulf;
Delegation for relations with the countries of Central America and Mexico;

SCHLEICHER, Ursula
Vice-Chairman Committee on Constitutional Affairs;
Chairman Delegation to the EU-Armenia, EU-Azerbaijan and EU-Georgia Parliamentary Cooperation Committees;

SCHMID, Gerhard
Vice-President of the EP;
Committee on Citizens' Freedoms and Rights, Justice and Home Affairs;
Delegation to the EU-Czech Republic Joint Parliamentary Committee;

SCHMITT, Ingo
Committee on Regional Policy, Transport and Tourism;
Delegation for relations with the countries of Central America and Mexico;

SCHNELLHARDT, Horst
Committee on the Environment, Public Health and Consumer Policy;
ACP-EU Joint Parliamentary Assembly;

SCHRÖDER, Ilka
Committee on Citizens' Freedoms and Rights, Justice and Home Affairs;
Delegation for relations with countries of South-East Europe;

SCHRÖDER, Jürgen
Committee on Foreign Affairs, Human Rights, Common Security and Defence Policy;
Delegation for relations with Canada;

SCHROEDTER, Elisabeth
Committee on Foreign Affairs, Human Rights, Common Security and Defence Policy;
Vice- Chairman Delegation to the EU-Ukraine and the EU-Moldova Parliamentary Cooperation Committees and Delegation for relations with Belarus;

SCHULZ, Martin
Committee on Citizens' Freedoms and Rights, Justice and Home Affairs;
Delegation to the EU-Armenia, EU-Azerbaijan and EU-Georgia Parliamentary Cooperation Committees;

SCHWAIGER, Konrad
Committee on Industry, External Trade, Research and Energy;
Vice-President ACP-EU Joint Parliamentary Assembly;

SOMMER, Renate
Committee on Regional Policy, Transport and Tourism;
Delegation to the EU-Turkey Joint Parliamentary Committee;

STAUNER, Gabriele
Committee on Budgetary Control;
Delegation to the EU-Russia Parliamentary Co-operation
Committee;

STOCKMANN, Ulrich
Committee on Regional Policy, Transport and Tourism;
Delegation for relations with Israel;

THEATO, Diemut
Chairman Committee on Budgetary Control;
Delegation to the EU-Romania Joint Parliamentary Committee;

UCA, Feleknas
Committee on Culture, Youth, Education, the Media and Sport;
Committee on Women's Rights and Equal Opportunities;
Delegation to the EU-Turkey Joint Parliamentary Committee;

WALTER, Ralf
Committee on Budgets;
Vice-Chairman Delegation to the EU-Latvia Joint Parliamentary
Committee;

WEILER, Barbara
Committee on Employment and Social Affairs;
Delegation to the EU-Malta Joint Parliamentary Committee;

WENZEL-PERILLO, Brigitte
Committee on Budgets;
Delegation for relations with South Africa;

WIELAND, Rainer
Committee on Legal Affairs and the Internal Market;
Committee on Petitions;
ACP-EU Joint Parliamentary Assembly;

VON WOGAU, Karl
Committee on Foreign Affairs, Human Rights, Common
Security and Defence Policy;
Delegation for relations with the Mashreq countries and the Gulf;
Delegation for relations with the NATO Parliamentary Assembly;

WÜRMELING, Joachim
Committee on Legal Affairs and the Internal Market;
Delegation to the EU-Malta Joint Parliamentary Committee;

ZIMMERLING, Jürgen
Committee on Development and Co-operation;
ACP-EU Joint Parliamentary Assembly;

ZISSENER, Sabine
Committee on Culture, Youth, Education, the Media and Sport;
Committee on Women's Rights and Equal Opportunities;
Delegation for relations with the Palestinian Legislative Council;
Delegation to the EU-Armenia, EU-Azerbaijan and EU-Georgia
Parliamentary Cooperation Committees;

GREECE

ALAVANOS, Alexandros
Committee on Culture, Youth, Education, the Media and Sport;
Delegation for relations with countries of South-East Europe;

ALYSSANDRAKIS, Konstantinos
Committee on Industry, External Trade, Research and Energy;
Vice-Chairman Delegation to the EU-Cyprus Joint
Parliamentary Committee;

AVEROFF, Ioannis
Committee on Budgets;
ACP-EU Joint Parliamentary Assembly;
Delegation to the EU-Bulgaria Joint Parliamentary Committee;

BAKOPOULOS, Emmanouil
Committee on Regional Policy, Transport and Tourism;
Delegation for relations with Switzerland, Iceland and Norway;

BALTAS, Alexandros
Committee on Foreign Affairs, Human Rights, Common
Security and Defence Policy;
Vice-Chairman Delegation to the EU-Bulgaria Joint
Parliamentary Committee;

DIMITRAKOPOULOS, Giorgos
Vice-President of the EP;
Committee on Constitutional Affairs;

FOLIAS, Christos
Committee on Agriculture and Rural Development;
Chairman Delegation for relations with Switzerland, Iceland
and Norway;
Delegation to the EU-Ukraine and the EU-Moldova
Parliamentary Cooperation Committees and Delegation for
relations with Belarus;

HATZIDAKIS, Konstantinos
Committee on Regional Policy, Transport and Tourism;
Delegation to the EU-Armenia, EU-Azerbaijan and EU-Georgia
Parliamentary Cooperation Committees;

KARAMANOU, Anna
Committee on Employment and Social Affairs;
Chairman Committee on Women's Rights and Equal
Opportunities;
ACP-EU Joint Parliamentary Assembly;
Delegation for relations with countries of South-East Europe;

KATIFORIS, Giorgos
Committee on Economic and Monetary Affairs;
Delegation to the EU-Turkey Joint Parliamentary Committee;

KORAKAS, Efstratios
Committee on Foreign Affairs, Human Rights, Common
Security and Defence Policy;
Delegation for relations with the NATO Parliamentary
Assembly;

KOUKIADIS, Ioannis
Vice-Chairman Committee on Legal Affairs and the Internal Market;
Committee on Petitions;
Vice-Chairman Delegations to the EU-Kazakhstan, EU-Kyrgyzstan and EU-Uzbekistan Parliamentary Cooperation Committees and for relations with Tadjikistan, Turkmenistan and Mongolia;

KOULOURIANOS, Dimitrios
Committee on Agriculture and Rural Development;
Delegation to the EU-Bulgaria Joint Parliamentary Committee;
Vice-Chairman Delegation to the EU-Armenia, EU-Azerbaijan and EU-Georgia Parliamentary Cooperation Committees;

KRATSA-TSAGAROPOULOU, Rodi
Committee on Employment and Social Affairs;
Committee on Women's Rights and Equal Opportunities;
Delegation for relations with countries of South-East Europe;

MALLIORI, Minerva Melpomeni
Committee on the Environment, Public Health and Consumer Policy;
Delegation to the EU-Russia Parliamentary Co-operation Committee;

MARINOS, Ioannis
Committee on Economic and Monetary Affairs;
Committee on Petitions;
Committee on Fisheries;
Vice-Chairman Delegation to the EU-Cyprus Joint Parliamentary Committee;

MASTORAKIS, Emmanouil
Committee on Regional Policy, Transport and Tourism;
Delegation for relations with countries of South-east Europe;

PAPAYANNAKIS, Mihail
Committee on the Environment, Public Health and Consumer Policy;
Chairman Delegation to the EU-Hungary Joint Parliamentary Committee;

PATAKIS, Ioannis
Committee on Economic and Monetary Affairs;
Delegation for relations with countries of South-East Europe;

SOULADAKIS, Ioannis
Committee on Foreign Affairs, Human Rights, Common Security and Defence Policy;
Vice-Chairman Delegation to the EU-Romania Joint Parliamentary Committee;

TRAKATELLIS, Antonios
Committee on the Environment, Public Health and Consumer Policy;
Delegation for relations with Israel;

TSATSOS, Dimitris
Committee on Constitutional Affairs;
Delegation to the EU-Cyprus Joint Parliamentary Committee;

XARCHAKOS, Stavros
Committee on Culture, Youth, Education, the Media and Sport;
Committee on Petitions;
Delegation to the EU-Russia Parliamentary Co-operation Committee;

ZACHARAKIS, Christos
Vice-Chairman Committee on Foreign Affairs, Human Rights, Common Security and Defence Policy;
Delegation to the EU-Turkey Joint Parliamentary Committee;

ZORBA, Myrsini
Committee on Industry, External Trade, Research and Energy;
Delegation to the EU-Armenia, EU-Azerbaijan and EU-Georgia Parliamentary Cooperation Committees;

IRELAND

AHERN, Nuala
Committee on Industry, External Trade, Research and Energy;
Delegation for relations with the United States;

ANDREWS, Niall
Committee on Citizens' Freedoms and Rights, Justice and Home Affairs;
ACP-EU Joint Parliamentary Assembly;

BANOTTI, Mary
Quaestor of the EP;
Committee on Citizens' Freedoms and Rights, Justice and Home Affairs;
Vice-Chairman Delegation for relations with Japan;

COLLINS, Gerard
Committee on Regional Policy, Transport and Tourism;
Chairman Delegation for relations with South Africa;

COX, Patrick
President of the EP;

CROWLEY, Brian
Committee on Legal Affairs and the Internal Market;
Delegation for relations with the United States;

CUSHNAHAN, John
Committee on Foreign Affairs, Human Rights, Common Security and Defence Policy;
Delegation for relations with the countries of South Asia and the South Asia Association for Regional Cooperation (SAARC);

DE ROSSA, Proinsias
Vice-Chairman Committee on Petitions;
Committee on Employment and Social Affairs;
Delegation for relations with the Palestinian Legislative Council;

DOYLE, Avril
Committee on the Environment, Public Health and Consumer Policy;
Delegation for relations with South Africa;

FITZSIMONS, Jim
Committee on the Environment, Public Health and Consumer Policy;
Committee on Petitions;
Delegation for relations with the Mashreq countries and the Gulf;

HYLAND, Liam
Committee on Agriculture and Rural Development;
Delegation to the EU-Malta Joint Parliamentary Committee;

McCARTIN, John
Committee on Budgets;
Delegation for relations with China;

McKENNA, Patricia
Committee on the Environment, Public Health and Consumer Policy;
Committee on Fisheries;
Delegation for relations with the member states of ASEAN, South-East Asia and the Republic of Korea;

Ó NEACHTAIN, Seán
Committee on Fisheries;
Committee on Industry, External Trade, Research and Energy;
Delegation to the EU-Hungary Joint Parliamentary Committee;

SCALLON, Dana Rosemary
Committee on Regional Policy, Transport and Tourism;

ITALY

ANDRIA, Generoso
Committee on Budgetary Control;
Committee on Economic and Monetary Affairs;
Delegation for relations with the Palestinian Legislative Council;

ANGELILLI, Roberta
Committee on Citizens' Freedoms and Rights, Justice and Home Affairs;
Delegation for relations with the Mashreq countries and the Gulf;

BARTOLOZZI, Paolo
Committee on Legal Affairs and the Internal Market;
Delegation for relations with the countries of Central America and Mexico;

BERLATO, Sergio
Committee on Agriculture and Rural Development;
Vice-Chairman Delegation for relations with Australia and New Zealand;

BERTINOTTI, Fausto
Committee on Industry, External Trade, Research and Energy;

BIGLIARDO, Felice
Committee on Economic and Monetary Affairs;
Delegation for relations with Canada;

BODRATO, Guido
Committee on Industry, External Trade, Research and Energy;
Delegation to the EU-Slovak Republic Joint Parliamentary Committee;

BONINO, Emma
Committee on Foreign Affairs, Human Rights, Common Security and Defence Policy;
Delegation for relations with the Mashreq countries and the Gulf;

BORGHEZIO, Mario
Committee on Citizens' Freedoms and Rights, Justice and Home Affairs;
Delegation to the EU-Latvia Joint Parliamentary Committee;

BOSELLI, Enrico
Committee on Employment and Social Affairs;
Delegation for relations with China;

BRIENZA, Giuseppe
Committee on Citizens' Freedoms and Rights, Justice and Home Affairs;
Vice-President ACP-EU Joint Parliamentary Assembly;

BRUNETTA, Renato
Committee on Economic and Monetary Affairs;
Delegation for relations with countries of South-East Europe;

CAPPATO, Marco
Committee on Industry, External Trade, Research and Energy;
Delegation for relations with the United States;

CARRARO, Massimo
Committee on Industry, External Trade, Research and Energy;
Delegation to the EU-Slovenia Joint Parliamentary Committee;

CAVERI, Luciano
Chairman Committee on Regional Policy, Transport and Tourism;
Delegation for relations with the countries of South America and Mercosur;

CELLI, Giorgio
Committee on Agriculture and Rural Development;
Delegation to the EU-Bulgaria Joint Parliamentary Committee;

CESARO, Luigi
Committee on Development and Co-operation;
Delegation to the EU-Slovenia Joint Parliamentary Committee;

COCILOVO, Luigi
Committee on Employment and Social Affairs;
Committee on Regional Policy, Transport and Tourism;
Chairman Delegation to the EU-Malta Joint Parliamentary
Committee;

COSSUTTA, Armando
Committee on Constitutional Affairs;
Delegation for relations with Australia and New Zealand;

COSTA, Paolo
Committee on Constitutional Affairs;
Vice-Chairman Delegation to the EU-Slovenia Joint
Parliamentary Committee ;

COSTA, Raffaele
Committee on the Environment, Public Health and Consumer
Policy;
Delegation to the EU-Armenia, EU-Azerbaijan and EU-Georgia
Parliamentary Cooperation Committees;

DELL'ALBA, Gianfranco
Committee on Budgetary Control;
Delegation for relations with China;

DELLA VEDOVA, Benedetto
Committee on Economic and Monetary Affairs;
Delegation for relations with the countries of South Asia and
the South Asia Association for Regional Cooperation (SAARC);

DELL'UTRI, Marcello
Committee on Citizens' Freedoms and Rights, Justice and
Home Affairs;
Delegation to the EU-Ukraine and the EU-Moldova Parliamentary
Cooperation Committees and Delagation for relations with
Belarus;

DE MITA, Ciriaco
Committee on Constitutional Affairs;
Delegation to the EU-Russia Parliamentary Co-operation
Committee;

DI LELLO FINUOLI, Giuseppe
Committee on Citizens' Freedoms and Rights, Justice and
Home Affairs;
Committee on Petitions;
Delegation for relations with the countries of South America
and Mercosur;

DI PIETRO, Antonio
Committee on Budgetary Control;
Chairman Delegations to the EU-Kazakhstan, EU-Kyrgyzstan
and EU-Uzbekistan Parliamentary Cooperation Committees
and for relations with Tadjikistan, Turkmenistan and
Mongolia;

DUPUIS, Olivier
Committee on Constitutional Affairs;
Delegation for relations with the Member States of ASEAN,
south-east Asia and the Republic of Korea;
Delegation to the EU-Armenia, EU-Azerbaijan and EU-Georgia
Parliamentary Cooperation Committees;

EBNER, Michl
Committee on Agriculture and Rural Development;
Chairman Delegation to the EU-Slovenia Joint Parliamentary
Committee;

FATUZZO, Carlo
Committee on Employment and Social Affairs;
Delegation to the EU-Bulgaria Parliamentary Co-operation
Committee;

FAVA, Giovanni
Committee on Regional Policy, Transport and Tourism;
Delegation for relations with the countries of Central America
and Mexico;
ACP-EU Joint Parliamentary Assembly;

FERRI, Enrico
Committee on Employment and Social Affairs;
Delegation to the EU-Malta Joint Parliamentary Committee;

FIORI, Francesco
Committee on Agriculture and Rural Development;
Delegation for relations with the countries of South America
and Mercosur;

FORMENTINI, Marco
Committee on Employment and Social Affairs;
Delegation for relations with the Maghreb countries and the
Arab Maghreb Union;

GARGANI, Giuseppe
Chairman Committee on Legal Affairs and the Internal Market;
Delegation to the EU-Russia Parliamentary Cooperation
Committee;

GAWRONSKI, Jas
Committee on Foreign Affairs, Human Rights, Common
Security and Defence Policy;
Delegation for relations with the United States;

GEMELLI, Vitaliano
Chairman Committee on Petitions;
Committee on Development and Co-operation;
ACP-EU Joint Parliamentary Assembly;

GHILARDOTTI, Fiorella
Committee on Legal Affairs and the Internal Market;
Committee on Women's Rights and Equal Opportunities;
ACP-EU Joint Parliamentary Assembly;

GOBBO, Gian Paolo
Committee on Industry, External Trade, Research and Energy;
Delegation to the EU-Romania Joint Parliamentary Committee;

IMBENI, Renzo
Vice-President of the EP;
Committee on Culture, Youth, Education, the Media and Sport;
Delegation for relations with the United States;

LAVARRA, Vincenzo
Vice-Chairman Committee on Agriculture and Rural Development;
Committee on Fisheries;
Delegation to the EU-Malta Joint Parliamentary Committee
Delegation for relations with countires of South-East Europe;

LISI, Giorgio
Committee on Regional Policy, Transport and Tourism;
Committee on Fisheries;
Delegation for relations with countries of South-East Europe;

LOMBARDO, Raffele
Committee on Employment and Social Affairs;
Delegation to the EU-Turkey Joint Parliamentary Committee;

MANISCO, Lucio
Committee on Culture, Youth, Education, the Media and Sport;
Delegation for relations with the countries of Central America and Mexico;

MANTOVANI, Mario
Committee on Employment and Social Affairs;
Delegation for relations with China;

MARINI, Franco
Committee on Foreign Affairs, Human Rights, Common Security and Defence Policy;
Delegation for relations with the countries of South America and Mercosur;

MARTELLI, Claudio
Committee on Foreign Affairs, Human Rights, Common Security and Defence Policy;
Delegation for relations with countries of South-East Europe;

MASTELLA, Clemente
Committee on Employment and Social Affairs;
Vice-Chairman Delegation to the EU-Hungary Joint Parliamentary Committee;

MAURO, Mario
Vice-Chairman Committee on Culture, Youth, Education, the Media and Sport;
Delegation for relations with Australia and New Zealand;

MENNEA, Pietro-Paolo
Committee on Culture, Youth, Education, the Media and Sport;
Delegation for relations with countries of South-East Europe;

MENNITTI, Domenico
Committee on Culture, Youth, Education, the Media and Sport;
Chairman Delegation to the EU-Romania Joint Parliamentary Committee;

MESSNER, Reinhold
Committee on Foreign Affairs, Human Rights, Common Security and Defence Policy;
Delegation for relations with the countries of South Asia and the South Asia Association for Regional Co-operation (SAARC);

MORGANTINI, Luisa
Committee on Development and Co-operation;
Chairman Delegation for relations with the Palestinian Legislative Council;
Delegation for relations with the countries of South Asia and the South Asia Association for Regional Cooperation (SAARC);

MUSCARDINI, Cristiana
Committee on Foreign Affairs, Human Rights, Common Security and Defence Policy;
Delegation for relations with China;

MUSOTTO, Francesco
Committee on Regional Policy, Transport and Tourism;
ACP-EU Joint Parliamentary Assembly;

MUSSA, Antonio
Committee on Culture, Youth, Education, the Media and Sport;
Delegations to the EU-Kazakhstan, EU-Kyrgyzstan and EU-Uzbekistan Parliamentary Cooperation Committees and for relations with Tadjikistan, Turkmenistan and Mongolia;

MUSUMECI, Sebastiono (Nello)
Committee on Employment and Social Affairs;
Committee on Fisheries;
Delegation to the EU-Cyprus Joint Parliamentary Committee;

NAPOLETANO, Pasqualina
Committee on Foreign Affairs, Human Rights, Common Security and Defence Policy;
Vice-Chairman Delegation for relations with the Maghreb countries and the Arab Maghreb Union;

NAPOLITANO, Giorgio
Chairman Committee on Constitutional Affairs;
Delegation for relations with Israel;

NISTICO', Giuseppe
Committee on the Environment, Public Health and Consumer Policy;
Delegation to the EU-Bulgaria Joint Parliamentary Committee;

NOBILIA, Mauro
Committee on the Environment, Public Health and Consumer Policy;
Delegation to the EU-Slovak Republic Joint Parliamentary Committee;

PACIOTTI, Elena
Committee on Citizens' Freedoms and Rights, Justice and
Home Affairs;
Committee on Women's Rights and Equal Opportunities;

PANNELLA, Marco
Committee on Development and Co-operation;
ACP-EU Joint Parliamentary Assembly;

PASTORELLI, Paolo
Committee on Industry, External Trade, Research and Energy;
Delegation for relations with China;

PISICCHIO, Giuseppe
Committee on Budgets;
Vice-Chairman Delegation for relations with the Maghreb
countries and the Arab Maghreb Union;

PITTELLA, Giovanni
Committee on Budgets;
Delegation for relations with Australia and New Zealand;

PODESTÀ, Guido
Vice-President of the EP;
Committee on Budgets;
Delegation for relations with Switzerland, Iceland and Norway;

POLI BORTONE, Adriana
Committee on Regional Policy, Transport and Tourism;
Delegation for relations with the countries of South Asia and
the South Asia Association for Regional Cooperation (SAARC);
Delegation for relations with countries of South-East Europe;

PROCACCI, Giovanni
Committee on Agriculture and Rural Development;
Delegation for relations with China;

RUFFOLO, Giorgio
Committee on Culture, Youth, Education the Media and Sport;
Delegation to the EU-Russia Parliamentary Cooperation
Committee;

RUTELLI, Francesco
Committee on Citizens' Freedoms and Rights, Justice and
Home Affairs;
Delegation for relations with the United States;

SACCONI, Guido
Vice-Chairman Committee on the Environment, Public Health
and Consumer Policy;
Committee on Petitions;
Delegation to the EU-Turkey Joint Parliamentary Committee;

SANTINI, Giacomo
Vice-Chairman Committee on Citizens' Freedoms and Rights,
Justice and Home Affairs;
Delegation for relations with the countries of South America
and Mercosur;

SARTORI, Amalia
Committee on Foreign Affairs, Human Rights, Common
Security and Defence Policy;
Committee on Women's Rights and Equal Opportunities;
Vice-Chairman Delegation to the EU-Bulgaria Joint
Parliamentary Committee;

SBARBATI, Luciana
Committee on Budgets;
Committee on Petitions;
Delegation for relations with Israel;

SCAPAGNINI, Umberto
Committee on Industry, External Trade, Research and Energy;
Delegation for relations with the Palestinian Legislative Council;

SEGNI, Mariotto
Committee on Constitutional Affairs;
Vice-Chairman Delegation for relations with the countries of
Central America and Mexico;

SPERONI, Francesco
Committee on Foreign Affairs, Human Rights, Common
Security and Defence Policy;
ACP-EU Joint Parliamentary Assembly;

TAJANI, Antonio
Committee on Constitutional Affairs;
Delegation for relations with Israel;

TRENTIN, Bruno
Committee on Economic and Monetary Affairs;
Delegation for relations with the Palestinian Legislative
Council;

TURCHI, Franz
Vice-Chairman Committee on Budgets;
Delegation for relations with Israel;

TURCO, Maurizio
Committee on Citizens' Freedoms and Rights, Justice and
Home Affairs;
Delegation for relations with countries of South-East Europe;

VATTIMO, Gianni
Committee on Culture, Youth, Education, the Media and Sport;
Delegation for relations with South Africa;

VELTRONI, Valter
Committee on Citizens' Freedoms and Rights, Justice and
Home Affairs;

VINCI, Luigi
Committee on Foreign Affairs, Human Rights, Common
Security and Defence Policy;
ACP-EU Joint Parliamentary Assembly;

VOLCIC, Demetrio
Committee on Foreign Affairs, Human Rights, Common
Security and Defence Policy;
Vice-Chairman Delegation to the EU-Armenia, EU-Azerbaijan
and EU-Georgia Parliamentary Cooperation Committees;

ZAPPALÀ, Stefano
Committee on Legal Affairs and the Internal Market;
Vice-Chairman Delegation for relations with the NATO
Parliamentary Assembly;

LUXEMBOURG

FLESCH, Colette
Committee on Development and Cooperation
Committee on Industry, External Trade, Research and Energy;
ACP-EU Joint Parliamentary Assembly;

GOEBBELS, Robert
Committee on Economic and Monetary Affairs;
ACP-EU Joint Parliamentary Assembly;

LULLING, Astrid
Committee on Economic and Monetary Affairs;
Committee on Women's Rights and Equal Opportunities;
ACP-EU Joint Parliamentary Assembly;

POOS, Jacques
Quaestor of the EP;
Committee on Foreign Affairs, Human Rights, Common
Security and Defence Policy;
Delegation for relations with the Maghreb countries and the
Arab Maghreb Union;

SANTER, Jacques
Committee on Foreign Affairs, Human Rights, Common
Security and Defence Policy;
Delegation for relations with the countries of South Asia and
the South Asia Association for Regional Co-operation (SAARC);

TURMES, Claude
Committee on Industry, External Trade, Research and Energy;
Delegation to the EU-Russia Parliamentary Cooperation
Committee;

NETHERLANDS

BELDER, Bastiaan
Committee on Foreign Affairs, Human Rights, Common
Security and Defence Policy;
Delegation for relations with the Member States of ASEAN,
south-east Asia and the Republic of Korea;
Vice-Chairman Delegation for relations with the United States;

VAN DEN BERG, Margrietus
Vice-Chairman Committee on Development and Co-operation;
ACP-EU Joint Parliamentary Assembly;
Delegation for relations with the countries of Central America
and Mexico;

BLOKLAND, Hans
Committee on Economic and Monetary Affairs;
Committee on the Environment, Public Health and Consumer
Policy;
Vice-Chairman Delegation to the EU-Slovak Republic Joint
Parliamentary Committee;
Delegation to the European Economic Area Joint
Parliamentary Committee (EEA);

BOOGERD-QUAAK, Johanna
Vice-Chairman Committee on Citizens' Freedoms and Rights,
Justice and Home Affairs;
Delegation for relations with the Palestinian Legislative Council;

VAN DEN BOS, Bob
Committee on Foreign Affairs, Human Rights, Common
Security and Defence Policy;
ACP-EU Joint Parliamentary Assembly;

BOUWMAN, Theodorus
Chairman Committee on Employment and Social Affairs;
Delegation for relations with Japan;

BUITENWEG, Kathalijne
Committee on Budgets;
Delegation for relations with South Africa;

VAN DEN BURG, Ieke
Committee on Employment and Social Affairs;
Delegation for relations with Japan;

CORBEY, Dorette
Committee on the Environment, Public Health and Consumer
Policy;

VAN DAM, Rijk
Vice-Chairman Committee on Regional Policy, Transport and
Tourism;
Committee on Budgetary Control;
Delegation for relations with Israel;
Delegation for relations with the countries of South Asia and
the South Asia Association for Regional Cooperation (SAARC);

DOORN, Lambert
Committee on Legal Affairs and the Internal Market;
Delegation for relations with the member states of ASEAN,
South-East Asia and the Republic of Korea;

VAN HULTEN, Michiel
Committee on Budgetary Control;

LAGENDIJK, Joost
Committee on Foreign Affairs, Human Rights, Common Security and Defence Policy;
Chairman Delegation to the EU-Turkey Joint Parliamentary Committee;
Delegation for relations with South-East Europe;

MAAT, Albert Jean
Vice-Chairman Committee on Agriculture and Rural Development;
Delegations to the EU-Kazakhstan, EU-Kyrgyzstan and EU-Uzbekistan Parliamentary Cooperation Committees and for relations with Tadjikistan, Turkmenistan and Mongolia;

MAATEN, Jules
Committee on the Environment, Public Health and Consumer Policy;
Delegation for relations with the member states of ASEAN, South-East Asia and the Republic of Korea;

MAIJ-WEGGEN, Hanja
Committee on Constitutional Affairs;
ACP-EU Joint Parliamentary Assembly;

MANDERS, Toine
Committee on Legal Affairs and the Internal Market;
ACP-EU Joint Parliamentary Assembly;

MARTENS, Maria
Committee on Culture, Youth, Education, the Media and Sport;
Committee on Women's Rights and Equal Opportunities;
Delegation for relations with the countries of South Asia and the South Asia Association for Regional Co-operation (SAARC);

MEIJER, Erik
Committee on Regional Policy, Transport and Tourism;
Delegation to the EU-Slovak Republic Joint Parliamentary Committee;

MULDER, Jan
Committee on Budgets;
Delegation to the EU-Poland Joint Parliamentary Committee;

OOMEN-RUIJTEN, Ria
Committee on the Environment, Public Health and Consumer Policy;
Delegation for relations with South Africa;

OOSTLANDER, Arie
Committee on Foreign Affairs, Human Rights, Common Security and Defence Policy;
Delegation for relations with countries of South-East Europe;

PEIJS, Karla
Committee on Regional Policy, Transport and Tourism;
Delegation for relations with the United States;

PLOOIJ-VAN GORSEL, Elly
Committee on Industry, External Trade, Research and Energy;
Chairman Delegation for relations with China;

PRONK, Bartho
Committee on Employment and Social Affairs;
Delegation for relations with Switzerland, Iceland and Norway;

DE ROO, Alexander
Vice-Chairman Committee on the Environment, Public Health and Consumer Policy;
Delegation to the EU-Cyprus Joint Parliamentary Committee;

SANDERS-TEN-HOLTE, Marieke
Vice-Chairman Committee on Development and Co-operation;
Committee on Culture, Youth, Education, the Media and Sport;
Committee on Women's Rights and Equal Opportunities;
ACP-EU Joint Parliamentary Assembly;

SWIEBEL, Joke
Committee on Citizens' Freedoms and Rights, Justice and Home Affairs;
Committee on Women's Rights and Equal Opportunities;
Delegation for relations with Australia and New Zealand;

VAN VELZEN, W G
Committee on Industry, External Trade, Research and Energy;
Delegation to the EU-Poland Joint Parliamentary Committee;

VERMEER, Adriaan
Committee on Regional Policy, Transport and Tourism;
Vice-Chairman Delegation to the EU-Estonia Joint Parliamentary Committee;

WIERSMA, Jan
Committee on Foreign Affairs, Human Rights, Common Security and Defence Policy;
Committee on Petitions;
Chairman Delegation to the EU-Ukraine and the EU-Moldova Parliamentary Cooperation Committees and Delegation for relations with Belarus;
Delegation for relations with the NATO Parliamentary Assembly;

PORTUGAL

ALMEIDA GARRETT, Teresa
Committee on Constitutional Affairs;
Delegation for relations with the countries of South America and Mercosur;

BASTOS, Regina
Committee on Employment and Social Affairs;
Women's Rights and Equal Opportunities;
Delegations to the EU-Ukraine and the EU-Moldova Parliamentary Cooperation Committees and for relations with Belarus;

CAMPOS, Antonio
Committee on Agriculture and Rural Development;

european parliament

CANDAL, Carlos
Committee on Legal Affairs and the Internal Market;
Delegation for relations with the member states of ASEAN,
South-East Asia and the Republic of Korea;

CARRILHO, Maria
Committee on Development and Co-operation;
Chairman Delegation for relations with the countries of South
Asia and the South Asia Association for Regional Cooperation
(SAARC);

CASACA, Paulo
Vice-Chairman Committee on Budgetary Control;
Delegation for relations with Switzerland, Iceland and Norway;

COELHO, Carlos
Committee on Citizens' Freedoms and Rights, Justice and
Home Affairs;
Delegation to the EU-Czech Republic Joint Parliamentary
Committee;

CUNHA, Arlindo
Committee on Agriculture and Rural Development;
Committee on Fisheries;
ACP-EU Joint Parliamentary Assembly;

DAMIÃO, Elisa Maria
Committee on Employment and Social Affairs;
Delegation for relations with Canada;

FIGUEIREDO, Ilda
Committee on Employment and Social Affairs;
Delegation for relations with the Mashreq countries and the Gulf;

GRAÇA MOURA, Vasco
Vice-Chairman Committee on Culture, Youth, Education the
Media and Sport;

LAGE, Carlos
Committee on Fisheries;
Delegations to the EU-Kazakhstan, EU-Kyrgyzstan and EU-
Uzbekistan Parliamentary Cooperation Committees and for
relations with Tadjikistan, Turkmenistan and Mongolia;

MARINHO, Luis
Committee on Constitutional Affairs;
Delegation for relations with the countries of South America
and Mercosur;

MARQUES, Sérgio
Committee on Regional Policy, Transport and Tourism;
Delegation for relations with Australia and New Zealand;

MIRANDA, Joaquim
Chairman Committee on Development and Co-operation;
ACP-EU Joint Parliamentary Assembly;

MOREIRA DA SILVA, Jorge
Committee on the Environment, Public Health and Consumer
Policy;
Delegation to the EU-Russia Parliamentary Cooperation
Committee;

PACHECO PEREIRA, José
Vice-President of the EP;
Committee on Foreign Affairs, Human Rights, Common
Security and Defence Policy;
Delegation for relations with the United States;

PISCARRETA, Joaquim
Committee on Budgets;
Delegation to the EU-Lithuania Joint Parliamentary Committee;
Vice-Chairman Delegation for relations with the Member
States of ASEAN, South-East Asia and the Republic of Korea;

QUEIRÓ, Luis
Committee on Foreign Affairs, Human Rights, Common
Security and Defence Policy;
Delegation for relations with the countries of South America
and Mercosur;

RIBEIRO E CASTRO, José
Committee on Citizens' Freedoms and Rights, Justice and
Home Affairs;
ACP-EU Joint Parliamentary Assembly;

DOS SANTOS, Manuel António
Committee on Budgets;
Delegation for relations with the Maghreb countries and the
Arab Maghreb Union;

SOARES, Mário
Committee on Foreign Affairs, Human Rights, Common
Security and Defence Policy;

SOUSA PINTO, Sérgio
Committee on Citizens' Freedoms and Rights, Justice and
Home Affairs;
Delegation for relations with Australia and New Zealand;

TORRES MARQUES, Helena
Committee on Economic and Monetary Affairs;
Committee on Women's Rights and Equal Opportunities;
ACP-EU Joint Parliamentary Assembly;

VAIRINHOS, Joaquim
Committee on Regional Policy, Transport and Tourism;
ACP-EU Joint Parliamentary Assembly;

SPAIN

APARICIO SÁNCHEZ, Pedro
Committee on Culture, Youth, Education, the Media and Sport;
Delegation for relations with the countries of Central America and Mexico;

AVILÉS PEREA, Maria Antonia
Committee on Budgetary Control;
Committee on Women's Rights and Equal Opportunities;
Delegation for relations with the Palestinian Legislative Council;

AYUSO GONZÁLES, Maria del Pilar
Committee on the Environment, Public Health and Consumer Policy;
ACP-EU Joint Parliamentary Assembly;

BARÓN CRESPO, Enrique
Chairman Group of the Party of European Socialists;
Committee on Constitutional Affairs;

BAUTISTA OJEDA, Carlos
Committee on Agriculture and Rural Development;
Delegation for relations with the Maghreb countries and the Arab Maghreb Union;

BAYONA DE PEROGORDO, Juan José
Committee on Budgetary Control;
Delegation to the EU-Armenia, EU-Azerbaijan and EU-Georgia Parliamentary Cooperation Committees;

BERENGUER FUSTER, Luis
Committee on Industry, External Trade, Research and Energy;
Delegation for relations with the member states of ASEAN, South-East Asia and the Republic of Korea;

CAMISÓN ASENSIO, Felipe
Committee on Regional Policy, Transport and Tourism;
Committee on Petitions;
Delegation for relations with the member states of ASEAN, South-East Asia and the Republic of Korea;

CARNERO GONZÁLEZ, Carlos
Committee on Constitutional Affairs;
Delegation to the EU-Turkey Joint Parliamentary Committee;

CERCAS, Alejandro
Committee on Employment and Social Affairs;
Delegation for relations with Israel;

CERDEIRA MORTERERO, Carmen
Committee on Citizens' Freedoms and Rights, Justice and Home Affairs;
Delegation for relations with the countries of South America and Mercosur;

COLOM I NAVAL, Joan
Vice-President of the EP;
Committee on Budgets;
Delegation for relations with China;

DÍEZ GONZÁLEZ, Rosa
Committee on Foreign Affairs, Human Rights, Common Security and Defence Policy;
Delegation for relations with the Maghreb countries and the Arab Maghreb Union;

DÜHRKOP DÜHRKOP, Bárbara
Committee on Budgets;
Delegation to the EU-Ukraine and the EU-Moldova Parliamentary Cooperation Committees and Delegation for relations with Belarus;
Delegation to the European Economic Area (EEA) Joint Parliamentary Committee;

FERNÁNDEZ MARTÍN, Fernando
Committee on Development and Co-operation;
ACP-EU Joint Parliamentary Assembly;

FERRER, Concepció
Committee on Industry, External Trade, Research and Energy;
Vice-President ACP-EU Joint Parliamentary Assembly;

GALEOTE QUECEDO, Gerardo
Committee on Foreign Affairs, Human Rights, Common Security and Defence Policy;
Chairman Delegation for relations with the Maghreb countries and the Arab Maghreb Union;
Delegation for relations with Israel;

GARCÍA-MARAGALLO Y MARFIL, José Manuel
Vice-Chairman Committee on Economic and Monetary Affairs;
Delegation for relations with the countries of Central America and Mexico;

GARCÍA-ORCOYEN TORMO, Cristina
Committee on the Environment, Public Health and Consumer Policy;
Delegation to the European Economic Area Joint Parliamentary Committee (EEA);

GARRIGA POLLEDO, Salvador
Committee on Budgets;
Delegation for relations with the Maghreb countries and the Arab Maghreb Union;

GASÒLIBA I BÖHM, Carles-Alfred
Committee on Economic and Monetary Affairs;
Delegation for relations with the countries of South America and Mercosur;

GIL-ROBLES GIL-DELGADO, José María
Committee on Constitutional Affairs;
Committee on Legal Affairs and the Internal Market;
Chairman Delegation to the EU-Bulgaria Joint Parliamentary
Committee;

GONZÁLEZ ÁLVAREZ, Laura
Committee on the Environment, Public Health and Consumer Policy;
Committee on Petitions;
Delegation for relations with the countries of Central America
and Mexico;

GOROSTIAGA ATXALANDABASO, Koldo
Committee on Employment and Social Affairs;
Committee on Women's Rights and Equal Opportunities;
Delegation for relations with the countries of Central America
and Mexico;

GUTIÉRREZ-CORTINES, Cristina
Committee on the Environment, Public Health and Consumer Policy;
Vice-Chairman Delegation for relations with Israel;

HERRANZ GARCÍA, María Esther
Committee on Budgets;
Delegation to the EU-Lithuania Joint Parliamentary Committee;

HERNÁNDEZ MOLLAR, Jorge
Chairman Committee on Citizens' Freedoms and Rights,
Justice and Home Affairs;
Vice-Chairman Delegation for relations with the Mashreq
countries and the Gulf;

IZQUIERDO COLLADO, Juan de Dio
Committee on Regional Policy, Transport and Tourism;
Delegation for relations with the Palestinian Legislative Council;

IZQUIERDO ROJO, María
Committee on Agriculture and Rural Development;
Delegation to the EU-Malta Joint Parliamentary Committee;

JOVÉ PEREZ, Salvador
Committee on Agriculture and Rural Development;
Committee on Fisheries;
Delegation for relations with China;

MARSET CAMPOS, Pedro
Committee on Foreign Affairs, Human Rights, Common
Security and Defence Policy;
Vice-Chairman Delegation for relations with the countries of
South America and Mercosur;

MARTÍNEZ MARTÍNEZ, Miguel Angel
Committee on Development and Co-operation;
Vice-President ACP-EU Joint Parliamentary Assembly;

MAYOL I RAYNAL, Miguel
Committee on Economic and Monetary Affairs;
Delegation for relations with the countries of Central America
and Mexico;

MEDINA ORTEGA, Manuel
Committee on Legal Affairs and the Internal Market;
Delegation for relations with the countries of South America
and Mercosur;

MÉNDEZ DE VIGO, Iñigo
Committee on Constitutional Affairs;

MENDILUCE PEREIRO, José
Committee on Culture, Youth, Education, the Media and Sport;
ACP-EU Joint Parliamentary Assembly;

MENÉNDEZ DEL VALLE, Emilio
Committee on Foreign Affairs, Human Rights, Common
Security and Defence Policy;
Vice-Chairman Delegation for relations with the Palestinian
Legislative Council;
ACP-EU Joint Parliamentary Assembly;

MIGUÉLEZ RAMOS, Rosa
Vice-Chairman Committee on Fisheries;
Committee on Regional Policy, Transport and Tourism;
Delegation for relations with Switzerland, Iceland and Norway;

MONSONÍS DOMINGO, Enrique

NARANJO ESCOBAR, Juan
Committee on Budgets;

NOGUEIRA ROMÁN, Camilo
Committee on Regional Policy, Transport and Tourism;
Delegation for relations with the United States;

OBIOLS I GERMÀ, Raimon
Committee on Foreign Affairs, Human Rights, Common
Security and Defence Policy;
Delegation for relations with the countries of Central America
and Mexico;

OJEDA SANZ, Juan
Committee on Culture, Youth, Education, the Media and Sport;
Delegation for relations with South-East Europe;

OREJA ARBURÚA, Marcelino
Committee on Citizens' Freedoms and Rights, Justice and
Home Affairs;
Delegation for relations with the Palestinian Legislative Council;

ORTUONDO LARREA, Josu
Committee on Regional Policy, Transport and Tourism;
Delegation for relations with the countries of South America
and Mercosur;

PERÉZ ÁLVAREZ, Manual
Committee on Employment and Social Affairs;
Committee on Fisheries;
Delegation for relations with Canada;

PÉREZ ROYO, Fernando
Committee on Economic and Monetary Affairs;
Delegation for relations with South Africa;

POMÉS RUIZ, Jose Javier
Committee on Regional Policy, Transport and Tourism;
Delegation for relations with the countries of Central America and Mexico;

PUERTA, Alonso
Vice-President of the EP;
Committee on Regional Policy, Transport and Tourism;
Delegation for relations with the countries of Central America and Mexico;

REDONDO JIMÉNEZ, Encarnacion
Committee on Agriculture and Rural Development;
Delegation for relations with the countries of South America and Mercosur;

RIDRUEJO, Mónica
Committee on Economic and Monetary Affairs;
Delegation for relations with countries of South-East Europe;

RIPOL Y MARTÍNEZ DE BEDOYA, Carlos
Committee on Regional Policy, Transport and Tourism;
Delegation for relations with the countries of Central America and Mexico;

RODRÍGUEZ RAMOS, María
Vice-Chairman Committee on Agriculture and Rural Development;
Committee on Women's Rights and Equal Opportunities;
Delegation for relations with Canada;

SALAFRANCA SÁNCHEZ-NEYRA, José Ignacio
Committee on Foreign Affairs, Human Rights, Common Security and Defence Policy;
Delegation for relations with the countries of South America and Mercosur;

SAUQUILLO PÉREZ DEL ARCO, Francisca
Committee on Development and Co-operation;
ACP-EU Joint Parliamentary Assembly;

SORNOSA MARTÍNEZ, Maria
Committee on the Environment, Public Health and Consumer Policy;
Committee on Petitions;
Delegation to the EU-Czech Republic Joint Parliamentary Committee;

TERRÓN I CUSÍ, Anna
Committee on Citizens' Freedoms and Rights, Justice and Home Affairs;
Delegation for relations with the Mashreq countries and the Gulf;

VALDIVIELSO DE CUÉ, Jaime
Vice-Chairman Committee on Industry, External Trade, Research and Energy;
Delegation to the EU-Russia Parliamentary Cooperation Committee;

VALENCIANO MARTÍNEZ-OROZCO, María
Committee on the Environment, Public Health and Consumer Policy;
Committee on Women's Rights and Equal Opportunities;
ACP-EU Joint Parliamentary Assembly;

VALLVÉ, Joan
Committee on Foreign Affairs, Human Rights, Common Security and Defence Policy;

VARELA SUANZES-CARPEGNA, Daniel
Committee on Fisheries;
Delegation for relations with Japan;

VIDAL-QUADRAS ROCA, Alejo
Vice-President of the EP;
Committee on Industry, External Trade, Research and Energy;
ACP-EU Joint Parliamentary Assembly;

WESTENDORP Y CABEZA, Carlos
Chairman Committee on Industry, External Trade, Research and Energy;
Delegation for relations with the United States;

ZABELL, Theresa
Vice-Chairman Committee on Culture, Youth, Education, the Media and Sport;
Delegation to the EU-Malta Joint Parliamentary Committee;

SWEDEN

ANDERSSON, Jan
Committee on Employment and Social Affairs;
Chairman Delegation for relations with Japan;

ARVIDSSON, Per-Arne
Committee on Foreign Affairs, Human Rights, Common Security and Defence Policy;
Delegation to the EU-Czech Republic Joint Parliamentary Committee;

CEDERSCHIÖLD, Charlotte
Vice-President of the EP;
Committee on Citizens' Freedoms and Rights, Justice and Home Affairs;
Delegation for relations with the United States;

ERIKSSON, Marianne
Vice-Chairman Committee on Women's Rights and Equal
Opportunities;
Committee on Industry, External Trade, Research and Energy;
Delegation for relations with the Maghreb countries and the
Arab Maghreb Union;

FÄRM, Göran
Committee on Budgets;
Delegation for relations with countries of South-East Europe;

GAHRTON, Per
Committee on Foreign Affairs, Human Rights, Common
Security and Defence Policy;
Chairman Delegation for relations with China;

GRÖNFELDT BERGMAN, Lisbeth
Committee on Economic and Monetary Affairs;
Delegation to the EU-Lithuania Joint Parliamentary Committee;

HEDKVIST PETERSEN, Ewa
Committee on Regional Policy, Transport and Tourism;
Delegation to the EU-Russia Parliamentary Co-operation
Committee;

KARLSSON, Hans
Committee on Industry, External Trade, Research and Energy;
Committee on Women's Rights and Equal Opportunities;
Delegation to the EU-Estonia Joint Parliamentary Committee;

MALMSTRÖM, Cecilia
Committee on Foreign Affairs, Human Rights, Common
Security and Defence Policy;
Vice-Chairman Delegation to the EU-Hungary Joint
Parliamentary Committee;
Delegation for relations with the countries of Central America
and Mexico;

OLSSON, Karl Erik
Committee on Agriculture and Rural Development;
Delegation to the EU-Czech Republic Joint Parliamentary
Committee;

PAULSEN, Marit
Committee on the Environment, Public Health and Consumer
Policy;
Delegation for relations with Australia and New Zealand;

SACRÉDEUS, Lennart
Committee on Employment and Social Affairs;
Delegation to the EU-Ukraine and the EU-Moldova
Parliamentary Cooperation Committees and Delegation for
relations with Belarus;

SANDBERG-FRIES, Yvonne
Committee on the Environment, Public Health and Consumer
Policy;
Delegation for relations with the Member States of ASEAN,
south-east Asia and the Republic of Korea;

SCHMID, Herman
Committee on Employment and Social Affairs;
Delegation for relations with the United States;

SCHMIDT, Olle
Committee on Economic and Monetary Affairs;
Delegation to the EU-Slovak Republic Joint Parliamentary
Committee;
Delegation for relations with Japan;

SCHÖRLING, Inger
Committee on the Environment, Public Health and Consumer
Policy;
ACP-EU Joint Parliamentary Assembly;

SJÖSTEDT, Jonas
Committee on the Environment, Public Health and Consumer
Policy;
ACP-EU Joint Parliamentary Assembly;

STENMARCK, Per
Committee on Budgets;
Chairman Delegation to the EU-Estonia Joint Parliamentary
Committee;

THEORIN, Maj
Committee on Development and Co-operation;
Vice-President ACP-EU Joint Parliamentary Assembly;

WACHTMEISTER, Peder
Committee on the Environment, Public Health and Consumer
Policy;
Delegation to the EU-Poland Joint Parliamentary Committee;

WIJKMAN, Anders
Vice-Chairman Committee on Development and Co-operation;
ACP-EU Joint Parliamentary Assembly;

UNITED KINGDOM*

ADAM, Gordon
Committee on Agriculture and Rural Development;
Chairman Delegation to the EU-Lithuania Joint Parliamentary
Committee;
Delegation to the EU-Ukraine and the EU-Moldova
Parliamentary Cooperation Committees and Delegation for
relations with Belarus;

ATKINS, Sir Robert
Committee on Industry, External Trade, Research and Energy;
Delegation for relations with South Africa;

* addresses for UK MEPs pp. 93-100

ATTWOOLL, Elspeth
Committee on Employment and Social Affairs;
Committee on Fisheries;
Delegation for relations with Canada;

BALFE, Richard
Quaestor of the EP;
Committee on Development and Co-operation;
ACP-EU Joint Parliamentary Assembly;

BEAZLEY, Christopher
Committee on Culture, Youth, Education, the Media and Sport;
Chairman Delegation to the EU-Estonia Joint Parliamentary Committee;

BETHELL, Lord
Committee on Citizens' Freedoms and Rights, Justice and Home Affairs;
Vice-Chairman Delegation to the EU-Russia Joint Parliamentary Committee;

BOOTH, Graham

BOWE, David
Committee on the Environment, Public Health and Consumer Policy;
Delegation for relations with China;

BOWIS, John
Committee on Development and Cooperation;
Committee on the Environment, Public Health and Consumer Policy;
Vice-Chairman Delegations to the EU-Kazakhstan, EU-Kyrgyzstan and EU-Uzbekistan Parliamentary Cooperation Committees and for relations with Tadjikistan, Turkmenistan and Mongolia;
ACP-EU Joint Parliamentary Assembly;

BRADBOURN, Philip
Committee on Regional Policy, Transport and Tourism;
Delegation for relations with Canada;

BUSHILL-MATTHEWS, Philip
Committee on Employment and Social Affairs;
Delegation for relations with the Mashreq countries and the Gulf;

CALLANAN, Martin
Committee on the Environment, Public Health and Consumer Policy;
Delegations to the EU-Kazakhstan, EU-Kyrgyzstan and EU-Uzbekistan Parliamentary Cooperation Committees and for relations with Tadjikistan, Turkmenistan and Mongolia;
ACP-EU Joint Parliamentary Assembly;

CASHMAN, Michael
Committee on Citizens' Freedoms and Rights, Justice and Home Affairs;
Delegation to the EU-Bulgaria Joint Parliamentary Committee;

CHICHESTER, Giles
Committee on Industry, External Trade, Research and Energy;
Delegation for relations with Australia and New Zealand;

CLEGG, Nick
Committee on Industry, External Trade, Research and Energy;
Delegation for relations with the Maghreb countries and the Arab Maghreb Union;

CORBETT, Richard
Committee on Constitutional Affairs;
Delegation for relations with the member states of ASEAN, South-East Asia and the Republic of Korea;
Delegations to the EU-Kazakhstan, EU-Kyrgyzstan and EU-Uzbekistan Parliamentary Cooperation Committees and for relations with Tadjikistan, Turkmenistan and Mongolia;

CORRIE, John
Committee on Development and Co-operation;
Vice-President ACP-EU Joint Parliamentary Assembly;

DAVIES, Chris
Committee on the Environment, Public Health and Consumer Policy;
Delegation to the EU-Cyprus Joint Parliamentary Committee;

DEVA, Nirj
Committee on Development and Co-operation;
Delegation for relations with the Member States of ASEAN, South-East Asia and the Republic of Korea;

DOVER, Den
Committee on Budgets;
Vice-Chairman Delegation to the EU-Malta Joint Parliamentary Committee;

DUFF, Andrew
Committee on Constitutional Affairs;
Vice-Chairman Delegation to the EU-Turkey Joint Parliamentary Committee;

ELLES, James
Committee on Budgets;
Delegation to the EU-Cyprus Joint Parliamentary Committee;

EVANS, Jill
Vice-Chairman Committee on Women's Rights and Equal Opportunities;
Committee on Employment and Social Affairs;
Delegation to the EU-Lithuania Joint Parliamentary Committee;

EVANS, Jonathan
Committee on Economic and Monetary Affairs;
Delegation for relations with Japan;

european parliament

EVANS, Robert
Vice-Chairman Committee on Citizens' Freedoms and Rights,
Justice and Home Affairs;
Delegation for relations with the countries of South Asia and
the South Asia Association for Regional Co-operation (SAARC);

FARAGE, Nigel
Committee on Fisheries;
Delegation to the EU-Malta Joint Parliamentary Committee;

FORD, Glyn
Committee on Foreign Affairs, Human Rights, Common
Security and Defence Policy;
Committee on Petitions;
Delegation for relations with Japan;
Delegations to the EU-Kazakhstan, EU-Kyrgyzstan and EU-
Uzbekistan Parliamentary Cooperation Committees and for
relations with Tadjikistan, Turkmenistan and Mongolia;

FOSTER, Jacqueline
Committee on Regional Policy, Transport and Tourism;
ACP-EU Joint Parliamentary Assembly;

GILL, Neena
Committee on Budgets;
Vice-Chairman Delegation for relations with the countries of
South Asia and the South Asia Association for Regional
Cooperation (SAARC);

GOODWILL, Robert
Committee on the Environment, Public Health and Consumer
Policy;
Committee on Women's Rights and Equal Opportunities;
Delegation to the EU-Ukraine and the EU-Moldova
Parliamentary Cooperation Committees and Delegation for
relations with Belarus;

HANNAN, Daniel
Committee on Constitutional Affairs;
Delegation for relations with the countries of Central America
and Mexico;

HARBOUR, Malcolm
Committee on Legal Affairs and the Internal Market;
Delegation for relations with Japan;

HEATON-HARRIS, Christopher
Committee on Budgetary Control;
Delegation for relations with the NATO Parliamentary Assembly;

HELMER, Roger
Committee on Industry, External Trade, Research and Energy;
Delegation for relations with the member states of ASEAN,
South-East Asia and the Republic of Korea;

HONEYBALL, Mary
Committee on Economic and Monetary Affairs;
Committee on Women's Rights and Equal Opportunities;
Delegation to the EU-Cyprus Joint Parliamentary Committee;

HOWITT, Richard
Committee on Development and Co-operation;
ACP-EU Joint Parliamentary Assembly;

HUDGHTON, Ian
Committee on Budgets;
Committee on Fisheries;
Delegation to the European Economic Area (EEA) Joint
Parliamentary Committee;

HUGHES, Stephen
Committee on Employment and Social Affairs;
Delegation to the EU-Russia Parliamentary Co-operation
Committee;

HUHNE, Chris
Committee on Economic and Monetary Affairs;
Delegation for relations with the Member States of ASEAN,
South-East Asia and the Republic of Korea;

HUME, John
Committee on Regional Policy, Transport and Tourism;

INGLEWOOD, Lord
Committee on Legal Affairs and the Internal Market;
Committee on Constitutional Affairs;
Vice-Chairman Delegation for relations with China;

JACKSON, Caroline
Chairman Committee on the Environment, Public Health and
Consumer Policy;

KHANBHAI, Bashir
Committee on Industry, External Trade, Research and Energy;
ACP-EU Joint Parliamentary Assembly;
Delegation to the EU-Armenia, EU-Azerbaijan and EU-Georgia
Parliamentary Cooperation Committees;

KINNOCK, Glenys
Committee on Development and Co-operation;
Co-President ACP-EU Joint Parliamentary Assembly;

KIRKHOPE, Timothy
Committee on Citizens' Freedoms and Rights, Justice and
Home Affairs;
Vice-Chairman Delegation to the European Economic Area
Joint Parliamentary Committee (EEA);

LAMBERT, Jean
Committee on Employment and Social Affairs;
Committee on Petitions;
Delegation to the EU-Malta Parliamentary Co-operation
Committee;

LUCAS, Caroline
Committee on Industry, External Trade, Research and Energy;
ACP-EU Joint Parliamentary Assembly;

Brussels tel +32 22 84 21 11 • Strasbourg tel +33 3 88 17 40 01

LUDFORD, Baroness Sarah
Committee on Citizens' Freedoms and Rights, Justice and Home Affairs;
Delegation for relations with countries of South-East Europe;

LYNNE, Liz
Committee on Employment and Social Affairs;
Delegation for relations with the countries of South Asia and the South Asia Association for Regional Co-operation (SAARC);

MacCORMICK, Professor Sir Neil
Committee on Legal Affairs and the Internal Market;
Delegation to the EU-Romania Joint Parliamentary Committee;

MARTIN, David
Vice-President of the EP;
Committee on Economic and Monetary Affairs;
Delegation for relations with Canada;

McAVAN, Linda
Committee on Foreign Affairs, Human Rights, Common Security and Defence Policy;

McCARTHY, Arlene
Committee on Legal Affairs and the Internal Market;
ACP-EU Joint Parliamentary Assembly;

McMILLAN-SCOTT, Edward
Committee on Budgets;
Delegation to the EU-Poland Joint Parliamentary Committee;

McNALLY, Eryl
Committee on Industry, External Trade, Research and Energy;
Delegation for relations with the countries of South America and Mercosur;

MILLER, Bill
Vice-Chairman Committee on Legal Affairs and the Internal Market;
Delegation to the EU-Latvia Joint Parliamentary Committee;

MORAES, Claude
Committee on Employment and Social Affairs;
Vice-Chairman Delegation for relations with South Africa;

MORGAN, Eluned
Committee on Budgetary Control;
Delegation for relations with the Mashreq countries and the Gulf;

MURPHY, Simon
Committee on Budgets;
Delegation to the EU-Slovak Republic Joint Parliamentary Committee;

NEWTON-DUNN, Bill
Committee on Citizens' Freedoms and Rights, Justice and Home Affairs;
Delegation for relations with the Palestinian Legislative Council;
Delegation to the EU-Armenia, EU-Azerbaijan and EU-Georgia Parliamentary Cooperation Committees;
Delegation to the EU-Russia Parliamentary Cooperation Committee;

NICHOLSON, James
Committee on Regional Policy, Transport and Tourism;
Chairman Delegation for relations with the United States;

NICHOLSON OF WINTERBOURNE, Baroness
Vice-Chairman Committee on Foreign Affairs, Human Rights, Common Security and Defence Policy;
Delegation for relations with the Mashreq countries and the Gulf;

O'TOOLE, Barbara
Committee on Culture, Youth, Education, the Media and Sport;
Delegation to the EU-Poland Joint Parliamentary Committee;

PAISLEY, Rev. Ian
Committee on Development and Co-operation;
Delegation to the EU-Estonia Joint Parliamentary Committee;

PARISH, Neil
Committee on Agriculture and Rural Development;
Delegation for relations with Israel;

PERRY, Roy
Vice-Chairman Committee on Petitions;
Committee on Culture, Youth, Education, the Media and Sport;
Delegation for relations with the Palestinian Legislative Council;

PROVAN, James
Vice-President of the EP;
Committee on Women's Rights and Equal Opportunities;
Committee on Employment and Social Affairs;
Delegation to the EU-Slovenia Joint Parliamentary Committee;

PURVIS, John
Committee on Industry, External Trade, Research and Energy;
Vice-Chairman Committee on Economic and Monetary Affairs;
Delegation for relations with the Mashreq countries and the Gulf;

READ, Mel
Committee on Industry, External Trade, Research and Energy;
Delegation for relations with the United States;

SIMPSON, Brian
Committee on Regional Policy, Transport and Tourism;
Delegation for relations with Switzerland, Iceland and Norway;

SKINNER, Peter
Committee on Economic and Monetary Affairs;
Delegation for relations with the United States;

STEVENSON, Struan
Chairman Committee on Fisheries;
Delegation for relations with China;

STIHLER, Catherine
Committee on the Environment, Public Health and Consumer Policy;
Committee on Fisheries;
Delegation to the EU-Hungary Joint Parliamentary Committee;

STOCKTON, Earl of
Committee on Petitions;
Delegation for relations with the countries of South Asia and the South Asia Association for Regional Cooperation (SAARC);

STURDY, Robert
Committee on Agriculture and Rural Development;
Temporary Committee on foot and mouth disease;
Chairman Delegation for relations with Australia and New Zealand;

SUMBERG, David
Committee on Foreign Affairs, Human Rights, Common Security and Defence Policy;
Delegation for relations with the United States;

TANNOCK, Charles
Committee on Foreign Affairs, Human Rights, Common Security and Defence Policy;
Delegation to the EU-Slovak Republic Joint Parliamentary Committee;
Delegation to the EU-Ukraine and the EU-Moldova Parliamentary Cooperation Committees and Delegation for relations with Belarus;

TITFORD, Jeffrey
Committee on Budgetary Control;

TITLEY, Gary
Committee on Industry, External Trade, Research and Energy;
Delegation to the European Economic Area (EEA) Joint Parliamentary Committee;

VAN ORDEN, Geoffrey
Vice-Chairman Committee on Foreign Affairs, Human Rights, Common Security and Defence Policy;
Delegation to the EU-Turkey Joint Parliamentary Committee;

VILLIERS, Theresa
Committee on Economic and Monetary Affairs;
Delegation to the EU-Cyprus Joint Parliamentary Committee;

WALLIS, Diana
Committee on Legal Affairs and the Internal Market;
Vice-Chairman Delegation for relations with Switzerland, Iceland and Norway;
Delegation to the European Economic Area Joint Parliamentary Committee (EEA);

WATSON, Graham

WATTS, Mark
Committee on Regional Policy, Transport and Tourism;
Vice-Chairman Delegation to the EU-Malta Joint Parliamentary Committee;

WHITEHEAD, Philip
Committee on the Environment, Public Health and Consumer Policy;
Delegation to the EU-Czech Republic Joint Parliamentary Committee;

WYN, Eurig
Committee on Culture, Youth, Education, the Media and Sport;
Delegation to the EU-Czech Republic Joint Parliamentary Committee;

WYNN, Terence
Chairman Committee on Budgets;
Delegation for relations with Australia and New Zealand;

contact details for uk meps by region

east midlands

Conservative

Mr Christopher HEATON-HARRIS MEP
Blaby Conservative Association
35 Lutterworth Road
Blaby, Leicester LE8 4DW
Tel: 0845 234 0059
Tel/Fax: 0183 272 0098 (Constituency Secretary)
E-mail: cheaton@europarl.eu.int

Mr Roger HELMER MEP
Blaby Conservative Association
35 Lutterworth Road
Blaby, Leicester LE8 4DW
Tel: 0845 234 0059/0116 277 9992
Fax: 0116 278 6664
E-mail: rhelmer@europarl.eu.int

Labour

Mrs Mel READ MEP
East Midlands Labour MEPs - Regional Centre
23 Barratt Lane
Attenborough
Nottingham NG9 6AD
Tel: 0115 922 0624
Fax: 0115 922 0621
E-mail: readm@labmeps-emids.fsnet.co.uk

Mr Phillip WHITEHEAD MEP
East Midlands Labour MEPs - Regional Centre
23 Barratt Lane
Attenborough
Nottingham NG9 6AD
Tel: 0115 922 0624
Fax: 0115 922 0621
E-mail: whiteheadp@labmeps-emids.fsnet.co.uk

Liberal Democrat

Mr Nicholas CLEGG MEP
17-21 High Street
Ruddington
Nottinghamshire NG11 6DT
Tel: 0115 846 0661/2
Fax: 0115 846 1769
E-mail: ld_eastmidland@cix.co.uk

Mr Bill NEWTON-DUNN MEP
10 Church Lane
Navenby
Lincoln LN5 0EG
Tel: 0152 281 0812
E-mail: wnewton@europarl.eu.int

eastern

Conservative

Mr Christopher BEAZLEY MEP
c/o Hertford & Stortford Conservative Association
4a Swains Mill
Crane Mead, Ware
Hertfordshire SG12 9PY
Tel: 0192 046 3064
Fax: 0192 046 3064
E-mail: cbeazley@europarl.eu.int

Mr Bashir KHANBHAI MEP
57 Peninsula Cottage
Staitheway Road
Wroxham
Norfolk NR12 8RN
Tel: 0032 2 284 7953
Fax: 0032 2 284 9953
E-mail: bkhanbhai@europarl.eu.int

Mr Robert STURDY MEP
153 St Neots Road
Hardwick
Cambridge CB3 7QJ
Tel: 0195 421 1790
Fax: 0195 421 1786
E-mail: rsturdy@tory.org
E-mail: rsturdy@europarl.eu.int

Mr Geoffrey VAN ORDEN MEP
Conservative Office
88 Rectory Lane
Chelmsford CM1 1RF
Tel: 0124 534 5141 / 5188
Tel: 00 32 2 284 5332 (Brussels)
Fax: 0124 526 9757
Fax: 00 32 2 284 9332 (Brussels)
E-mail: gvanorden@europarl.eu.int

Labour

Mr Richard HOWITT MEP
The Labour European Office
The Labour Hall
Collingwood Road
Witham
Essex CM8 2EE
Tel: 0137 650 1700
Fax: 0137 650 1900
E-mail: richard.howitt@geo2.poptel.org.uk

Mrs Eryl McNALLY MEP
European Office
270 St Albans Road
Watford
Herts WD24 6PE
Tel: 0192 324 2102
Fax: 0192 324 2063
E-mail: emcnally@europarl.eu.int

Liberal Democrat

Mr Andrew DUFF MEP
Orwell House
Cowley Road
Cambridge CB4 0PP
Tel: 0122 356 6700
Fax: 0122 356 6698
E-mail: mep@andrewduffmep.org

UK Independence Party

Mr Jeffrey TITFORD MEP
Rooms 1 & 2, Rochester House
145 New London Road
Chelmsford
Essex CM2 0QT
Tel: 0124 526 6466/525 1651
Fax: 0124 525 2071
or
European Parliament
Room ASP 7H342
B-1047 Brussels
E-mail: ukipeast@globalnet.co.uk
E-mail: jtitford@aspects.net

london

Conservative

Mr Richard BALFE MEP
28 Honeyden Road
Sidcup
Kent DA14 5LX
Tel: 0208 302 1405
Fax: 0208 302 1427
E-mail: rbalfe@honeyden.fsnet.co.uk

Lord BETHELL MEP
Conservative Central Office
32 Smith Square
London SW1P 3HH
Tel: 0207 821 1687
Fax: 0184 423 7821
E-mail: nikbeth@aol.com

Mr John BOWIS OBE MEP
PO Box 262
New Malden
Surrey KT3 4EA
Tel: 0208 949 2555
Fax: 0208 395 7463
E-mail: johnbowis@aol.com
E-mail: jbowis@europarl.eu.int

Dr Charles TANNOCK MEP
Conservative Central Office
32 Smith Square
London SW1P 3HH
Tel: 0207 984 8235/8231
Fax: 0207 984 8292
E-mail: ctannock@europarl.eu.int
E-mail: ctannock@conservatives.com

Mrs Theresa VILLIERS MEP
Conservative Central Office
32 Smith Square,
London SW1P 3HH
Tel: 0207 984 8227
Fax: 0207 984 8292
E-mail: tvilliers@conservatives.com

Labour

Mr Robert EVANS MEP
101 High Street
Feltham
Middx TW13 4HG
Tel: 0208 890 1818
Fax: 0208 890 1628
E-mail: robertevans.mep@btclick.com
E-mail: r.evans.mep@geo2.poptel.org.uk

Mrs Mary HONEYBALL MEP
Labour European Office
16 Charles Square
London N1 6HP
Tel: 0207 253 1810
Fax: 0207 253 1812
E-mail: mhoneyball@europarl.eu.int
E-mail: mary@honeyballmep.fsnet.co.uk

Mr Claude MORAES MEP
65 Barnsbury Street
London N1 1EJ
Tel: 0207 609 5005
Fax: 0207 609 3005
E-mail: cmoraes@europarl.fsnet.co.uk

Liberal Democrat

Baroness Sarah LUDFORD MEP
London Liberal Democrat European Office
36 St Peter's Street
London N1 8JT
Tel: 0207 288 2526
Fax: 0207 288 2581
E-mail: sludford@europarl.eu.int
E-mail: sludfordmep@cix.co.uk

Green

Mrs Jean LAMBERT MEP
Suite 58
The Hop Exchange
24 Southwark Street
London SE1 1TY
Tel: 0207 407 6269
Fax: 0207 234 0183
E-mail: jeanlambert@greenmeps.org.uk
E-mail: jelambert@europarl.eu.int

north east

Conservative

Mr Martin CALLANAN MEP
22 Osborne Road
Jesmond
Newcastle-upon-Tyne NE2 2AD
Tel: 0191 240 2600
Fax: 0191 240 2612
E-mail: mcallanan@europarl.eu.int

Labour

Dr Gordon ADAM MEP
7 Palmersville
Great Lime Road
Forest Hall
Newcastle-upon-Tyne NE12 9HN
Tel: 0191 280 2929
Fax: 0191 256 6067

Mr Stephen HUGHES MEP
North East Euro Constituency Office
Room 4/38
County Hall
Durham DH1 5UR
Tel: 0191 384 9371
Fax: 0191 384 6100
E-mail: alma@mep.u-net.com

Dr Barbara O'TOOLE MEP
7 Palmersville
Great Lime Road
Forest Hall
Newcastle-upon-Tyne NE12 9HN
Tel: 0191 256 6066
Fax: 0191 256 6067
E-mail: botoolemep2@aol.com
or
European Parliament
Room ASP 13G257
B-1047 Brussels
Tel: 00 32 22 84 53 62/73 62
Fax: 00 32 22 84 93 62
E-mail: botoole@europarl.eu.int

north west

Conservative

Rt Hon Sir Robert ATKINS MEP
Manor House
Lancaster Road
Garstang
Lancashire PR3 1JA
Tel: 0199 560 2225
Fax: 0199 560 5690
E-mail: ratsmep@aol.com

Mr Den DOVER MEP
30 Countess Way
Euxton
Chorley
Lancashire PR7 6PT
Tel: 0125 727 3183
Fax: 0032 2 284 9787
E-mail: ddover@europarl.eu.int

european parliament

Mrs Jacqueline FOSTER MEP
European Parliament
B-1047 Brussels
Belgium
Tel: 0032 2 284 5957
Fax: 0032 2 284 9957
E-mail: jfoster@europarl.eu.int

Lord INGLEWOOD MEP
Hutton-in-the-Forest
Penrith
Cumbria CA11 9TH
Tel: 0176 848 4500
Fax: 0176 8484 571
E-mail: linglewood@europarl.eu.int

Mr David SUMBERG MEP
North West Regional Office
9 Montford Enterprise Centre
Wynford Square, Salford M5 2SN
Tel: 0161 745 7880
Fax: 0161 737 1980
E-mail: dsumberg@europarl.eu.int

Labour
Mrs Arlene McCARTHY MEP
Express Networks
1 George Leigh Street
Manchester M4 5DL
Tel: 0161 906 0801
Fax: 0161 906 0802
E-mail: arlene.mccarthy@easynet.co.uk

Mr Brian SIMPSON MEP
Gilbert Wakefield House
67 Bewsey Street
Warrington WA2 7JQ
Tel: 0192 565 4074
Fax: 0192 565 4077
E-mail: briansimpson@lab.u-net.com

Mr Gary TITLEY MEP
Euro Office
16 Spring Lane
Radcliffe
Manchester M26 2TQ
Tel: 0161 724 4008
Fax: 0161 724 4009
E-mail: contact@gary-titley-mep.new.labour.org.uk

Mr Terry WYNN MEP
Lakeside, Alexandra Park
Prescot Road
St Helens WA10 3TT
Tel: 0174 445 1609
Fax: 0174 42 9832
E-mail: terry-wynn.labour@virgin.net

Liberal Democrat
Mr Chris DAVIES MEP
87A Castle Street
Edgeley
Stockport SK3 9AR
Tel: 0161 477 7070
Fax: 0161 477 7007
E-mail: chrisdaviesmep@cix.co.uk

south east

Conservative
Mr Nirj DEVA MEP
169B Kennington Road
London SE11 6SF
Tel: 0207 642 8880
Fax: 0207 642 8879
E-mail: nirjdevamep@hotmail.com
E-mail: ndeva@europarl.eu.int

Mr James ELLES MEP
European Parliament
B-1047 Brussels
Belgium
Tel: 0032 2 284 5951
Fax: 0032 2 284 9951
E-mail: jelles@europarl.eu.int

Mr Daniel HANNAN MEP
Conservative Central Office
32 Smith Square
London SW1P 3HH
Tel: 0207 984 8238/8239
Fax: 0207 984 8207
E-mail: office@hannan.co.uk

Mr Roy PERRY MEP
Tarrants Farmhouse
Maurys Lane
West Wellow
Romsey
Hampshire SO51 6DA
Tel: 0179 432 2472
Fax: 0179 432 3498
E-mail: royperry@europe.com

Mr James PROVAN MEP
Middle Lodge
Barns Green
nr Horsham
West Sussex RH13 7NL
Tel: 0140 373 3700
Fax: 0140 373 3588
E-mail: jamesprovan@europarl.eu.int

Labour

Mr Peter SKINNER MEP
99 Kent Road
Dartford
Kent DA1 2AJ
Tel: 0163 440 9222
Fax: 0163 440 9333
E-mail: peterskinnermep@southeastoffice.fsnet.co.uk

Mr Mark WATTS MEP
Euro Office
29 Park Road
Sittingbourne
Kent ME10 1DR
Tel: 0179 547 7880
Fax: 0179 543 7224
E-mail: mfwatts1@aol.com

Liberal Democrat

Mr Chris HUHNE MEP
Liberal Democrat Office
European Parliament
2 Queen Anne's Gate
London SW1H 9AA
Tel: 0207 227 4319
Fax: 0207 233 3959
E-mail: chuhneoffice@cix.co.uk

Baroness NICHOLSON of WINTERBOURNE MEP
Room ASP 10G209
European Parliament
B-1047 Brussels
Belgium
Tel: 0032 2 284 7625
Fax: 0032 2 284 9625
E-mail: enicholson@europarl.eu.int

UK Independence Party

Mr Nigel FARAGE MEP
The Old Grain Store
Church Lane
Lyminster
Nr Littlehampton
West Sussex BH17 7QJ
Tel: 0190 388 5573
Fax: 0190 388 5574
E-mail: nfarage@europarl.eu.int
E-mail: ukipse@Dukip.org

Greens

Dr Caroline LUCAS MEP
Suite 58
The Hop Exchange
24 Southwark Street
London SE1 1TY
Tel: 0207 407 6281
Fax: 0207 234 0183
E-mail: carolinelucas@greenmeps.org.uk
or
European Parliament
Room ASP 8G269
B-1047 Brussels
Belgium
Tel: 00 32 22 84 51 53
Fax: 00 32 22 84 91 53
E-mail: clucas@europarl.eu.int

south west

Conservative

Mr Giles CHICHESTER MEP
48 Queen Street
Exeter EX4 3SR
Tel: 0139 249 1815
Fax: 0139 249 1588
E-mail: giles@gileschichestermep.org.uk

Dr Caroline JACKSON MEP
14 Bath Road
Swindon
Wiltshire SN1 4BA
Tel: 0179 342 2663
Fax: 0179 342 2664
E-mail: cj@carolinejackson.demon.co.uk

Mr Neil PARISH MEP
16 Northgate
Bridgwater
Somerset TA6 3EU
Tel: 0127 842 3110
Fax: 0127 843 1034
E-mail: martin.r.perry@tesco.net
E-mail: nparish@europarl.eu.int

The Earl of STOCKTON MEP
Glenthorne House
131 Coronation Road
Bristol BS3 1RE
Tel: 0117 953 7260
Fax: 0117 953 7261
E-mail: alexanderstockton@tory.org

european parliament

Labour

Mr Glyn FORD MEP
South West Labour Party
1 Newfoundland Court
Newfoundland Street
Bristol BS2 9AP
Tel: 0117 924 6399
Fax: 0117 924 8599
E-mail: penny_richardson@new.labour.org.uk

Liberal Democrat

Mr Graham WATSON MEP
Bagehot's Foundry
Beard's Yard
Bow Street, Langport
Somerset TA10 9PS
Tel: 0145 825 9176/825 2265
Fax: 0145 825 3430/825 9174
E-mail: euro_office@cix.co.uk

UK Independence Party

Mr Graham BOOTH MEP
41 Oyster Bend, Paignton
Devon TQ4 6NL
Tel/Fax: 0180 355 7433
Email: gbooth@ukip.org

west midlands

Conservative

Mr Philip BRADBOURN OBE MEP
Radclyffe House, 66-68 Hagley Road
Edgbaston
Birmingham B16 8PF
Tel: 0845 606 0239
Fax: 0121 456 5989

Mr Philip BUSHILL-MATTHEWS MEP
The Manor House
Harbury, Leamington Spa
Warwickshire CV33 9HX
Tel: 0192 661 2476
Fax: 0192 661 3168
E-mail: bushillm@aol.com

Mr John CORRIE MEP
West Midlands Region
Radclyffe House, 66-68 Hagley Road
Edgbaston
Birmingham B16 8PF
Tel: 0845 606 0239
Fax: 0121 456 5989
E-mail: jacorrie@compuserve.com

Mr Malcolm HARBOUR MEP
Manor Cottage
Manor Road
Solihull
West Midlands B91 2BL
Tel: 0121 711 3158
Fax: 0121 711 3159
E-mail: Manor_Cottage@compuserve.com

Labour

Mr Michael CASHMAN MEP
West Midlands Labour European Office
Terry Duffy House, Thomas Street
West Bromwich B70 6NT
Tel: 0121 569 1923
Fax: 0121 525 0949
E-mail: jkeenan@michaelcashmanmep.org.uk

Mrs Neena GILL MEP
West Midlands Labour European Office
Terry Duffy House, Thomas Street
West Bromwich B70 6NT
Tel: 0121 569 1921
Fax: 0121 525 0949
E-mail: contact@neena-gill-mep.new.labour.org.uk

Mr Simon MURPHY MEP
West Midlands Labour European Office
Terry Duffy House, Thomas Street
West Bromwich B70 6NT
Tel: 0121 569 1920
Fax: 0121 525 0949
E-mail: Tony-Carroll@new.labour.co.uk

Liberal Democrat

Mrs Liz LYNNE MEP
55 Ely Street
Stratford-upon-Avon
Warwickshire CV37 6LN
Tel: 0178 926 6354
Fax: 0178 926 6848
E-mail: lizlynne@cix.co.uk

yorkshire and the humber

Conservative

Mr Robert GOODWILL MEP
Southwood Farm
Terrington
York YO60 6QB
Tel: 0165 364 8459
Fax: 0165 364 8225
E-mail: r.goodwill@farmline.com

northern ireland

Democratic Unionist Party
Rev. Ian PAISLEY MEP
256 Ravenhill Road
Belfast BT6 8GF
Tel: 0289 045 4255
Fax: 0289 045 7783

Social Democratic and Labour Party
Mr John HUME MEP
5 Bayview Terrace
Derry BT48 7EE
Tel: 0287 126 5340
Fax: 0287 136 3423

Ulster Unionist Party
Mr James NICHOLSON MEP
429 Holywood Road
Belfast BT4 2LN
Tel: 0289 076 5504
Fax: 0289 076 9419

Mr Timothy KIRKHOPE MEP
7 Dewar Close
Collingham, Wetherby
West Yorkshire LS22 5JR
Tel: 0193 757 4649
Fax: 0193 757 4651
E-mail: timothy@leedsne.demon.co.uk

Mr Edward McMILLAN-SCOTT MEP
1 Ash Street
Poppleton Road
York YO26 4UR
Tel: 0190 478 1999
Fax: 0190 478 1998
E-mail: emcmillan@europarl.eu.int

Labour
Mr David BOWE MEP
2 Blenheim Terrace
Leeds LS2 9JG
Tel: 0113 245 8993
Fax: 0113 244 2782
E-mail: mail@davidbowe.demon.co.uk

Mr Richard CORBETT MEP
2 Blenheim Terrace
Leeds LS2 9JG
Tel: 0113 245 8978
Fax: 0113 245 8992
E-mail: richard@corbett-euro.demon.co.uk

Mrs Linda McAVAN MEP
79 High Street
Wath-upon-Dearne S63 7QB
Tel: 0170 987 5665
Fax: 0170 987 4207
E-mail: lindamcavan@lindamcavanmep.org.uk

Liberal Democrat
Mrs Diana WALLIS MEP
Land of Green Ginger
Hull HU1 2EA
Tel: 0148 260 9943
Fax: 0148 260 9951
E-mail: diana@dianawallismep.org.uk

wales

Conservative
Mr Jonathan EVANS MEP
4 Penlline Road, Whitchurch
Cardiff CF14 2XS
Tel: 0292 061 6031
Fax: 0292 0613539
E-mail: jevans@europarl.eu.int

Labour
Mrs Glenys KINNOCK MEP
Labour European Office
The Coal Exchange
Mount Stewart Square
Cardiff CF10 6EB
Tel: 0292 048 5305
Fax: 0292 048 4534
E-mail: gkinnock@europe-wales.new.labour.org.uk

Mrs Eluned MORGAN MEP
Labour European Office
The Coal Exchange
Mount Stewart Square
Cardiff CF10 6EB
Tel: 0292 048 5305
Fax: 0292 048 4534
E-mail: emorgan@europe-wales.new.labour.org.uk

Plaid Cymru
Mrs Jill EVANS MEP
20 Chester Street
Wrexham LL13 8BG
Tel: 0197 831 1564
Fax: 0197 831 1574
or
3 Hill Street
Haverfordwest SA61 1QQ
Tel: 0143 777 9042
Fax: 0143 777 9048
E-mail: jievans@europarl.eu.int

Mr Eurig WYN MEP
70 High Street
Bangor LL57 1NR
Tel: 0124 835 2306
Fax: 0124 836 1260
E-mail: ewyn@europarl.eu.int

scotland

Scottish Conservative and Unionist Party
Mr Struan STEVENSON MEP
SCCO, 83 Princes Street
Edinburgh EH2 2ER
Tel: 0131 247 6890
Fax: 0131 247 6891
E-mail: sstevenson@europarl.eu.int
E-mail: ssteve@aol.com

Mr John PURVIS CBE MEP
Gilmerton, St Andrews
Fife KY16 8NB
Tel: 0133 447 5830
Fax: 0133 447 7754
E-mail: purvisco@compuserve.com
E-mail: jpurvis@europarl.eu.int

Labour
Mr David MARTIN MEP
PO Box 27030
Edinburgh EH10 7YP
Tel: 0131 654 1606
Fax: 0131 654 1607
E-mail: martin@martinmep.com

Mr Bill MILLER MEP
John Smith House, 145-165 West Regent Street
Glasgow G2 4RZ
Tel: 0141 221 3024
Fax: 0141 221 4912
E-mail: BMillerMEP@aol.com

Mrs Catherine STIHLER MEP
Constituency Office
Music Hall Lane
Dunfermline Five KY12 7NG
Tel: 0138 373 1890
Fax: 0138 373 1835
E-mail: cstihler@europarl.eu.int

Liberal Democrat
Mrs Elspeth ATTWOOLL MEP
Suite 1, 2nd floor
Olympic House
142 Queen Street
Glasgow G1 3BU
Tel: 0141 243 2421
Fax: 0141 243 2451
E-mail: eattwooll@europarl.eu.int
E-mail: info@scotlibdem.fsnet.co.uk

Scottish National Party
Mr Ian HUDGHTON MEP
70 Rosemount Place
Aberdeen AB25 2XJ
Tel: 0122 462 3150
Fax: 0122 462 3160
E-mail: ihudghton@europarl.eu.int
or
8 Old Glamis Road
Dundee DD3 8HP
Tel: 0138 290 3206
Fax: 0138 290 3205

Professor Sir Neil MacCORMICK MEP
107 McDonald Road
Edinburgh EH7 4NW
Tel: 0131 525 8918
Fax: 0131 525 8933
E-mail: NMacCormick@europarl.eu.int
E-mail: nmacmes@snp.sol.co.uk
or
31 Combie Street
Oban
Argyll PA34 4HS

european commission

introduction

The Commission consists of the college of Commissioners and a civil service of some 17,000 Eurocrats organised into 35 directorates-general and other specialised services.

The Commission has three main functions:

- to initiate legislation
- to act as the guardian of EU Treaties
- to act as the Union's executive body

initiator of legislation

The Commission has the sole right of initiative in the field of European Union legislation. Most of the Commission's proposals have a clear legal base in the treaties or in the amendments to the treaties. These activities range from trade, industry and social policies to agriculture, the environment, energy, regional development and development co-operation. As the European Union has developed over the years, the Commission has acquired new responsibilities. The Single European Act of 1986, incorporating the first significant update of the founding treaties, the Maastricht Treaty on European Union (1992) and the Amsterdam Treaty (1997) all confirm and expand both the scope of the Union and the areas of Commission responsibility. These include the environment, education, health, consumer affairs, the development of trans-European networks, research and development policy, culture and economic and monetary union.

Legislative process

- Before it issues an item of draft legislation, the Commission carries out extensive preliminary soundings and discussions with representatives of governments, industry, the trade unions, special interest groups and, where necessary, technical experts.

- The Commission takes the principle of subsidiarity into account in its proposals, initiating legislation only in areas where the EU is better placed than individual Member States to take effective action.

- Once a Commission proposal has been submitted to the Council of Ministers and the European Parliament, the three institutions work together to produce a satisfactory result.

- The Commission also works closely with the Union's two consultative bodies, the Economic and Social Committee and the Committee of the Regions, and consults them on most items of draft legislation.

- In agreement with the Commission, the Council can amend a proposal by a qualified majority. If the Commission does not agree the change requires unanimity. The European Parliament shares the power of co-decision with the Council in most areas and has to be consulted in others. When revising its proposals the Commission is required to take Parliament's amendments into consideration.

- Although the Commission makes the proposals, all major decisions on important legislation are taken by the ministers of the Member States in the Council of the European Union, in co-decision (or, in some cases, consultation) with the democratically elected European Parliament.

guardian of eu treaties

The Commission acts as the guardian of the EU treaties to ensure that EU legislation is applied correctly by the Member States. It can institute legal proceedings against Member States or businesses that fail to comply with European law and, as a last resort, bring them before the European Court of Justice. It can also impose fines on individuals or companies, notably when they act in breach of the European Union's competition rules.

Firms and the Member States may also appeal to the Court of Justice; for example, they may appeal against fines imposed by the Commission.

executive body to the eu

The Commission is European Union's executive body, responsible for implementing and managing policy. This involves issuing rules for the implementation of certain treaty Articles and administering budget appropriations earmarked for Community operations. The bulk of these fall within one or other of the major Funds: the European Agricultural Guidance and Guarantee Fund, the European Social Fund, the European Regional Development Fund and the Cohesion Fund.

The Commission's management of the EU budget is scrutinised by the Court of Auditors.

In some areas like competition, agriculture and trade policy, the Commission has considerable autonomy to take decisions without submitting proposals to the Council of Ministers, either because of its specific powers under the EU Treaties or by delegated authority from the Council.

The Commission also negotiates trade and co-operation agreements with outside countries and groups of countries on behalf of the Union. More than 100 countries around the world have such accords with the European Union. The Lomé Convention links the European Union with developing countries of Africa, the Caribbean and Pacific (ACP). The Commission also negotiated the Uruguay Round trade liberalisation accord and the creation of the World Trade Organisation (WTO) on the Union's behalf.

administration

The Commission is the biggest of the European institutions. It has a staff of about 17,000 people, roughly half of the total employed by the European institutions.

The Union has 11 official languages, and about one fifth of the Commission staff work in the translation and interpreting services. Citizens of the Union must have access to the texts adopted at EU level in their own language.

The Commission consists of 35 directorates-general and specialised services. They are each headed by a director-general, who is equivalent in rank to the top civil servant in a government ministry. The directors-general report to a Commissioner, each of whom has the political and operational responsibility for one or more DGs.

commissioners and their responsibilities

Website: http://europa.eu.int/comm/commissioners/index_en.htm

President Romano PRODI (Head of Private Office Stefano MANSERVISI): Secretariat-General, Legal Service, Press and Communication DG

Vice-President Neil KINNOCK (Head of Private Office Gert-Jan KOOPMAN): Personnel and Administration DG, Administrative Reform, Inspectorate-General, Joint Interpreting and Conference Service, Translation Service

Vice-President Loyola DE PALACIO (Head of Private Office Daniel CALLEJA CRESPO): Transport and Energy DG, Relations with the European Parliament, Relations with the Committee of Regions, the Economic and Social Committee and the European Ombudsman

Mario MONTI (Head of Private Office Marc VAN HOOF): Competition DG

Franz FISCHLER (Head of Private Office Corrado PIRZIO BIROLI): Agriculture DG, Fisheries DG

Erkki LIIKANEN (Head of Private Office Heikki SALMI): Enterprise DG, Information Society DG

Frits BOLKESTEIN (Head of Private Office Laurs NØRLUND): Internal Market DG, Taxation and Customs Union DG

Philippe BUSQUIN (Head of Private Office Daniel JACOB): Research DG, Joint Research Centre

Pedro SOLBES MIRA (Head of Private Office Luis PLANAS PUCHADES): Economic and Financial Affairs DG, Eurostat

Poul NIELSON (Head of Private Office Claus SØRENSEN): Development DG, Humanitarian Aid Office (ECHO)

Günter VERHEUGEN (Head of Private Office Heinz-Peter TEMPEL): Enlargement DG

Chris PATTEN (Head of Private Office Anthony CARY): External Relations DG, EuropeAid Co-operation Office

Pascal LAMY (Head of Private Office Pierre DEFRAIGNE): Trade DG

David BYRNE (Head of Private Office Martin POWER): Health and Consumer Protection DG

Michel BARNIER (Head of Private Office Christina ROGER): Regional Policy DG, Institutional Reform

Viviane REDING (Head of Private Office Gregory PAVLGER): Education and Culture DG, Publications Office

Michaele SCHREYER (Head of Private Office Rolf Eckart GUTH): Budget DG, Financial Control DG, European Anti-Fraud Office

Margot WALLSTRÖM (Head of Private Office Rolf ANNERBERG): Environment DG

Antonio VITORINO (Head of Private Offfice Antonio CAVACO SERVINHO): Justice and Home Affairs DG

Anna DIAMANTOPOULOU (Head of Private Office Giorgos GLYNOS): Employment and Social Affairs DG

The 20 members of the Commission are drawn from the 15 EU countries, but they each swear an oath of independence. Commissioners are nominated for a renewable five-year term. The previous Commission under Jacques Santer resigned before its term expired so the current Prodi Commission will serve for slightly over five years: from September 1999 until 22 January 2005.

At present two Commissioners come from each of the 'big' Member States (Germany, Spain, France, Italy and the United Kingdom) and one from each of the 'smaller' ones (Belgium, Denmark, Greece, Ireland, Luxembourg, the Netherlands, Austria, Portugal, Finland and Sweden).

It is proposed under the Treaty of Nice that from 2005 the Commission will comprise one national per Member State, in preparation for EU enlargement. Once the Union reaches 27 Member States, there will be fewer Commissioners than Member States. The Council will have to take a unanimous decision on the exact number of Commissioners and decide on a system of rotation that will be fair to all countries.

The **President of the Commission** is chosen by EU Heads of State or Government meeting in the European Council and acting by qualified majority. The European Parliament must approve the appointment. In agreement with the new President, the Council decides on the other 19 members of the Commission from those proposed by each Member State. The President and the other members-designate are subject to a collective vote of approval by the European Parliament. These selection procedures are laid out by the Treaty of Nice, which entered into force on 1 February 2003 after ratification by all Member States. The Treaty also enhances the powers of the Commission's President. The President of the Commission participates alongside the Heads of State or Government of the Member States at the twice-yearly meetings of the European Council.

working methods

The work of the Commission is co-ordinated by its Secretariat-General. The Commission meets once a week to adopt proposals, finalise policy papers and take other decisions required of it. It deals with routine matters via simplified written procedures. Where necessary decisions are taken by majority vote.

Each Commissioner has his or her own private office or 'cabinet', in addition to the staff of the directorates-general for which they are responsible. Cabinets consist of six officials who serve as the bridge between the Commissioner and the DGs.

The Commission has important responsibilities for aid and development programmes in third countries. It has been given the task of managing the PHARE and TACIS programmes of financial and technical assistance to the countries of Central and Eastern Europe and to the Republics of the former Soviet Union.

The Commission is answerable to the European Parliament which has the power to dismiss it by a vote of censure or no confidence. The Commission attends all sessions of the European Parliament and must explain and justify its policies if so requested by members of the house. It must reply to written or oral questions put by MEPs.

contact details

General: http://europa.eu.int/comm/index_en.htm
Directorates-General and Services: http://europa.eu.int/comm/dgs_en.htm

E-mail format: firstname.surname@cec.eu.int
When the first name and/or surname are composed of more than one word, the different words are linked by a hyphen. Queries: address-information@cec.eu.int

Belgium
Postal address: Rue de la Loi 200, B-1049 Brussels, Belgium
Tel: +32 22 99 11 11
Fax numbers are listed separately below under each DG/Service
Telex: 21877 COMEU B

Luxembourg
Bâtiment Jean Monnet, Rue Alcide De Gasperi, L-2920 Luxembourg
Phone: +352 43 01-1
Telex: 3423, 3446, 3476 COMEUR LU

Commission Representations are to be found in all Member States' capitals and in some major regional cities. In the UK Commission Representations are as follows:

United Kingdom
England
8 Storey's Gate
London SW1P 3AT
Tel: 0207 973 1992
Fax: 0207 973 1900
Head of Representation: Jim DOUGAL
Deputy Head: Ian BARBER
Website: http://www.cec.org.uk

Northern Ireland
Windsor House, 9/15 Bedford Street
Belfast BT2 7EG
Tel: 0289 024 0708
Fax: 0299 024 8241
Head of Representation: Edward MCVEIGH

Scotland
9 Alva Street
Edinburgh EH2 4PH
Tel: 0131 225 2058
Fax: 0131 226 4105
Head of Representation: Elizabeth HOLT

Wales
2 Caspian Point, Caspian Way
Cardiff CF10 4QQ
Tel: 0292 089 5020
Fax: 0292 089 5035
Head of Representation: Vacant

directorates-general and services

AGRICULTURE DIRECTORATE-GENERAL

Fax: +32 22 96 42 67

Website: http://europa.eu.int/comm/dgs/agriculture /index_en.htm

Commissioner Franz FISCHLER
Director-General José Manuel SILVA RODRIGUEZ
Deputy Director-General (responsible for Directorates E, F and G) Joachim HEINE
Deputy Director-General (responsible for Directorates B, C and D) Fabrizio BARBASO
Deputy Director-General (responsible for Directorates H, I and J) Jean-Luc DEMARTY
Deputy Director-General (responsible for the analysis of aspects of CAP) David ROBERTS
Assistants to the Director-General Josefine LORIZ-HOFFMANN, Nicolas VERLET

Internal Audit
Head of Unit Antonio MICELI

Directorate A.I
International Affairs (WTO)
Director - Mary MINCH
1 WTO/OECD/USA/Canada - João PACHECO
2 Europe/newly independent states - Sven BERGLUND

Directorate A.II
International Affairs (Enlargement)
Director - Alexander TILGENKAMP
1 Latin America / Mediterranean countries / Gulf countries / CEECs / W. Balkans - Helmut STADLER
2 Enlargement - Rudolf MOEGELE

Directorate B
Relations with other institutions; communication and equality
Director - José Manuel SUOSA UVA
1 Information policy on agriculture and rural development -

Eugène LEGUEN DE LACROIX
2 Promotion of agricultural products - Fabio GENCARELLI
3 Agricultural product quality policy - Isabelle PEUTZ
4 Relations with other Community institutions and agricultural NGOs - Rudolf STROHMEIER

Directorate C
Markets in crop products
Director - Russell MILDON
1 Cereals, oilseeds and protein plants; management of food aid - John BENSTED-SMITH
2 Rice, animal feed, non-food uses, cereal substitutes and dried fodder - Susanne NIKOLAJSEN
3 Olive oil, olives, fibre plants and sugar - Jean-Marc GAZAGNES
4 Fresh and processed fruit and vegetables - Tomás GARCÍA AZCARATE

Directorate D
Markets in livestock products; specialised crops and wine
Director - Lars Christian HOELGAARD
1 Milk products - Herman VERSTEIJLEN
2 Beef/veal, pigmeat, sheepmeat and poultry - Jean-Jacques JAFFRELOT
3 Bananas, tobacco, hops, potatoes and other specialised crops - Aldo LONGO
4 Wine, alcohol and derived products - Maurizio CHIAPPONE

Directorate E
Rural development programmes
Director - Michele PASCA-RAYMONDO
1 Spain, Sweden, United Kingdom, Finland - Jean-François HULOT
2 Greece, Italy, Portugal - Balthazar HUBER
3 Belgium, Denmark, France, Austria - Angel CARRO CASTRILLO
4 Germany, Ireland, Luxembourg, Netherlands - Markus HOLZER

Directorate F
Horizontal aspects of rural Development; SAPARD
Director - Nikiforos SIVENAS
1 Environment and forestry - Leopold MAIER
2 Financial coordination of rural development - Bernard CAISSO
3 Consistency of rural development - Robertus PETERS
4 SAPARD programmes - Alan WILKINSON

Directorate G
Economic analysis and evaluation
Director - Dirk AHNER
1 Studies and overall approach - Bruno BUFFARIA
2 Quantitative analysis, forecasts, statistics and studies - Saverio TORCASIO
3 Analysis of the situation of agricultural holdings - Keijo HYVÖNEN
4 Evaluation of measures applicable to agriculture - Hilkka SUMMA

Directorate H
Agricultural legislation
Director - Wolfgang BURTSCHER
1 Agricultural law - Klaus-Dieter BORCHARDT
2 Competition - Michael ERHART
3 Supervision of the application of agricultural legislation, infringements and complaints - Luis Alfonso DE MIGUEL ROLÍN
4 Horizontal aspects relating to trade; simplification of agricultural legislation - François VITAL
5 Co-ordination of procedures and joint secretariat of management committees - Jan VERSTRAETE

Directorate I
Resource management
Director - Prosper DE WINNE
1 Budget management - Irini PAPADIMITRIOU
2 Assistance and central financial control - Bernard CAISSO
3 Information technology - Georgios VLAHOPOULOS
4 Financial management of EAGGF-Guarantee Section - Jens SCHAPS
5 Personnel and administration - Juan Luis FERNÁNDEZ MARTÍN
6 Activity-based management and IRMS - Søren KISSMEYER-NIELSEN

Directorate J
Audit of agricultural expenditure
Director - Chantelle HEBETTE
Adviser (secretariat of the conciliation body) - Richard ETIEVANT
Adviser - Gerrit VERHELST
1 Co-ordination of horizontal questions concerning the clearance of accounts; financial audit - Michele OTTATI
2 Audit of expenditure on market measures - Hans-Erwin BARTH
3 Integrated administration and control system (IACS) and audit of direct aid - Richard ETIEVANT
4 Audit of rural development expenditure - Paul WEBB

COMPETITION DIRECTORATE-GENERAL

Fax: General: +32 22 95 01 28
State aid: +32 22 96 12 42
Antitrust: +32 22 95 01 28
Mergers: +32 22 96 43 01

Website: http://europa.eu.int/comm/dgs/competition/index_en.htm

Commissioner Mario MONTI
Director-General Philip LOWE
Deputy Director-General (responsible for mergers: Directorate B) Claude CHENE
Deputy Director-General (responsible for antitrust activities: Directorates C to F; antitrust reform and security issues) Gianfranco ROCCA
Deputy Director-General (responsible for State aid: Directorates G and H) Vacant
Adviser hors classe (responsible for enlargement, the follow-up to the Doha conference, communication, ethics and relations with the Court of Auditors) Jean-François PONS
Assistants to the Director-General Nicola PESARESI, Linsey MCCALLUM

Internal Audit
Head of Unit Johan VANDROMME

Hearing Officer Helmuth SCHRÖTER

Staff, budget, administration, information
Head of Unit Stefaan DEPYPERE

Information technology
Head of Unit Javier Juan PUIG SAQUES

Rue de la Loi 200, B-1049 Brussels • Tel +32 22 99 11 11

Directorate A
Competition policy, co-ordination, international affairs and relations with other institutions
Director - Kirtikumar MEHTA
Advisers - Juan RIVIÈRE MARTI, Georgios ROUNIS
1 General competition policy, economic and legal aspects - Oliver GUERSENT
2 Legislative and regulatory proposals; relations with the Member States - Emil PAULIS
3 General policy and legislation, co-ordination and transparency of State aid - Robert HANKIN
4 International affairs - Blanca GALINDO RODRIGUEZ

Directorate B
Merger Task Force
Director - Götz DRAUZ
1 Operating Unit I - Claude RAKOVSKY
2 Operating Unit II - Francisco Enrique GONZALEZ DIAZ
3 Operating Unit III - Dietrich KLEEMANN
4 Operating Unit IV - Paul MALRIC SMITH
5 Unit responsible for monitoring implementation - Wolfgang MEDERER

Directorate C
Information, communication and multimedia
Director - Jürgen MENSCHING
1 Post and telecommunications; Information society co-ordination - Pierre BUIGUES
2 Media and music publishing - Herbert UNGERER
3 Information industries and consumer electronics - Cecilio MADERO VILLAREJO

Directorate D
Services
Director - Lowri EVANS
1 Financial services (banking and insurance) - Bernhard FREISS
2 Transport - Joos STRAGIER

3 Distributive trades and other services - Anne-Margrete WACHTMEISTER

Directorate E
Cartels, basic industries and energy
Director - Ángel TRADACETE COCERA
1 Cartels Unit I - Georg-Klaus DE BRONNET
2 Cartels Unit II - Nicola ANNECCHINO
3 Basic industries - Yves DEVELLENNES
4 Energy, water and steel - Michael ALBERS

Directorate F
Capital and consumer goods industries
Director - Sven NORBERG
1 Textiles, cosmetics and other consumer goods; mechanical and electrical engineering and other manufacturing industries - Fin LOMHOLT
2 Motor vehicles and other means of transport - Eric VAN GINDERACHTER
3 Agricultural, food and pharmaceutical products - Luc GYSELEN

Directorate G
State aid I
Director - Loretta DORMAL-MARINO
1 Regional aid - Wouter PIEKE
2 Horizontal aid - Jean-Louis COLSON
3 Business taxation, coordination of the enlargement task force, follow-up of decisions - Reinhard WALTHER

Directorate H
State aid II
Director - Humbert DRABBE
1 Steel, non-ferrous metals, mining, shipbuilding, motor vehicles and synthetic fibres - Maria REHBINDER
2 Textiles, paper, chemical, pharmaceutical and electronics industries, mechanical engineering and other manufacturing sectors - Jorma PIHLATIE
3 Public undertakings and services - Ronald FELTKAMP

ECONOMIC AND FINANCIAL AFFAIRS DIRECTORATE-GENERAL

Fax: +32 22 96 48 85

Website: http://europa.eu.int/comm/dgs/economy_finance/index_en.htm

Commissioner Pedro SOLBES MIRA
Director-General Klaus REGLING
Director-Secretary of the Economic and Financial Committee and of the Economic Policy Committee Günter GROSCHE
Deputy Director-General (responsible for Directorates B, C and E) António José CABRAL
Chief Adviser (responsible for coordination in fields specifically designated by the Director-General) Henry Joly DIXON
Director (responsible for relations with the EBRD; based in London) Philippe PETIT-LAURENT
Adviser (responsible for matters relating to financial engineering; based in Luxembourg) Vacant
Assistant to the Director-General Stefan PFLÜGER

Internal Audit
Acting Head of Unit Brian PHILLIPS

Directorate A
Economic studies and research
Acting Director - Jürgen KRÖGER
Study advisers - Heikki OKSANEN, Karl PICHELMANN, Jon Lars JONUNG
Economic advisers - Fabrizio CORICELLI, Philippe MILLS, Harry HUIZINGA, Fernando BALLABRIGA CLAVERÍA, Vacant, Vacant
1 Econometric models and medium-term studies - André Louis DRAMAIS
2 Economic databases and statistical co-ordination - Frank SCHÖNBORN
3 Business surveys - Peter WEISS

Directorate B
National economies
Director - Vacant
Adviser (responsible for public finance) - Mervyn JONES
1 Member States I: Germany, Austria, Portugal, and Finland - Vacant
2 Member States II: Belgium, Greece, France, Luxembourg, and the Netherlands - Mirella TIELEMAN-GARGARI
3 Member States III: Spain, Ireland, Italy - Lucio PENCH
4 Member States IV: Denmark, Sweden, and United Kingdom - José Luis ROBLEDO FRAGA
5 Forecasts and economic situation - Filip KEEREMAN

Rue de la Loi 200, B-1049 Brussels • Tel +32 22 99 11 11

Directorate C
Economy of the euro zone and the Union
Director - Servass DEROOSE
Adviser (multilateral surveillance) - Christian GHYMERS
1 Monetary affairs within the euro zone and the other Member States; ERM 2 - Vacant
2 Public finance, with particular reference to the eurozone - Elena FLORES GUAL
3 Co-ordination of economic policies within the Member States and the euro zone - Vacant
4 Transition issues related to EMU - Johan VERHAEVEN
5 Financial markets and financial intermediaries - John BERRIGAN
6 Financial integration and capital movements - Sotirios KOLLIAS

Directorate D
International questions
Director - Alexander ITALIANER
Adviser (coordinating financial aid to non-member countries)* - Vassili LELAKIS
Adviser (budget questions within the pre-accession countries) - Alain MORISSET
1 Economic affairs and related issues within the accession countries - Alexandra CAS GRANJE
2 Economic affairs within the G7 countries and related multilateral issues; trade policy; external aspects of EMU - Johan BARAS
3 Economic affairs within the Asian and Latin-American countries and within Russia and the newly independent states - Peter BEKX
4 Economic affairs within Mediterranean and Western Balkan non-member countries; development policy; links with multilateral banks - Barbara KAUFFMAN

Directorate E
Economic evaluation service
Director - Jan Høst SCHMIDT
1 Employment, taxation and co-ordination of structural reforms - Mary McCARTHY

* Alternate director at the EBRD

2 Internal market and national products and services markets; competition policy; analysis of competitiveness - Fabienne ILZKOVITZ
3 Structural funds and Common Agricultural Policy - Carole GARNIER
4 Environment, transport and energy policies - Manfred BERGMANN

Directorate L
Financial operations, programme management and liaison with the EIB group
Director - Robert McGLUE
1 New financial instruments and liaison with the EIB group and the other international financial institutions - Jean-Marie MAGNETTE
2 Programme management (SMEs) - Judith ELLES
3 Loan and infrastructure programme management - Peter REICHEL
4 Accounting and budget mangement - Robert VAN DER STAR
5 Cash management and market operations - James McGING
6 Risk capital and SME financing - Maria Kristiina RAADE§

Direction R
Resources
Director - Alexandra CAS GRANJE
Adviser (responsible for relations witht the European Parliament) - Antonio ESPINO
Adviser (responsible for horizontal administrative issues) - Enrique JUARISTI MARTÍNEZ
Adviser - Sylvain SIMONETTI
1 Human resources and administration - Sylvain SIMONETTI†
2 Budgetary resources and internal control - Jean-Claude SCHUTZ
3 Interinstitutional relations; strategic planning and evaluation - Bernard NAUDTS
4 Information and communication - Peter BLACKIE
5 Management of IT resources - Pierre HIRN

§ Based in Luxembourg
† Based in Luxembourg

EDUCATION AND CULTURE DIRECTORATE-GENERAL

Fax: +32 22 95 60 85

Website: http://europa.eu.int/comm/dgs/education_culture/index_en.htm

Commissioner Viviane REDING
Director-General Nikolaus VAN DER PAS
Chief Advisers Otto DIBELIUS, Jean-Michel BAER
Assistants to the Director-General Marc JORNA, David HUGHES

Interinstitutional - co-ordination - evaluation
Acting Head of Unit Monique LEENS-FERRANDO

Audit
Head of Unit Carlo PETTINELLI

Directorate A
Education
Director - David COYNE
1 Lifelong learning policy development - Angélique VERLI
2 Higher education: Socrates, Erasmus, Jean Monnet - Marianne HILDEBRAND
3 School education: Socrates, Comenius - Bertrand DELPLEUCH
4 Socrates: coordination and horizontal actions - Anders HINGEL
5 Tempus programme: co-operation with the USA and Canada - Martin WESTLAKE

Directorate B
Vocational training
Director - Michel RICHONNIER
1 Development of vocational training policy - Gordon CLARK
2 Implementation of the Leonardo da Vinci programme - Marta Maria LOURENÇO FERREIRA
3 Application and dissemination of innovation - Alice COPETTE
4 Language policy - Sylvia VLAEMINCK

Directorate C
Culture, audiovisual policy and sport
Director - Vacant
1 Audiovisual policy - Jean-Eric DE COCKBORNE

2 Culture: policy and framework programme - Antonios KOSMOPOULOS
3 Audiovisual support (MEDIA) - Jacques DELMOLY
4 Multimedia: culture, education, training - Maruja GUTIÉRREZ DÍAZ
5 Sport - Jaime ANDREU ROMEO

Directorate D
Youth, civil society, communication
Director - Joao VALE DE ALMEIDA
1 Youth - Pierre MAIRESSE
2 Visits, traineeships, partnerships with civil society - Harald HARTUNG
3 Central Library - Ana MELICH JUSTE
4 Communication - Alain DUMORT

Directorate E
Resources
Director - Gilbert GASCARD
1 Human resources, administration - Christine BOON-FALLEUR
2 Budget programming and co-ordination - Pascal LEJEUNE
3 Finance and on-site monitoring - Franco BISCONTIN
4 Informatics - Simon SMITH

EMPLOYMENT AND SOCIAL AFFAIRS DIRECTORATE-GENERAL

Fax: +32 22 95 65 07

Website: http://europa.eu.int/comm/dgs/employment_social/index_en.htm

Commissioner Anna DIAMONTOPOULOU
Director-General Odile QUINTIN
Deputy Director-General Karl-Johan LONNROTH
Assistant to Director-General Erick Stefan OLSSON

SPP and interinstitutional relations
Head of Unit Jordi CURELL GOTOR

Internal audit
Head of Unit Emilio DALMONTE

Advisers Group
Economy and speechwriting John MORLEY
Social issues Paolo BACCHIELLI
Information Richard NOBBS

Directorate A
Employment strategy and European Social Fund (ESF) policy development and co-ordination
Director - Antonis KASTRISSIANAKIS
1 Employment analysis - Georg FISCHER
2 Employment strategy - Hélène CLARK-DAGEVILLE
3 Employment services - Johan TEN GEUZENDAM
4 ESF policy co-ordination; employment local development - Xavier PRATS MONNE

Directorate B
National employment and social inclusion monitoring and ESF Operations I
Director - Peter Stub JØRGENSEN
1 Italy, Portugal, Malta, Romania - Michel LAINE
2 Belgium, Luxembourg, France, Netherlands, Czech Republic, Slovakia - Walter FABER
3 Denmark, Sweden, Finland, Estonia, Latvia, Lithuania - Philippe HATT
4 Community Initiatives - Stephen WESTON

Directorate C
National employment and social inclusion monitoring and ESF Operations II
Director - Sven KJELLSTROM
1 Spain, Greece, Cyprus - Lea VERSTRAETE
2 Germany, Austria, Poland, Slovenia, Turkey - Georges KINTZELE
3 United Kingdom and Ireland, Bulgaria, Hungary - Vassiliki KOLOTOUROU
4 Article 6 ESF and readaptation - Antonella SCHULT-BRAUCKS

Directorate D
Adaptability, social dialogue and social rights
Director - Bernhard JANSEN
1 Interprofessional social dialogue; industrial relations; adaptation to change - Jackie MORIN
2 Sectorial social dialogue, Relations with ILO and social clauses - Fay DEVONIC
3 Labour law and work organisation - Rosendo GONZALEZ DORREGO
4 Anti-discrimination, Fundamental Social Rights and Civil Society (Article 13) - Barbara NOLAN
5 Health, safety and hygiene at work - José Ramón BIOSCA DE SAGASTUY

Directorate E
Social protection and social integration
Director - Jérôme VIGNON
1 Social and demography analysis - Constantinos FOTAKIS

2 Social protection and social inclusion policies - Armindo SILVA
3 Free movement of workers and co-ordination of social security schemes - Rob CORNELISSEN
4 Integration of people with disabilities - GOELEN-VANDEBROK

Directorate F
Management of resources
Director - Raoul PRADO
Adviser (auditor training policy, methodological refinement and the specific requirements of federal States in the Union) - Franz-Peter VEITS
1 Personnel and administration - René GUTH
2 Budget, financial co-ordination and accounts - Brendan SINNOTT
3 System audits and ex post controls - Marc OOSTENS
4 IT and workflow - Jean-François LEBRUN

Directorate G
Horizontal and international issues
Director - Luisella PAVAN-WOOLFE
1 Equality for women and men - Marie DONNELLY
2 Enlargement and international co-operation - Jean-Paul TRICART
3 Knowledge Society - Robert STRAUSS
4 Communication - Giorgio CLAROTTI
5 Evaluation - Santiago LORANCA GARCÍA

Rue de la Loi 200, B-1049 Brussels • Tel +32 22 99 11 11

ENERGY AND TRANSPORT
DIRECTORATE-GENERAL

Bâtiment CUB, Plateau de Kirchberg, L-2920 Luxembourg
Fax: +32 22 95 01 50

Website: http://europa.eu.int/comm/dgs/energy_transport/index_en.html

Commissioner Loyola DE PALACIO
Director-General François LAMOUREUX
Deputy Director-General (responsible for co-ordination of nuclear activities, supervision of Directorates H and I) Fernando DE ESTEBAN ALONSO
Principal Adviser (reporting to the Director-General) Jorgen HENNINGSEN
Adviser (reporting to the Deputy Director-General, responsible for technical analysis) Gaston LANDRESSE
Assistants to the Director-General Laurent MUSCHEL, Cesare ONESTINI

Internal audit
Head of Unit Alessandro D'ATRI

Directorate A
General affairs and resources
Director - Dominique RISTORI
1 Financial resources and activity-based management - Dirk BECKERS
2 Personnel, training and information technology - Gerhard SCHUMANN-HITZLER
3 Interinstitutional relations, enlargement and international relations - Patrick LAMBERT
4 Internal market, public service, competition and user rights - Marie WOLFCARIUS
5 Information and communication - Roberto SALVARANI

Directorate B
Trans-European networks - Energy and transport
Director - Alfonso GONZÁLEZ FINAT

1 Sectoral economy - John REES
2 TEN policy and technological development - Edgar THIELMANN
3 Management of TEN projects - Eleni KOPANEZOU
4 Sustainable development - Pirjo-Liisa KOSKIMÄKI

Directorate C
Conventional sources of energy
Director - Pedro Miguel DE SAMPAIO NUNES
Adviser (promoting a dialogue between producers and consumers in the field of energy) - Johannes MATERS
1 Safeguarding internal and external energy sources - Cristóbal BURGOS ALONSO
2 Electricity and Gas - Christopher JONES
3 Coal and oil - Vicente LUQUE CABAL

Directorate D
New sources of energy and demand management
Director - Günther HANREICH
Adviser (SAVE and Altener: preparing revision of the future framework programme for energy) - Enzo MILLICH
1 Regulatory policy, promotion of new sources of energy and demand management - Luc WERRING
2 New and renewable sources of energy - Karl KELLNER
3 Energy management - Gonzalo MOLINA IGUARTA
4 Clean transport - Kevin LEYDON

Directorate E
Inland transport
Director - Heinz HILBRECHT
1 Road transport - Dirk VAN VRECKEM
2 Rail transport and interoperability - Jean-Arnold VINOIS
3 Road safety and technology - Dimitrios THEOLOGITIS
4 Satellite navigation systems (Galileo); intelligent transport - Olivier ONIDI

Directorate F
Air transport
Director - Michel AYRAL
Adviser (coordinating security and safety measures) - Claude PROBST
1 Economic regulation - Peter FAROSS
2 Air traffic management - Bernard VAN HOUTTE
3 Airport policy and safety - Eckard SEEBOHM
4 Airport safety - Michel AYRAL
5 Air transport agreements - Ludolf VAN HASSELT

Directorate G
Maritime transport
Director - Fotis KARAMITSOS
1 Maritime policy and technology - Jean TRESTOUR
2 Maritime safety - Willem DE RUITER
3 Short sea shipping and port policy - Wolfgang ELSNER
4 Intermodality and logistics - Stefan TOSTMANN

esa - euratom supply agency

(Attached for administrative purposes to the Energy and Transport DG)
Acting Director-General Christian WAETERLOOS

Nuclear fuels supply contracts and research
Head of Unit María Dolores CARRILLO DORADO

Directorate H
Nuclear safety and safeguards
Director - Christian WAETERLOOS
1 Euratom coordination and nuclear safety - Nina COMMEAU-YANNOUSSIS
2 Nuclear energy, waste management and transport - Derek TAYLOR
3 Safeguards and non-proliferation - Stamatios TSALAS

Directorate I
Nuclear inspections
Director - Christian CLEUTINX
1 Logistics and information techonology - Winfried KLOECKNER
2 Verification and reprocessing plants - José SANTOS BENTO
3 Verification of fabrication and enrichment plants - Heinrich KSCHWENDT
4 Verification of reactors and of storage and other facilities - Klaus GRIGOLEIT

euratom safeguards office

Director Christian WAETERLOOS
1 **Inspection I** Head of Unit - Stamatios TSALAS
2 **Inspection II** Head of Unit - Gaston LANDRESSE
3 **Accounting and auditing** Head of Unit - José SANTOS BENTO
4 **Basic concepts** Head of Unit - Winfried KLOECKNER
5 **Informatics** Head of Unit - Heinrich KSCHWENDT

ENTERPRISE DIRECTORATE-GENERAL

Fax: +32 22 95 97 92

Website: http://europa.eu.int/comm/dgs/enterprise/index_en.htm

Commissioner Erkki LIIKANEN
Director-General Jean-Paul MINGASSON
Deputy Director-General (responsible for Directorates B, C and F) Heinz ZOUREK
Deputy Director-General (responsible for Directorates D, E and G) Vacant
Assistant to the Director-General Valère MOUTARLIER

Audit
Head of Unit Claes SONNERBY

Directorate R
Resources
Director - Belinda PYKE
1 Financial resources - Jean-Luc ABRIVARD
2 Human resources - Michel COOMANS
3 Informatics - Wilfried BEURMS
4 Information and communication - Geneviève PONS-DELADRIÈRE

Directorate A
Enterprise policy
Director - David WHITE
1 Development of enterprise policy - Didier HERBERT
2 External aspects of enterprise policy - Philippe JEAN
3 Enterprise aspects of relations with the candidate countries

and neighbouring countries - Peter WRAGG
4 Enterprise aspects of competition - Geert DANCET
5 Competitiveness analysis and benchmarking - Tassos BELESSIOTIS
6 Co-ordination of enterprise policy - Renate WEISSENHORN

Directorate B
Promotion of entrepreneurship and SMEs
Director - Timo SUMMA
1 Improving business support measures - Karl Georg DOUTLIK
2 Business co-operation and Community business support network development - Jacques McMILLAN
3 Crafts, small businesses, co-operatives and mutuals - Francesco IANNIELLO
4 Access to finance - Albrecht MULFINGER

Directorate C
Innovation
Director - Giulio GRATA
1 Innovation Policy - Jean-Noël DURVY
2 Projects and methodologies - John TSALAS
3 Networks and services - Vacant
4 Communication and awareness - Kurt KÖNIG
5 Administrative support - Luc BRIOL

Directorate D
Services, commerce, tourism, E-business and IDA
Director - Pedro ORTÚN-SILVÁN
1 Business services and distributive trades; enterprise aspects of social policy - Ole GULDBERG
2 Networks between public administrations (IDA) - Manuela FINETTI
3 Tourism - Reinhard KLEIN
4 E-business; ICT industries and services - Reinhard BÜSCHER

Directorate E
Environmental aspects of enterprise policy, resource-based and specific industries
Director - Patrick HENNESSY
1 Environmental aspects of enterprise policy - Michel CATINAT
2 Steel, non ferrous metals and other materials - Liliana BRYKMAN
3 Chemicals - Reinhard SCHULTE-BRAUCKS

4 Forest based industries - Kim HOLMSTRÖM
5 Textiles, leather, toys - Luis Filipe GIRAO
6 Aerospace, defence, rail and maritime industries - Constantin ANDROPOULOS

Directorate F
Single market: management and legislation for consumer goods
Director - Paul WEISSENBERG
1 Notifications and infringements - Sabine LECRENIER
2 Pharmaceuticals: regulatory framework and market authorisations - Philippe BRUNET
3 Biotechnology, competitiveness in pharmaceuticals, cosmetics - Abraao CARVALHO
4 Food industry - Andreas MENIDIATIS
5 Automotive industry - Per-Ove ENGELBRECHT

Directorate G
Single market: regulatory environment, standardisation and new approach
Director - Evangelos VARDAKAS
1 Legislative co-ordination and simplification; mutual recognition - Colette COTTER
2 Standardisation - Norbert ANSELMANN
3 Mechanical and electrical engineering, radio and telecom terminal equipment industries - Luis MONTOYA MORÓN
4 Pressure equipment, medical devices, metrology - Cornelis BREKELMANS
5 Construction - Vincente LEOZ ARGÜELLES

ENVIRONMENT DIRECTORATE-GENERAL

Avenue de Beaulieu 5, B-1160 Brussels
Centre Wagner, Plateau de Kirchberg, L-2920 Luxembourg
Fax: General: +32 22 99 03 07

Website: http://europa.eu.int/comm/dgs/environment/index_en.htm

Commissioner Margot WALLSTRÖM
Director-General Catherine DAY
Deputy Director-General (responsible for Directorates B and C) Jean-François VERSTRYNGE
Assistant to the Director-General Elizabeth GOLBERG
Assistant to the Deputy Director-General Pierre SCHELLEKENS

Internal Audit
Head of Unit Jan Julius GROENENDAAL

Strategic programming; policy co-ordination and evaluation
Head of Unit Emer DALY

Directorate A
Sustainable development and policy support
Director - David LAWRENCE
1 Communication and civil society - Ylva TIVEUS
2 Sustainable development of resources - Marianne KLINGBEIL
3 Environmental governance - Ludwig KRÄMER
4 Interinstitutional matters - Paulus BROWER

Directorate B
Environmental quality of natural resources
Director - Prudencio PERERA MANZANEDO
1 Water, sea and soil protection - Patrick MURPHY
2 Nature and bio-diversity - Nicholas HANLEY
3 Territorial dimension - Michael HAMELL
4 Civil protection and environmental accidents - Prudencio PERERA MANZANEDO

Directorate C
Environment and Health
Director - Jos DELBEKE
1 Air and Noise - Peter GAMMELTOFT
2 Biotechnology - Vacant
3 Chemical substances - Eva HELLSTEN
4 Biotechnology and pesticides - Hervé MARTIN

Directorate D
Implementation and enforcement
Director - Ruth FROMMER-RINGER
1 LIFE - Bruno JULIEN

2 Application of Community law - Georges KREMLIS
3 Industry and implementation of instruments - Pia BUCELLA

Directorate E
Global questions and international affairs
Director - Christoph BAIL
1 Climate change - Soledad BLANCO MANGUDO
2 International matters, trade and environment - Julio GARCÍA BURGUES
3 Development and the environment, the Mediterranean - Christoph BAIL

Directorate F
Resource management
Director - Viola GROEBNER
1 Human resources; administration - Hans DE JONG
2 Budget and finance - Glyn OWEN
3 Information and technology - Thomas CUNNINGHAM

Directorate G
Sustainable development and integration
Acting Director - Catherine DAY
1 Sustainable development and economic analysis - David LAWRENCE
2 Industry - Herbert AICHINGER
3 Research, science and innovation - David LAWRENCE
4 Sustainable territorial dimension - Claude ROUAN

FISHERIES DIRECTORATE-GENERAL

Fax: +32 22 95 25 69

Website: http://europa.eu.int/comm/dgs/fisheries/index_en.htm

Commissioner Franz FISCHLER
Director-General Holmquist JÖRGEN
Assistant to the Director-General Emmanouil PAPAIOANNOU

Resources
Head of Unit John MALLETT

Audit and evaluation
Head of Unit Vacant

Directorate A
Conservation policy
Director - John FARNELL
Adviser - David ARMSTRONG
1 Management of stocks - Ole TOUGAARD
2 Management of fleets - Jean-Claude CUEFF
3 Environment and health - Armando ASTUDILLO GONZALEZ
4 Research and scientific analysis - Willem-Jan BRUGGE

Directorate B
External policy and markets
Director - César DEBEN ALFONSO
1 General matters in the field of external relations - Serge BESELIER
2 International and regional arrangements - Edward SPENCER
3 Bilateral agreements - Stephanos SAMARAS
4 Common organisation of markets and trade - Friedrich WIELAND

Directorate C
Structural policy
Director - Manuel ARNAL MONREAL
Adviser - Jacques SOENENS
1 General aspects of structural policy - Monique PARIAT
2 Greece, France, Ireland, Italy, Portugal and Finland - Pedro TARNO FERNÁNDEZ
3 Belgium, Denmark, Germany, Spain, Luxembourg, Netherlands, Austria, Sweden and United Kingdom - Christoph NORDMANN
4 Aquaculture - Constantin VAMVAKAS

Directorate D
Horizontal policy
Director - Emilio MASTRACCHIO
1 Internal co-ordination, relations with the other institutions and dialogue with industry and organisations - Baudouin SURY
2 Communications and information - Chiara GARIAZZO
3 Legal issues - Paul NEMITZ
4 Monitoring and licences - Giorgio GALLIZIOLI
5 Inspection - Harm KOSTER

Rue de la Loi 200, B-1049 Brussels • Tel +32 22 99 11 11

HEALTH AND CONSUMER PROTECTION DIRECTORATE-GENERAL

Fax: +32 22 96 62 98

Website: http://europa.eu.int/comm/dgs/health_consumer/index_en.htm

Commissioner David BYRNE
Director-General Robert COLEMAN
Deputy Director-General Jaana HUSU-KALLIO
Adviser Jens NYMAND CHRISTENSEN
Adviser (responsible for animal disease eradication issues) Jan-Peter PAUL
Assistants to the Director-General Dirk STAUDENMAYER, Vacant

Audit and Evaluation
Head of Unit Vacant

Directorate A
General affairs
Director - Theodius LENNON
1 Co-ordination and institutional relations - Matthew HUDSON
2 Legal Affairs - Paul REMITS
3 Financial, human and other resources - Daniel JANSSENS
4 Information; systems and publications - Marie-Paule BENASSI

Directorate B
Consumer affairs
Director - Agnes PANTELOURI
1 Policy analysis and development; relations with consumer organisations; international questions - Véronique ARNAULT
2 Consumers' legal, economic and other interests, redress and administrative co-operation - Carina TORNBLOM
4 Product and service safety - Bernardo DELOGU
5 Financial services - Thierry VISSOL

Directorate C
Scientific opinions
Director - Vacant
Adviser - Vacant
1 Monitoring and dissemination of scientific opinions - Carlo BERLINGIERI
2 Management of Scientific Committees; scientific co-operation and networks - Peter WAGSTAFFE

Directorate D
Food safety: production and distribution chain
Director - Paola TESTORI
Adviser (Consumer information) - Jean-Jacques RATEAU
1 Animal nutrition - Willem PENNING
2 Biological risks - Eric POUDELET
3 Chemical and physical risks; surveillance - Patricia BRUNKO
4 Food law and biotechnology - Patrick DEBOYSER

Directorate E
Food safety, plant health, animal health and welfare, international questions
Director - Alejandro CHECCHI LANG
Adviser (vetinary and phytosanitary issues in relation to enlargement) - Saara REINIUS
1 Plant health - Goffredo DEL BINO
2 Animal health and welfare, zootechnics - Bernard VAN GOETHE

3 International food, veterinary and phytosanitary questions - Michael SCANNEL

Directorate F
Food and Veterinary Office (Ireland)
Grange, Dunsany, Co Meath, Ireland
Tel: +353 4 66 17 00
Fax: +353 4 66 18 79
Director - Michael GAYNOR
1 Quality, planning and development - Saara REINIUS
2 Food of animal origin: mammals - Stephen HUTCHINS
3 Food of animal origin: birds and fish - Jacky LE GOSLES
4 Food and plant origin, plant health; processing and distribution - Michael FLÜH
5 Animal nutrition, import controls, residues - Carlos ALVAREZ ANTOLÍNEZ

Directorate G
Public Health (Luxembourg)
Bâtiment Euroforum, L-2920 Luxembourg
Director - Fernand SAUER
1 Policy analysis and development; international questions - Bernard MERKEL
2 Cancer, drug dependence and pollution-related diseases - Matti RAJALA
3 Health promotion, health monitoring and injury prevention - John RYAN
4 Communicable, rare and emerging diseases - Ronald HAIGH

INFORMATION SOCIETY DIRECTORATE-GENERAL

Avenue de Beaulieu, B-1160 Brussels
Rue des Nerviens, B-1040 Brussels
Plateau de Kirchberg, L-2920 Luxembourg
Fax: +32 22 96 88 80

Website: http://europa.eu.int/comm/dgs/information_society/index_en.htm

Commissioner Erkki LIIKANEN
Director-General Fabio COLASANTI
Deputy Director-General (Brussels) Peter ZANGL
Adviser Cristopher WILKINSON
Adviser (at the disposal of the Greek President) Simon BENSASSON
Adviser to the Deputy Director-General Spyros KONIDARIS
Assistants to the Director-General Tonnie DE KOSTER, Armaud RAUCH

Internal audit
Head of Unit Christian DUBS

IST Operations
Head of Unit Vacant

Directorate R
Integrated management of resources and horizontal questions
Director - Bernard LIBERTALIS
1 Human resources* - Gianmarco DI VITA
2 Budgetary resources* - Walter SCHWARZENBRUNNER
3 Co-ordination and planning - José COTTA
4 Information technology services* - Bas DE BRUIJN
5 Development and application of Information Systems -
Massimo LUCIOLLI
*Parts of these units are based in Luxembourg

Directorate A
IST: Systems and services for the citizen
Director - Pedro Miguel DE SAMPAIO NUNES
Adviser - Michael NIEBEL
1 Analysis, policy planning, eEurope - Anne BUCHER
2 Strategy for IST research activities - Gerard COMYN
3 Information and communication - Pierrette PELCHATE
4 Evaluation of policy and programmes - Peter JOHNSTON
5 Interinstitutional relations - Pierre BOCKSTAEL
6 Regional and societal aspects - Giangaleazzo CAIROLI

european commission

Directorate B
Communications services: policy and regulatory framework
Director - Bernd LANGEHEINE
1 Regulatory framework - Peter SCOTT
2 Implementation of the regulatory framework - Peter RODFORD
3 Mobile and satellite communications - Rupert NIEPOLD
4 Internet-related services - George PAPAPAVLOU
5 International aspects - Paul VERHOEF

Directorate C
IST: New methods of work and electronic commerce
Director - Rosalie ZOBEL
1 Microelectronics - Rainer ZIMMERMAN
2 Peripherals, sub-systems and microsystems - Dirk BEERNAERT
3 Integrated systems - Vacant
4 Applications relating to health - Jean-Claude HEALY
5 Transport and the environment - André VITS
6 eGovernment - Vacant

Directorate D
IST: Content, multimedia tools and market
Director - Frans DE BRUINE
Adviser - Stephan PASCALL
1 Mobile and personal communications and systems, including satellite-related systems and services - João AUGUSTO
2 Simulation and visualisation technologies - Augusto DE ALBUQUERQUE

3 Technologies and engineering for software, systems and services - Jacobus BUS
4 Information security and confidentiality, intellectual property - Gerald SANTUCCI
5 Electronic matters - Jesús VILLASANTE
6 Trans-European telecommunications networks - Vacant

Directorate E
Essential IST technologies and infrastructures
Director - Horst FORSTER
1 Interfaces and cognition - Giovanni VARILE
2 Development of knowledge and content creation - Roberto CENCIONI
3 Formation improved by technology - Patricia MANSON
4 Information market - Javier HERNANDEZ-ROZ
5 Cultural heritage applications - Bernard SMITH

Directorate F
IST: Integration and implementation - networks and future technologies
Director - Vacant
Adviser - Luis RODRÍGUEZ ROSELLO
1 Future and emerging technologies - Thierry VAN DER PYL
2 GRID systems for the resolution of complex problems - Wolfgang BOCH
3 Research networks - Spyros KONIDARIS
4 New working environments - Bror SALMELIN
5 Applications for the disabled and the elderly - Per Axel BLIXT

130   Rue de la Loi 200, B-1049 Brussels • Tel +32 22 99 11 11

INTERNAL MARKET DIRECTORATE-GENERAL

Fax: +32 22 95 65 00

Website: http://europa.eu.int/comm/dgs/internal_market/index_en.htm

Commissioner Frits BOLKESTEIN
Director-General Alexander SCHAUB
Deputy Director-General (responsible for Directorates B and D; the application of Community law and parliamentary affairs) Thierry STOLL
Chief Adviser Paul WATERSCHOOT
Hearing Officer Pascale VAN OUTRYVE
Assistants Martin MERLIN, Nathalie DE BASALDUA LEMARCHAND

Directorate A
Functioning and impact of the single market; co-ordination; data protection
Director - Jacqueline MINOR
1 Human and financial resources - Vacant
2 Information-related technology and treatment of documents - Suzanne JESSEL PICOURY
3 Internal and external communication - Anthony DEMPSEY

Directorate B
Public procurement policy
Director - Susan BINNS
Adviser - Dag Sverker HÅKAN
1 Single market: functioning and co-ordination - Gerrit Gerard DE GRAAF
2 Activity-based management, legal and institutional affairs - Pascal LEARDINI
3 Economic analysis and evaluation - Francisco de Asís CABALLERO SANZ
4 Internal market: external dimension - Johannes HOOIJER

Directorate C
Free movement of goods, regulated professions and postal services
Director - Vacant
Adviser - Ulf BRUEHANN
1 Removal of trade barriers for goods (articles 28 to 30 of the Treaty) - Ghyslaine GUISOLPHE
2 Postal services - Fernando TOLEDANO GASCA
3 Regulated professions (qualifications) - Jonathon STOODLEY

Directorate D
Financial institutions
Director - Bertrand CARSIN
1 Formulation of public procurement, concessions and PPP law; surveillance and application for Belgium, Greece, Spain, France, Ireland, Luxembourg, Portugal and United Kingdom; ACPC and Public Procurement Advisory - Vittoria ALLIATA-FLOYD
2 Formulation of public procurement, concessions and PPP law; surveillance and application for Denmark, Germany, Italy, Netherlands, Austria, Finland and Sweden; relations with other Community policies - Pamela BRUMTER-CORET
3 Public procurement: international relations, enlargement, economic aspects, electronic procedures; SIMAP - Panayotis STAMATOPOULOS

Directorate E
Services, electronic commerce, intellectual and industrial property and the media
Director - Guido BERARDIS
1 Services - Margot FRÖHLINGER
2 Industrial property - Erik NOOTEBOOM
3 Intellectual property - Jörg REINBOTHE
4 Media in the Information Society - Philippe THÉBAULT

Directorate F
Financial markets
1 Financial services: politics and the dispersal of information - Irmfried SCHWIMANN
2 Banking - Patrick PEARSON
3 Insurance - David DEACON
4 Retail issues and payment systems - Udo BADER

Directorate G
Financial markets
Director - David WRIGHT
1 Financial instruments - José María FOMBELLIDA PRIETO
2 Securities and investment services providers - Pierre DELSAUX
3 Financial reporting and company law - Gianluigi CAMPOGRANDE
4 Compatibility and audit - Karel VAN HULLE

JOINT RESEARCH CENTRE

Fax: +32 22 95 01 46

Website: http://www.jrc.cec.eu.int

Commissioner Philippe BUSQUIN

Director-General Finbarr McSWEENEY

Deputy Director-General (with special responsibility for nuclear activities, the comprehensive decommissioning programme and the interaction between the Directorate for Science Strategy and the Directorate for Resources) Roland SCHENKEL

Principal Adviser (reporting to the Director-General on the domain of research and technology, especially on the improvement of links with european research organisations) Jean-Marie MARTIN

Assistants to the Director-General Freddy DEZEURE, (responsible for scientific matters) Dimosthenis SARIGIANNIS

Development of the organisation
Head of Unit Freddy DEZEURE

Management support
Head of Unit Michael FAHY

Internal audit
Head of Unit Freddy DEZEURE

Secretariat of the Board of Governors
Adviser Piedad GARCIÁ DE LA RASILLA Y PINEDA

Euratom project and the dismantlement of obsolete matter
Head of Unit Pierre FRIGOLA

Supplementary programme
Head of Unit Marc BECQUET

Directorate A
Science Strategy (Brussels)
Director - David WILKINSON
1 Work programme - Jean-Paul MALINGREAU
2 ERA, innovation and evaluation - Robin MIEGE
3 Anticipation of users' needs and enlargement - Giancarlo CARATTI DI LANZACCO
4 Information and public relations - Gülperi VURAL

Directorate B
Resources Directorate (Ispra)
I-21020 Ispra (Varese)

Tel: +39 3 32 78 98 28
Fax: +39 3 32 78 91 52
Director - Jean-Pierre VANDERSTEEN
Adviser - Adriano ENDRIZZI
1 Human resources - Jean-Pierre VANDERSTEEN
2 Budget and programming of resources (Brussels) - Eric FISCHER
3 Analytical accounting and finances - Peter CHURCHILL
4 Technical services - Dolf VAN HATTEM
5 Knowledge management - Richard ROSS
6 Management support - Albert JERABEK
7 Initiation and supervision of reform - Kenneth WEAVING

Rue de la Loi 200, B-1049 Brussels • Tel +32 22 99 11 11

Directorate C
Ispra department reporting to the Director of ISIS (Ispra)
Adviser - Ettore CARUSO
1 Nuclear decommissioning and waste management -
Giacinto TARTAGLIA
2 Safety, security and radiological protection - Celso OSIMANI

Directorate D
Institute for Reference Materials and Measurements (Geel)
Steenweg op Retie, B-2240 Geel, Belgium
Tel: +32 14 57 12 11 Fax: +32 14 58 42 73
Director - Alejandro HERRERO MOLINA
1 Management support - Marc WELLENS
2 Reference materials - Hendrik EMONS
3 Analytical chemistry - Adela RODRÍGUEZ FERNÁNDEZ
4 Isotope measurements - Philip TAYLOR
5 Neutron physics - Philip RULLHUSEN
6 Informatics and electronics - Stefan NONNEMAN
7 Commercialisation of materials and reference methods and
scientific liaison - Doris FLORIAN
8 Animal feed and nutrition - Elke ANKLAM

Directorate E
Institute for Transuranium Elements (Karlsruhe)
D-76125 Karlsruhe, Germany
Tel: +49 72 47 95 10 Fax: +49 72 47 95 15 90
Director - Gerard LANDER
Adviser - Serge CRUTZEN
1 Management support - Jean-Pierre MICHEL
2 Hot cell technology - Jean-Paul GLATZ
3 Materials research - Claudio RONCHI
4 Nuclear fuels - Didier HAAS
5 Nuclear chemistry - Klaus LUETZENKIRC
6 Actinides research - Gerard LANDER
7 Nuclear safety and infrastructure - Werner WAGNER

Directorate F
Institute for Advanced Materials (Petten)
Westerduinweg 3, 1755 ZG Petten (N.-H.), Netherlands
Tel: +31 2 24 56 56 56 Fax: +31 2 24 56 33 93
Director - Kari TÖRRÖNEN
Adviser (ERA dimension) - Roger HURST
1 Management support - Patrice LEMAITRE
2 Clean energies - Juha-Pekka HIRVONEN
3 High-flux reactor and reactor applications - Joël GUIDEZ
4 Nuclear safety - Horst WEISSHAEUPL
5 Scientific and technical support to TACIS and PHARE -
Michel BIETH
6 Scientific and technical support - Marc STEEN

Directorate G
Institute for the Protection and Security of the Citizen (Ispra)
I-21020 Ispra (Varese)
Tel: +39 03 32 78 91 11 Fax: +39 03 32 78 99 23
Director - Jean-Marie CANDIOU

1 Management support - James GRAY
2 Cybersecurity and new technologies for combating fraud -
Martyn DOWELL
3 Monitoring agriculture with remote sensing - Jacques
DELINCÉ
4 Technological and economic risk management - Alfredo
LUCIA
5 European laboratory for Structural Assessment - Michel
GERADIN
6 Humanitarian Security - Alois SIEBER
7 Non-proliferation and nuclear safeguards - André
POUCET

Directorate H
Institute for Environment and Sustainability (Ispra)
I-21020 Ispra (Varese)
Tel: +39 03 32 78 91 11 Fax: +39 03 32 78 92 22
Director - Manfred GRASSERBAUER
Acting Deputy Director - Jean MEYER-ROUX
Adviser (marine environment) - Peter SCHLITTENHARDT
1 Management support - Emanuela ROSSI
2 Climate Change - Frank RAES
3 Global vegetation monitoring - Alan BELWARD
4 Emissions and Health - Giovanni DE SANTI
5 Inland and Marine Waters - Steven EISENREICH
6 Soil and waste - Giovanni BIDOGLIO
7 Spatial planning - Jean MEYER-ROUX
8 Renewable energies - Heinz OSSENBRINK

Directorate I
Institute for Health and Consumer Protection (Ispra)
I-21020 Ispra (Varese)
Tel: +39 03 32 78 91 11 Fax: +39 03 32 78 95 36
Director - Cornelis VAN LEEUWEN
Adviser (in charge of health and environment interaction) -
Peter PÄRT
1 Management support - Bruno DE BERNARDI
2 Validation of biomedical testing methods - Michael
BALLS
3 Toxicology and chemical substances - Gerald VOLLMER
4 Biomedical materials and systems - Hermann STAMM
5 Physical and chemical exposures - Dimitrios KOTZIAS
6 Biotechnology and O.G.M. - Guy VAN DEN EEDE

Directorate J
Institute for Prospective Technological Studies (Seville)
World Trade Center, Isla de la Cartuja s/n, E-41092 Seville
Tel: +34 9 54 48 82 73 Fax: +34 9 54 48 82 74
Director - Per SØRUP
1 Management support - Claude TAHIR
2 Technologies for sustainable development - Per SØRUP
3 Technology, competitiveness, employment and society -
Gustav FAHRENKROG
4 Technologies for life science, information and
communication - Bernard CLEMENTS

JUSTICE AND HOME AFFAIRS DIRECTORATE-GENERAL

Fax: +32 22 96 74 81

Website: http://europa.eu.int/comm/dgs/justice_home/index_en.htm

Commissioner António VITORINO
Director-General Jonathan FAULL
Adviser Adrian FORTESCUE
Assistant (responsible for matters of policy) Telmo BALTAZAR

Policy and strategic planning, legal and institutional matters
Head of Unit Tung-Laï MARGUE

Internal Audit
Head of Unit Claire MAGNANT

Directorate A
Free movement of persons, citizenship, fundamental rights
Director - Gustaaf BORCHARDT
1 Free movement of persons, visa policy, external borders, Schengen - Giuseppe CALLOVI
2 Immigration and asylum (including European Refugee Fund) - Jean-Louis DE BROUWER
3 Judicial co-operation in civil matters - Mario Paulo TENREIRO
4 Co-ordination of drug abuse prevention - Liliana BRYKMAN
5 Citizenship, Charter on Fundamental Rights, racism and xenophobia, DAPHNE programme - Alain BRUN

Directorate B
Fight against crime and terrorism; enlargement, external relations
Director - Denise SORASIO
1 Police and customs co-operation; prevention of delinquency - Willem ALDERSHOFF
2 Fight against organised crime - Sönke SCHMIDT
3 Judicial co-operation in criminal matters - Gisèle VERNIMMEN
4 External relations and enlargement - Lotte KNUDSEN
5 Management of the Title VI programmes (Treaty on the European Union) - Jean-Jacques NUSS

Direction C
Resource management; communication; information networks
Acting Director - Carel EDWARDS
1 Human and financial resources, information technology, security - Carel EDWARDS
2 Information and communication - Gisela VANWERT
3 Large-scale information systems - Frank PAUL

Rue de la Loi 200, B-1049 Brussels • Tel +32 22 99 11 11

REGIONAL POLICY
DIRECTORATE-GENERAL

Fax: +32 22 95 61 49
Website: http://europa.eu.int/comm/dgs/regional_policy/index_en.htm

Commissioner Michel BARNIER
Acting Director-General Graham MEADOWS
Adviser Guy GRAUSER
Assistant (political matters) Vacant

Information and relations with the European Parliament, the Committee of the Regions and the
Economic and Social Committee
Head of Unit Thierry DAMAN
Internal Audit: audit and advice
Head of Unit Charles GROUTAGE

Directorate A
Conception, impact, co-ordination and evaluation of regional policies
Director - Jean-Charles LEYGUES
1 Conception and analysis, accession negotiations and spatial planning - Vacant
2 Co-ordination of regional, Cohesion Fund and other fund operations, conformity with other Community policies; strategic programming - Everardus HARTOG
3 Co-ordination of evaluation, regional impact of Community policies and additionality - Anastassios BOUGAS

Directorate B
Community initiatives and innovative schemes
Director - Elisabeth HELANDER
1 INTERREG - Esben POULSEN
2 URBAN and action in urban areas - Rudolf NIESSLER
3 Innovative action - Jean-Pierre BERG

Directorate C
Regional operations in Denmark, Germany, Ireland, Finland, Sweden and the United Kingdom
Director - José PALMA ANDRÉS
1 Ireland and United Kingdom - Manfred BESCHEL
2 Denmark, Finland and Sweden - Germán GRANDA ALVA
3 Germany - Michel-Éric DUFEIL

Directorate D
Regional operations in Belgium, Spain, Luxembourg, the Netherlands, Austria and Portugal
Director - Ranieri DI CARPEGNA
1 Spain - Rory McKENNA
2 Portugal - Marco ORANI
3 Belgium, Luxembourg, the Netherlands and Austria - Guido BERNARDINI

Directorate E
Regional operations in Greece, France and Italy
Director - Graham MEADOWS
1 Greece - Robert SHOTTON
2 Italy - Jack ENGWEGEN
3 France - Bernard LANGE
4 Co-ordination of matters concerning the outermost regions - Pascale WOLFCARIUS

Directorate F
ISPA and pre-accession measures
Director - Luis RIERA FIGUERAS
Adviser (overall co-ordination) - Eric UNTERWURZACHER
1 Co-ordination of ISPA activities and preparation for accession - Eric UNTERWURZACHER
2 Estonia, Latvia, Lithuania, Poland - Friedemann ALLGAYER
3 Czech Republic, Slovakia - Vacant
4 Bulgaria, Hungary, Romania, Slovenia - Jean-Marie SEYLER

Directorate G
Financial management, legal matters, monitoring, informatics and human resources
Director - Walter DEFFAA
Adviser (co-ordination and implementation of the administrative reform) - Ricardo GARCIA AYALA
1 Financial and budgetary management - Alain ROGGERI
2 Legal matters, procedures and relations with the Committees and the Council - Hans JANKOWSKI
3 Monitoring and audit of ERDF, relations with the Court of Auditors and OLAF - Kurt-Peter HÖTTE
4 Information technology - Marc BOTMAN
5 Human resources and training - Christopher TODD
6 Monitoring and audit of ERDF and ISPA - Nicholas MARTYN
7 Monitoring and audit of the Cohesion fund and co-ordination of the monitoring of the Structural Funds - Lena ANDERSSON PENCH

RESEARCH DIRECTORATE-GENERAL

Fax: +32 22 95 01 45
Website: http://europa.eu.int/comm/dgs/research/index_en.htm

Commissioner Philippe BUSQUIN
Director-General Achilleas MITSOS
Deputy Director-General (responsible for the European Research Area and in particular its international dimension) Hugh RICHARDSON
Deputy Director-General Vacant
Assistant to the Director-General Stavros CHATZIPANAGIOTOU
Chief Adviser (responsible for the international dimension of the European Research Area) - Vacant
Chief Advisers (research policy matters) Vacant, (nuclear fusion matters) Umberto FINZI, (research policy matters) Michel ANDRÉ, (economic matters) Vacant

Interinstitutional relations
Head of Unit Christian FISCHER-DIESKAU

Information and communication
Head of Unit Jürgen ROSENBAUM

Internal audit
Head of Unit Liliane DE WOLF

Space research policy and co-ordination
Head of Unit Luc TYTGAT

Planning, programming, evaluation
Head of Unit Brigit DE BOISSEZON

International scientific co-operation policy
Head of Unit Louis BELLEMIN

International scientific co-operation projects
Head of Unit Thomas ARNOLD

Directorate A
Co-ordination of Community activities
Director - Richard ESCRITT
1 Framework Programme - Allessandro DAMIANI
2 Support for the implementation of the research programmes - Graham STROUD
3 Aspects of regulation and cross-cutting - Robert Jan SMITS
4 Research and SMEs - Robert Jan SMITS
5 Links with other policies - Robert BURMANJER

Rue de la Loi 200, B-1049 Brussels • Tel +32 22 99 11 11

Directorate B
European research area: structural aspects
Director - Peter KIND
1 National research policies, intergovernmental co-operation - Clara DE LA TORRE
2 Centres and networks of excellence - Vacant
3 Research and innovation - Isi SARAGOSSI
4 Research infrastructures - Marco MALACARNE
5 Administration and finance; COST programme - Miroslav BURES

Directorate C
Science and society
Director - Rainer GEROLD
1 Governance, scientific reference systems and relations with the JRC - Roderick HURST
2 Relations with scientific advisory bodies - Roderick HURST
3 Ethical issues of research and science - Barbara RHODE
4 Public awareness of science; young people and science - Gregorio MEDRANO ASENSIO
5 Women and science - Nicole DEWANDRE

Directorate D
European research area: the human factor
Director - Raffaele LIBERALI
1 Mobility policy - Jocelyne GAUDIN
2 Marie Curie training fellowships - Georges BINGEN
3 Research training networks - Bruno Serge SCHMITZ
4 Promotion of scientific excellence - Rudolf MEIJER
5 International fellowships - Nicholas NEWMAN
6 Administration and finance - Robert KRENGEL

Directorate E
Life sciences: biotechnology, agricultural and food research
Director - Bruno HANSEN
1 Policy aspects - Étienne MAGNIEN
2 Health, food and environment - Liam BRESLIN
3 Agriculture, agribusiness, fisheries and forestry - Xabier GOENAGA BELDARRAIN
4 Cell factory - Alfredo AGUILAR ROMANILLOS
5 Administration and finance - Maria SOARES DE AIRES

Directorate F
Life sciences: health research
Director - Octavio QUINTANA TRIAS
1 Policy aspects - Timothy HALL
2 Infectious diseases - Alan VANVOSSEL
3 The ageing population; poverty-related diseases - Arndt HOEVELER
4 Generic activities and infrastructure - Manuel HALLEN
5 Administration and finance - Martine Marie WAUTERS

Directorate G
Industrial technologies
Director - Ezio ANDRETA
1 Policy aspects - Nicholas HARTLEY
2 Products, processes and organisations - Hervé PERO
3 Materials - Luisa PRISTA

4 Nanoscience and nanotechnology - Renzo TOMELLINI
5 Administration and finance - Megan RICHARDS
6 Coal smelted steel - Philippe VANNSON

Directorate H
Competitive and sustainable growth: transport research
Director - Jack METTHEY
1 Policy aspects - Luisa PRISTA
2 Inland transport and marine technology - Christos TOKAMANIS
3 Aeronautics - Herbert VON BOSE
4 Measurement and testing and infrastructure - Wiktor RALDOW
5 Administration and finance - Michael SUCKER

Directorate I
Environment
Director - Chris PATERMANN
1 Policy aspects - Pierre VALETTE
2 Global change - Anver GHAZI
3 Water management and quality - Andrea TILCHE
4 Biodiversity and marine ecosystems - Pierre MATHY
5 The city of tomorrow and cultural heritage - David MILES
6 Administration and finance - Martin BOHLE

Directorate J
Energy
Director - Pablo FERNÁNDEZ RUIZ
1 Policy aspects - Michel POIREAU
2 Clean energy systems - Ángel PÉREZ SAINZ
3 Improvement of energy efficiency - Barry ROBERTSON
4 Nuclear fission and radiation protection - Hans FORSSTROM
5 Joint development of fusion - Jean-Pierre RAGER
6 Fusion association agreements - Hardo BRUHNS
7 Administration and finance - Johannes SPOOR

Directorate K
Technology foresight and socio-economic research
Director - Jean-François MARCHIPONT
1 Strategic and political aspects: investment in research - Isi SARAGOSSI
2 Science and technology foresight; links with the IPTS - Paraskevas Dimitri CARACOSTAS
3 Competitiveness, economic analysis and indicators - Suleyman MULDUR
4 Socio-economic knowledge base - Andrew SORS
5 Administration and finance - Priscila FERNÁNDE-CANADAS

Directorate L
Resources
Director - Maria Manuela SOARES
1 Personnel policy and equal opportunities - Georges PAPAGEORGIOU
2 Budget and financial service - Stefan LEHNER
3 Training and in-house information - Michel STAVAUX
4 External audits - Eduard RILLE
5 Informatics - David GOULD

TAXATION AND CUSTOMS UNION DIRECTORATE-GENERAL

Fax: +32 22 95 07 56

Website: http://europa.eu.int/comm/dgs/taxation_customs/index_en.htm

Commissioner Frits BOLKESTEIN
Director-General Robert VERRUE
Assistant to Director-General Lilian BERTIN

Management of human and financial resources
Head of Unit Thierry VINOIS

Directorate A
General affairs
Director - Manuel ARNAL MONREAL
1 Relations with the institutions, internal co-ordination - Jean-Louis VERGNOLLE
2 Strategy, political and economic forward studies, evaluation - Bernard GRAND
3 Legal affairs and enforcement of Community provisions - Richard VAN RAAN
4 International affairs - Pierre FAUCHERAND

Directorate B
Customs policy
Director - Alexander WIEDOW
Advisor (customs policy with regard to WTO and G7) - Vacant
1 Customs legislation - Michael LUX
2 Modernisation of customs - John PULFORD
3 Economic aspects of customs and transit - Maria CABRAL
4 Rules of origin - Rosa María LÓPEZ JORRIN
5 Customs tariff - Luigi CASELLA

Directorate C
Tax policy
Director - Michel AUJEAN
1 Co-ordination of tax matters (Secretariat of the Tax Policy Group and the Code of Conduct Group) - Matthias MORS
2 Direct taxation - Philip KERMODE
3 VAT and other turnover taxes - Stephen BILL
4 Excise duties and transport, environment and energy taxes - Donato RAPONI
5 Economic analysis of taxation - Anne BUCHER

Directorate D
Programme management
Director - Marinus DE GRAAFF
1 Information, training, management of customs and tax co-operation programmes - Sebastian BIRCH
2 International technical assistance on customs and taxation - Thomas CARROLL
3 Information technology - Iosif DASCALU

Rue de la Loi 200, B-1049 Brussels • Tel +32 22 99 11 11

DEVELOPMENT DIRECTORATE-GENERAL

Rue de Genève 12, B-1140 Brussels
Fax: +32 22 99 28 72/73

Website: http://europa.eu.int/comm/dgs/development/index_en.htm

Commissioner Poul NIELSON
Director-General Jacobus RICHELLE
Deputy Director-General Vacant
Chief Adviser Friedrich HAMBURGER
Adviser hors classe (responsible for the EDF Committee, relations with the ACP countries and political and geographical issues) Athanassios THEODORAKIS
Assistant Vacant

Internal audit, relations with the Court of Auditors and the European Ombudsman, OLAF
Head of Unit Klaas EHBETS

Directorate A
General support and operational support
Director - Maria BARREIROS
1 Programming, strategic planning and finance - Jean-Pierre REYMONDET-COMMOY
2 Relations with the UN, member states and other OECD donors - Hugo SCHALLY
3 Relations with the EU institutions and ACP, civil society and NGOs - Paul MALIN
4 Human resources; information technology - Peter CRAIG McQUAIDE
5 Information and communication - Leonidas ANTONADOPOULOS

Directorate B
Development policy and sectoral questions
Director - Bernard PETIT
Adviser (matters relating to research and development and the information society - Amos TINCANI
Adviser (sustainable development questions) - Vacant
1 Development policy, coherence and forward studies - Françoise MOREAU
2 Economic co-operation and PRSP process - Gilles HERVIO

3 Social and human development - Lieve FRANSEN
4 Environment, rural development - Uwe WERBLOW
5 Transport and infrastructure, urban development - Antonio GARCÍO FRAGIO

Directorate C
Horn of Africa, East and Southern Africa, Indian Ocean, Pacific
Acting Director - Roger MOORE
Adviser (geographical questions) - Valeriano DÍAZ
1 Regional questions - Jean-Claude BOIDIN
2 Horn of Africa, East Africa and Indian Ocean - Roger MOORE
3 Southern Africa - Philippe DARMUZEY
4 Pacific - George GWYER

Directorate D
West and Central Africa, Caribbean, OCTs
Director - Friedrich HAMBURGER
Adviser (geographical questions) - Miguel FORCAT ICARDO
1 Regional questions and the OCTs - Gaspar FRONTINI CATTIVELLO
2 West Africa - Anna Silvia PIERGROSSI-FRASCHINI
3 Central Africa, the Great Lakes - Peter CHRISTIANSEN
4 Caribbean - Luis RITTO

ENLARGEMENT DIRECTORATE-GENERAL

Fax: +32 22 96 84 90

Website: http://europa.eu.int/comm/dgs/enlargement/index_en.htm

Commissioner Günter VERHEUGEN
Director-General Eneko LANDÁBURU ILLARRAMENDI
Chief Adviser Graham AVERY
Assistant to the Director-General Petros MAVROMICHALIS

Audit
Head of Unit Michael BERRISFORD

Information and interinstitutional relations
Head of Unit Wencesles DE LOBKOWICZ

Directorate A
Estonia, Latvia, Lithuania, Poland
Director - Françoise GAUDENZI
1 Poland team - Françoise GAUDENZI
2 Estonia team - Dirk LANGE
3 Latvia team - Manel CAMOS GRAU
4 Lithuania team - Vacant

Directorate B
Czech Republic, Hungary, Slovakia, Slovenia
Director - Pierre MIREL
1 Hungary team - Pierre MIREL
2 Czech Republic team - Rutger WISSELS
3 Slovakia team - Dirk MEGANCK
4 Slovenia team - Jaime GARCÍA LOMBARDERO

Directorate C
Bulgaria, Cyprus, Malta, Romania, Turkey
Director - Michael LEIGH
1 Bulgaria team - Morter JUNG-OLSEN
2 Cyprus team - Leopold MAURER

3 Malta team - Arhi PALOSUO
4 Romania team - Enrico GRILLO PASQUARELLI
5 Turkey team - Michael LEIGH

Directorate D
Negotiation, pre-accession, co-ordination and financial instruments
Director - Alfred Matthias RUETE
1 Negotiations and pre-accession, co-ordination - Ricardo PASCUAL BREMON
2 TAIEX - Bridget CZARNOTA
3 Co-ordination of financial instruments - Vincent DEGERT
4 Implementation and contracts - Helmuth LOHAN

Directorate E
Resources and finance
Director - Augusto BONUCCI
1 Resources - Laura MORETTI
2 Financial planification and execution - Carlos FILIPE
3 Evaluation - Goran SEGERLUND

Rue de la Loi 200, B-1049 Brussels • Tel +32 22 99 11 11

EUROPEAID CO-OPERATION OFFICE

Fax: +32 22 99 64 07

Website: http://europa.eu.int/comm/dgs/europeaid/index_en.htm

Commissioner Chris PATTEN
Director-General Giorgio BONACCI
Deputy Director-General Marc FRANCO
Chief Adviser Irma Margreta PETTERSON
Assistants to the Director-General Emma TOLEDANO LAREDO, Fabienne LEVY

Co-ordination, devolution
Head of Unit Carla MONTESI

Internal auditing
Head of Unit Rony SABAH

General programming, support to finance committees
Head of Unit Agnes LINDEMANS-MAES

Directorate A
Europe, Caucasus, Central Asia
Director - Per Brix KNUDSEN
Adviser - Guy DOUCET
1 Co-ordination for Europe - Per EKLUND
2 Economic reform, private sector - Barbara LÜCKE
3 Social development, institutional support - Colin WOLFE
4 Energy, transport, infrastructure - Dino SINIGALLIA
5 Nuclear safety - Guy DOUCET
6 Financial and contract management - Konstantin KONSTANTINOU

European Agency for Reconstruction
Director - Hugues MINGARELLI

Directorate B
Southern Mediterranean, Middle East
Director - Richard WEBER
1 Co-ordination for the Mediterranean region - Ana GONZALO CASTELLANOS
2 Economic co-operation - Marco MAZZOCCHI-ALEMANNI
3 Regional integration, institutional support - Basile PAPADOPOULOS
4 Social development (health, education) - Elisabeth FERET
5 Sustainable rural development, environment - Robert KREMER
6 Transport, infrastructure, water, energy - Vacant
7 Financial and contract management - José IZARRA AGUADO

Directorate C
Africa, Caribbean, Pacific
Director - José SILVA DOMINGOS
1 Co-ordination for the ACP countries - Mikael BARFORD
2 Economic co-operation - Jean-Louis LACUBE
3 Regional integration, Institutional support - Dominique DELLICOUR
4 Social development (health, education) - Riccardo GAMBINI
5 Sustainable rural development, environment - Hubertus ZIMMER
6 Transport, infrastructure - Gerald BARON
7 Financial and contract management - Geremia SCIANCA

Directorate D
Asia
Director - Erich MULLER
1 Co-ordination for Asia - Thomas McGOVERN
2 Economic co-operation - David MACRAE
3 Regional integration, institutional support - Alessandro MARIANI
4 Social development - Marianne WENNING
5 Sustainable rural development, infrastructure, environment - Vacant

Directorate E
Latin America
Director - Fernardo CARDESA GARCÍA
1 Co-ordination for Latin America - George KASIMATIS
2 Economic co-operation - Adrianus KOETSENRUIJTER
3 Regional integration, institutional support - Denis SALORD
4 Social development (health, education) - François NIZERY
5 Sustainable rural development, infrastructure, environment - José Luis TRIMIÑO PEREZ
6 Financial and contract management - Michel DE CONINCK

Directorate F
Horizontal operations and innovation
Director - Francesco DE ANGELIS
1 Innovation - César DEBEN ALFONSO
2 Co-financing with NGOs - Aristotelis BOURATSIS
3 Democracy, human rights - Timothy CLARKE
4 Environment, social development - Jan TEN BLOEMENDAL
5 Food security - Chantal HEBBERECHT
6 Financial and contract management - Andreas HECKER

Directorate G
Operational support
Director - Constantin STATHOPOULOS
1 Budget, monitoring of budget implementation - Jean-Louis VILLE
2 Finance, contracts, procurement notices - Raul MATEUS PAULA
3 Legal affairs, litigation - Ole SCOTT-LARSEN
4 External audit of operations - Michael KAGEL
5 Relations with international organisations, co-financing - Franco NICORA

Directorate H
General affairs
Director - Thierry DE SAINT-MAURICE
1 Personnel, training - Fermín J. MELENDRO ARNÁIZ
2 Individual experts - Catherine THEODOROU-KALOGIROU
3 Information systems, office automation - Jacques HAÏK
4 Relations with the other institutions - Martyn PENNINGTON
5 Information, communication - Santiago HERRERO VILLA
6 Evaluation - Jean-Louis CHOMEL

Rue de la Loi 200, B-1049 Brussels • Tel +32 22 99 11 11

EXTERNAL RELATIONS DIRECTORATE-GENERAL

Fax: +32 22 99 65 29

Website: http://europa.eu.int/comm/dgs/external_relations/index_en.htm

Commissioner Chris PATTEN
Director-General Guy LEGRAS
Deputy Director-General (CFSP, Multilateral affairs and North America, East Asia, Australia, New Zealand, EEA and EFTA [Directorates A, B and C]) Fernando VALENZUELA MARZO
Deputy Director-General (Europe and Central Asia, Middle East and South Mediterranean [Directorates D, E and F]) Vacant
Deputy Director-General (Asia, Latin America [Directorates G and H]) Vacant
Chief Adviser Ove JUUL JORGENSEN
Chief Adviser Vacant
Assistant to Director-General Rhoda Anette MANDLER

Inspection of the delegations
Head of Unit Tue ROHRSTED

Audit
Head of Unit Apostolos BLETSAS

Planning Service for External Relations
Head of Unit Helmut STEINEL

Economic Analysis
Head of Unit Michael GREEN

Directorate A
CFSP
Director - Lodewijk BRIET
1 European Correspondent - Philippe COESSENS
2 Legal and institutional matters for external relations; sanctions - Florika FINK-HOOIJER
3 Security policy - Lars-Erik LUNDIN
4 Conflict prevention, crisis management and ACP countries - Anna McLOUGHLIN

Directorate B
Multilateral relations and human rights
Director - Danièle SMADJA
1 Human rights and democratisation - Daniela NAPOLI
2 United Nations, Law of the Sea, Treaties office - Philippe WILLAERT
3 OSCE and Council of Europe - Gilbert DUBOIS

Directorate C
North America, East Asia, Australia, New Zealand, EEA, EFTA, San Marino, Andorra, Monaco
Director - Percy WESTERLUND
1 United States, Canada, NAFTA - Eric HAYES
2 Japan, Korea, Australia, New Zealand - Seamus GILLESPIE
3 EEA, EFTA, San Marino, Andorra, Monaco - Matthias BRINKMANN

Directorate D
Western Balkans
Director - Reinhard PRIEBE
1 Horizontal matters - Michael PERETTI
2 Federal Republic of Yugoslavia - Thérèse SOBIESKI
3 Albania, Bosnia and Herzegovina, Croatia, FYROM - David DALY

Directorate E
Eastern Europe, Caucasus, Central Asian Republics
Director - Hughes MINGARELLI
1 Horizontal matters - Alistair MacDONALD
2 Russia, Ukraine, Moldova, Belarus - Gerhard LOHAN
3 Caucasus and Central Asia (including Mongolia) - Kurt JUUL

Directorate F
Middle East, South Mediterranean
Director - Christian LEFFLER
1 Horizontal matters - Laura BAEZA
2 Barcelona Process, Gulf countries, Iran, Iraq and Yemen - Patrick LAURENT
3 Mashreq and Israel - Alan SEATTER
4 Maghreb - Robert VAN DER MEULEN

Directorate G
Latin America
Director - Francisco DA CÂMARA-GOMES
1 Horizontal matters - Tomás DUPLA DEL MORAL

2 Mexico, Central America - Victor ANDRÉS MALDONADO
3 Andean Pact - Astrid SCHOMAKER
4 Mercosur, Chile - Damián HERNÁNDEZ LÓPEZ

Directorate H
Asia (except Japan and Korea)
Director - Fokion FOTIADIS
1 Horizontal matters - Pierre AMILHAT
2 China, Hong Kong, Macao, Taiwan - Angelos PANGRATIS
3 India, Bhutan, Nepal - Laurence ARGIMON-PISTRE
4 Pakistan, Afghanistan, Sri Lanka, Bangladesh, Maldives - Marcus CORNARO
5 South East Asia - James MORAN

Directorate I
Headquarters resources, information, interinstitutional relations
Director - David LIPMAN
1 Human resources and administration - Eva GERNER
2 Financial and budgetary matters, relations with the Court of Auditors - Mark JOHNSTON
3 Information technology resources - Michael KEYMOLEN
4 Interinstitutional relations - Reinhold HACK
5 Information and communication - Saturnino MUÑOZ GÓMEZ

Directorate K
External service
Director - Christian FALKOWSKI
1 Personnel; planning of the development of the external service - Chantal GRAYKOWSKI-MASSANGIOLI
2 Rights and obligations - Catherine THEODOROU-KALOGIROU
3 Administration - Giuseppe ROSIN
4 Budget - Maria Luísa MERLA
5 Local staff - Antonius BRÜSER

Rue de la Loi, 200, B-1049 Brussels • Tel +32 22 99 11 11

HUMANITARIAN AID OFFICE (ECHO)

Fax: +32 22 95 45 78

Website: http://europa.eu.int/comm/dgs/humanitarian_aid/index_en.htm

Commissioner Poul NEILSON
Director Costanza ADINOLFI
Adviser (responsible for evaluation) Vacant
Adviser (responsible for information and communication) Giorgio GUARNERI
Assistant to Director Hervé DELPHIN

1 Africa, Caribbean, Pacific - Steffen STENBERG-JENSEN
2 Central and Eastern Europe, CIS - Cornelis WITTEBROOD
3 Asia, Latin America, Mediterranean, Middle East - Ruth ALBUQUERQUE
4 General affairs and relations with European institutions, other donors and international organisations; disaster preparedness; support for major crisis; statistics and database - Michel ARRION
5 Human resources; including training and contractual relations with NGO - René GUTH
6 Finance and audit - Vacant

TRADE DIRECTORATE-GENERAL

Fax: +32 22 99 10 29

Website: http://europa.eu.int/comm/dgs/trade/index_en.htm

Commissioner Pascal LAMY
Director-General Mogens Peter CARL
Deputy Director-General Pierre DEFRAIGNE
Assistant to Director-General Luc DEVIGNE

Directorate A
General affairs; resources; bilateral trade relations I
Director - Françoise LE BAIL
1 Human, administrative and financial resources; external service; programming - Bruno PRAGNELL
2 Trade analysis - Gustavo MARTÍN PRADA
3 Inter-institutional relations and communication policy - Olivier de LAROUSSILHE
4 Information technology - Philippe RUYS

Directorate B
Trade defence instruments
Director - Fritz-Harald WENIG
1 Trade defence instruments: general policy, complaints office - Peter KLEIN
2 Trade defence instruments: investigations I; Monitoring of third-country measures - Neil MACDONALD
3 Trade defence instruments: investigations II - Bruno ADINOLFI
4 Trade defence instruments: investigations III; Monitoring and follow-up of the implementation of measures in the Community - Dominique AVOT
5 Trade defence instruments: investigations IV - Vacant

Directorate C
Free trade agreements; agricultural trade questions; ACP; bilateral trade relations II
Director - Karl Friedrich FALKENBERG
1 Trade relations with ACP countries including South Africa - Ingo FEUSTEL
2 Agriculture, fisheries, sanitary and phytosanitary measures, biotechnology - Jens SCHAPS
3 Negotiations and management of free trade agreements, GSP - Lars Holger STANDERTSKJÖLD-NORDENSTAM

Directorate D
Co-ordination of WTO and OECD matters; services, dispute settlement, Trade Barriers Regulation
Director - Hervé JOUANJEAN
1 Co-ordination of WTO, OECD, TRTA, GATT - Raffaele PETRICCIONE
2 Trade in services (including e-commerce); GATS - João AGUIAR MACHADO
3 Dispute settlement and Trade Barriers Regulation - Ignacio GARCÍA BERCERO

Directorate E
Sectoral trade questions; market access; bilateral trade relations III
Director - Vacant
Adviser (export credits) - Allan DALVIN
1 Negotiation and management of textiles agreements; footwear - Fernando PERREAU DE PINNINCK
2 Steel, coal, shipbuilding, automotive, chemicals, and other industries - Salvatore SALERNO
3 Market access - Alistair STEWART

Directorate F
WTO: sustainable development, investment, standards, intellectual property, new technologies; bilateral trade relations IV
Director - Robert MADELIN
1 New technologies, intellectual property, public procurement - Paul VANDOREN
2 Investment, standards and certification, TBT - Philippe MEYER
3 Sustainable development (including trade and environment); co-ordination of dialogue with civil society - Rupert SCHLEGEMILCH

BUDGET DIRECTORATE-GENERAL

Fax: +32 22 95 95 85
Website: http://europa.eu.int/comm/dgs/budget/index_en.htm

Commissioner Michaele SCHREYER
Director-General Luis ROMERO REQUENA
Deputy Director-General Brian GRAY
Assistant to Director-Generanl Antoine QUERO MUSSOT
Adviser in charge of the Secretariat of the 'FUN' and ad hoc Tasks Vacant

Secretariat of the Audit Progress Committee Enrique LOBERA ALGÜELLES
Adviser Vacant

Relations with the European Parliament, the Court of Auditors and the Member States
Head of Unit Jacques VONTHRON

General co-ordination; human and budgetary resources
Acting Head of Unit Martine MATEO

Financial information systems
Head of Unit Jean-Pierre BUISSERET

IT infrastructure and user support
Head of Unit Vacant

Directorate A
Expenditure
Director - Fritz BRUCHERT
1 Budgetary procedure and synthesis, ABB and relations with the COBU - Éric PARADIS
2 Common agricultural policy and structural actions - Marc VANHEUKELEN

3 Internal policies - Louis- Jacques SANT'ANA CALAZANS
4 External policies - René VANDERMOSTEN
5 Administrative appropriations and allocation of IT resources - Philippe BERTRAND
6 Allocation of human resources - Silvano PRESA
7 Monitoring and reporting on budget implementation - Peter LAURSON

Directorate B
Own resources, evaluation and financial programming
Director - Marc OOSTENS
1 Multiannual financial framework; funding systems and forecasts; budgetary aspects of enlargements - Johan UREEL
2 Revenue management - Antti SUORTTI
3 Control of traditional own resources - Robert GIELISSE
4 Control of VAT and GNP-based resources and ACOR secretariat - Richard CONDON
5 Evaluation - Svend JAKOBSEN

Directorate C
Budget execution
Acting Director - Jörgen HOLMQUIST
1 Cash office and treasury management - Basil HOLDER
2 General accounting and recovery of debts - Jean-Marie COUSIN
3 Accounting and budget execution - Willy HOEBEECK

4 European Development Fund and Joint Research Centre accounts - Friedrich BRAEUER

Directorate D
Central Financial Service
Director - Philippe TAVERNE
1 Financial Regulations - Paraskevi GILCHRIST
2 Contracts, grants, ACPC and TAO Monitoring Unit - Philippe VANNSON
3 Financial Procedures and control systems - Herman MOSSELMANS
4 Help Desk, information and training in financial matters - Bruno KRÖLLER
5 User management of financial information systems - Adrian WINDOW
6 Assistance to the applicant countries in the field of financial management and control - Jürgen ANDERMANN

Rue de la Loi 200, B-1049 Brussels • Tel +32 22 99 11 11

FINANCIAL CONTROL DIRECTORATE-GENERAL

Fax: +32 22 95 01 41
Website: http://europa.eu.int/comm/dgs/financial_control/index_en.htm

Commissioner Michaele SCHREYER
Director-General (Financial Controller of the Commission) Edith KITZMANTEL
Assistant to the Director-General Stéphane LOPPARELLI

Personnel, administration, budget and information technology
Head of Unit Arturo CABALLERO BASSEDAS

Co-ordination, methodology and monitoring tools
Head of Unit Ludovic PROMELLE

Directorate A
Ex ante financial control
Director - Horst HÜNKE
Adviser (control of own resources) - Karl ELSNER
1 Internal policies, central administration JRC and Agencies - Udo HEIDER
2 Structural policies and common agricultural policy - Ricardo GARCÍA AYALA
3 External policies - Daniel VAN DER SPREE
4 Luxembourg transactions - Etienne HENTGEN

Rue de la Loi 200, B-1049 Brussels • Tel +32 22 99 11 11

european commission

GROUP OF POLICY ADVISERS

E-mail: group-advisers@cec.eu.int

Website: http://europa.eu.int/comm/dgs/policy_advisers/index_en.htm

Directly attached to President PRODI

Director Ricardo Franco LEVI
Assistant William FLOYD

Advisers
Peter SMITH
André SAPIR
Marco BUTI
Vacant
Vacant

Rue de la Loi 200, B-1049 Brussels • Tel +32 22 99 11 11

INTERNAL AUDIT SERVICE

E-mail: ias-europa@cec.eu.int

Website: http://europa.eu.int/comm/dgs/internal_audit/index_en.htm

Commissioner Neil KINNOCK
Director-General / Head of IAS (Internal Auditor of the Commission) Jules MUIS
Assistant to the Director-General Matthias WILL

Director / Deputy Head of IAS Antony WRIGHT

Administration and technology
Head of Unit Thomas ZIOLKOWSKI

Audit Supervisors
Américo CAVALHEIRO
Vijay BHARDWAJ
Arturo CABALLERO BASSEDAS
Pascal HALLEZ
Vacant

JOINT INTERPRETING AND CONFERENCE SERVICE

Fax: +32 22 95 95 84

Website http://europa.eu.int/comm/dgs/interpretation/index_en.htm

Commissioner Neil KINNOCK
Head of Service Marco BENEDETTI
Assistant to the Head of Service Carlos ALEGRÍA
Adviser (TQM/Inter-departmental consultations) Oscar DÖRFLINGER

Audit
Head of Unit José Antonio LÓPEZ SÁNCHEZ

Programming and evaluation, relations with the other institutions, information systems
Head of Unit Vacant

Directorate A
Interpreting and multilingualism
Director - Noël MUYLLE
Adviser (professional appraisal) - Jean-Pierre DELAVA
1 Multilingualism - Brian FOX
2 Danish language interpreting - Preben SAUGSTRUP
3 German language interpreting - Irene BOHN
4 Greek language interpreting - Alexandra PANAGAKOU
5 English language interpreting - Terence CLOUGH
6 Spanish language interpreting - Rafael GÁLVEZ VÍA
7 Finnish language interpreting - Veijo KRUTH
8 French language interpreting - Marie-Christine COLPAERT-LUX
9 Italian language interpreting - Luisa CASTELLANI
10 Dutch language interpreting - Elisabeth FREUDENSTEIN-

WEIJER
11 Portuguese language interpreting - Luís MACHADO
12 Swedish language interpreting - Annica ÖSTLUND

Directorate B
Meetings and resources
Director - David WALKER
1 Meetings - Wolter WITTEVEEN
2 Budget and finance - Vacant
3 Personnel management and career development - Elizabeth EGELUND-JØRGENSEN
4 New technologies related to conference interpreting - José ESTEBAN CAUSO
5 Conferences - Jupp HAMACHER

Rue de la Loi 200, B-1049 Brussels • Tel +32 22 99 11 11

LEGAL SERVICE

Fax: +32 22 96 30 86

Website: http://europa.eu.int/comm/dgs/legal_service/index_en.htm

Commissioner Romano PRODI
Director-General Michel PETITE
Deputy Director-General Giuliano MARENCO
Assistant to the Director-General William O'LEARY

Principal Legal Advisers

Richard WAINWRIGHT
Hans Peter HARTVIG
Marie-José JONCZY-MONTASTRUC
Claire-Françoise DURAND
José Luis IGLESIAS BUHIGUES
Francisco SANTAOLALLA GADEA
Frank BENYON
Dierk BOOSS
Jürgen GRÜNWALD
Pieter Jan KUIJPER

Legal Advisers

Dominique MAIDANI, Jean-Jacques BOUFLET (attached to the Commission Delegation to the UN and other international organisations in Geneva), Thomas Finbarr CUSACK, Eugenio DE MARCH, John FORMAN, Julian CURRALL, Jürgen GRÜNWALD, Hans Peter HARTVIG, Eric WHITE, Alain VAN SOLINGE, Viktor KREUSCHITZ, Xenophon YATAGANAS, Gérard ROZET, Jörn SACK, Christina TUFVESSON, Hendrik VAN LIER, Thomas VAN RIJN, Götz Eike ZUR HAUSEN, Enrico TRAVERSA, Vacant, Vacant

Legal Revisers Group

Head of group Bevis CLARK-SMITH

PERSONNEL AND ADMINISTRATION DIRECTORATE-GENERAL

Fax: +32 22 99 62 76

Website: http://europa.eu.int/comm/dgs/personnel_administration/index_en.htm

Commissioner Neil KINNOCK
Director-General Horst REICHENBACH
Adviser hors classe Santiago GÓMEZ REINO
Permanent Rapporteur Marina MANFREDI
Chief Adviser Rocco TANZILLI
Principal Adviser (responsible for specific projects in the area of administrative reform) Photius NANOPOULOS
Adviser (resposible for organisation and control) Eberhard BRANDT
Assistant to the Director-General Diane SCHMITT
Assistant to the Director-General (responsible for reform) Daniele DOTTO

Direction IDOC - Investigation and Disciplinary Office
Acting Director Mercedes DE SOLA DOMINGO

Statutory negotiations and surveillance of reform
Head of Unit Martin TERBERGER

Audit
Head of Unit Marc BELLENS

Social dialogue
Head of Unit Stefan HUBER

Administration (Ispra)
Head of Unit Francesco CIVILETTI

Directorate A
Staff Policy
Director - Irène SOUKA
1 General aspects of personnel policy - Klaus RUDUSCHHAUSER
2 SCOP: Professional Orientation and Career Development - Fernando GARCÍA FERREIRO
3 Statutory staff and seconded national experts - Roger FRY
4 Temporary employees: recruitment and administrative statutes - Roger FRY
5 Organigram and management staff - Ann d'HAEN-BERTIER
6 Career structure, evaluation and promotions - Marco MOULIGREAU
7 Training office - Guido VERVAET

Rue de la Loi 200, B-1049 Brussels • Tel +32 22 99 11 11

Directorate B
Rights and obligations; social welfare policy and actions
Director - Vacant
Adviser (co-ordination) - Luc LATOUCHE
1 Staff regulations - Adrian BARNETT
2 Appeal - Adrian BARNETT
3 Conditions of employment, rights and non-pecuniary obligations - Jean-Pierre GRILLO
4 Non-discrimination and equal opportunities - Ana LAISSY
5 Horizontal issues related to enlargement - Hans-Georg GERSTENLAUER

Directorate E
Health, hygeine and social policy; termination of rights
Acting Director - Fritz BRUCHERT
Adviser - Pedro DE MIGUEL GARCÍA
1 Social welfare policy and actions - Antonio SILVA MENDES
2 Personnel, statutes and social policy (Luxembourg) - Bernard REYNOLDS
3 Medical service (Luxembourg) - Thierry JADOT
4 Medical service (Brussels) - Gabriel MARTINEAU
5 Medical service (Ispra) - Paul Helmut ORTH
6 Health and safety at work - Franz TSCHISMARON

Directorate D
Resources
Director - Vacant
Adviser (relations with national public services) - Maurizio MANCINI
Adviser (data protection and computer security) - Patrice MARCELLI
Adviser (internal reform of budgetary procedures and financial circuits) - Oskar ZIPFEL
1 Finance and contract support - Hendrik VANTILBORGH
2 Relations with institutions, ABM and document development - Martin TERBERGER
3 Human resources administration and internal reform - Alain SCRIBAN
4 Information systems - Philippe BIERLAIRE
5 Internal communication and information - Nicholas BEARFIELD

Directorate DI
Informatics directorate
Director - Francisco GARCÍA MORÁN
1 Advice and technical evaluation - Jean-Pierre WEIDERT
2 Customer services and relations - Jean-Pierre LAMBOT
3 Office systems and technical support - José MARÍN NAVARRO
4 Information systems support (Brussels) - Karel DE VRIENDT
5 Telecommunications and networks - Marcel JORTAY
6 Data centre - Declan DEASY
7 IT finance, contracts and logistics - Francis PELTGEN
8 Integration of information systems and quality - Theodoros VASSILIADIS

Directorate DS
Security
Acting Director - Frank ASBECK
Adviser - Frank ASBECK
1 Protection (Luxembourg) - Hannu HYVÄRINEN
2 Evaluation and prevention - Jonathan LAMB
3 Inspection and advice - Willem KELLER
4 Data security - Leonardus VOORHAM

TRANSLATION SERVICE

(Based in Luxembourg)
Fax (Luxembourg): +352 43 03 32 99/53 19
Fax (Brussels): +32 22 95 65 03

Website: http://europa.eu.int/comm/dgs/translation/index_en.htm

Commissioner Neil KINNOCK
Director-General Michel VANDEN ABEELE
Chief Adviser Ranieri BOMBASSERI
Adviser (responsible for Luxembourg departments) Vacant
Adviser Vacant
Assistant to Director-General Carole ORY

Information and communications
Head of Unit Cornelis VAN DER HORST

Audit
Head of Unit Vacant

Directorate RL
Resources and Language Support
Director - Fernand THURMES
Adviser (evaluation of quality of freelance translations) -
Paloma HOFFMANN-VEVIA ROMERO
Adviser - Paola IOVINE-KRAUS
1 Resources - Basile KOUTSIVITIS
2 Information technology and development - Jean-Louis
COBBAERT
3 Analysis of needs and multilingual tools - Alain
REICHLING
4 Terminology and Language Support Services - Hubert
PAESMANS
- Language help desk (Brussels) - Diana JANK
- Language help desk (Luxembourg) - Roger BENNETT
- Eurodicautom - Augustin JIMINEZ
5 External translation - Juan José MARTÍNEZ GUILLÉN
6 Training - Rosanna CAO

Directorate TR
Translation
Director - Georges VLACHOPOULOS
Advisers - Paul ATKINS, Vacant
1 Planning and interinstitutional procedures - Vacant
2 Language co-ordination and quality assurance

Head of Department	Manuel DE OLIVEIRA BARATA
1 Danish	Peter AURØ
2 German	Reinhard HOHEISEL
3 English	Timothy MARTIN
4 Spanish	Amadeo SOLÀ GARDELL
5 French	Andrea BENDA
6 Greek	Constantinos SOTIRCHOS
7 Italian	Vacant
8 Dutch	Vacant
9 Portuguese	Maria DAS DORES SERRÃO
10 Finnish	Jyrki LAPPI-SEPPÄIÄ
11 Swedish	Kenneth LARSSON

Directorate TR/AB
Legal, economic and financial affairs, competition and information

Head of Department	Georges VLACHOPOULOS
1 Danish	Inga WALDSTRØM
2 German	Klaus MEYER-KOEKEN
3 English	William BYTHELL
4 Spanish	Jesús Manuel MARTÍNEZ GARCÍA
5 French	Elaine JABON
6 Greek	Georgios HANIOTAKIS
7 Italian	Claudio FISCHER
8 Dutch	Jean-Pierre STERCK
9 Portuguese	Maria Cristina DE PRETER
10 Finnish	Tiina LOHIKKO
11 Swedish	Lennart LUNDBERG

Directorate TR/C
Agriculture, fisheries, regional policy and cohesion

Head of Department	Svend BECH
1 Danish	Tove BLAABJERG-SØRENSEN
2 German	Raymond WALTZING
3 English	William FRASER
4 Spanish	Marta MANTE BARTRA
5 French	Christian SCOCARD
6 Greek	Dimitrios CHRONOPOULOS
7 Italian	Luigi MAGI
8 Dutch	Marc DE REU
9 Portuguese	Vitor SINDE
10 Finnish	Risto PITKÄNEN
11 Swedish	Inga ROTH

Directorate TR/D
External relations, customs union, development, enlargement, humanitarian aid

Head of Department	María Elena FERNÁNDEZ-MIRANDA
1 Danish	Derrick OLESEN
2 German	Raymund BERNERS
3 English	Gillian COLLEDGE
4 Spanish	Paloma DÍEZ PARDO
5 French	Alain MASSCHELEIN
6 Greek	Athanassios ANTOULAS
7 Italian	Marina SANTELLI
8 Dutch	Vacant
9 Portuguese	Maria Cecília CORTE REAL
10 Finnish	Risto NIEMINEN
11 Swedish	Annika WALLEN

Directorate TR/E
Research, telecommunications, energy, industry, environment and transport

Head of Department	Luigi VESENTINI
1 Danish	Preben FINK-JENSEN
2 German	Raymond REGH
3 English	Charles LUCAS
4 Spanish	Magdalena GUILLÓ FONTANILLS
5 French	Bruno LIBERT
6 Greek	Jean CARATZICOS
7 Italian	Adelia BERTETTO
8 Dutch	Luc VERDEGEM
9 Portuguese	Peter SOARES PINTO
10 Finnish	Paula OVASKA ROMANO
11 Swedish	Gertrud INGESTAD

Directorate TR/F
Social affairs, human resources, consumer policy

Head of Department	Elizabeth WAGNER
1 Danish	Poul ANDERSEN
2 German	Margret HEIMBECK
3 English	David CROWTHER
4 Spanish	Francisco VALERI COBO
5 French	Armand SPODEN
6 Greek	Spiridon BOCOLINIS
7 Italian	Marcello ANGIONI
8 Dutch	Antoine DE BRABANDER
9 Portuguese	Jorge HOMEM
10 Finnish	Mada KALLIOPUSKA
11 Swedish	Ewa ROSSING

Directorate TR/G
Statistics, enterprise policy, information market, innovation

Head of Department	Ludovicus DE PRINS
1 Danish	Bodil FRANSSEN
2 German	Elisabeth CONSTANT
3 English	Douglas JENKS
4 Spanish	Josep BONET
5 French	René FOUCART
6 Greek	Konstantinos ZACHARIS
7 Italian	Christiano GAMBARI
8 Dutch	Theo VAN DIJK
9 Portuguese	Helena DOMINGOS
10 Finnish	Päivi OLLILA
11 Swedish	Bengt HANER

EUROPEAN ANTI-FRAUD OFFICE

Tel: +32 22 96 66 88
Fax: +32 22 96 37 31

Website: http://europa.eu.int/comm/dgs/anti_fraud/index_en.htm

Commissioner Michaele SCHREYER
Director-General Franz-Hermann BRÜNER
Assistant to the Director-General (responsible for policy) Harald SPITZER
Assistant to the Director-General (responsible for operations) Jonathan REVILL

Administration, human resources and budget
Head of Unit Paolo MILLICH

Communication, public relations, co-ordination of training
Head of Unit Alessandro BUTTICÉ

External relations and support for candidate countries
Head of Unit Kjell LARSSON
Adviser (responsible for Poland) François BEULLENS

Magistrates, judicial advice and follow-up
Head of Unit Joaquín GONZÁLEZ GONZÁLEZ
OLAF Supervisory Committee
Committee Secretary Jean DARRAS

Directorate A
Policy, legislation and legal affairs
Director - Claude LECOU
Acting Adviser (general co-ordination and enlargement) - Luc SCHAERLAEKENS
1 Legislation, legal affairs and relations with the other institutions; Protection of the euro - Lothar KUHL
2 Work programmes, reports and consultative committee - Catherine VIEILLEDENT-MONFORT
3 Customs, indirect taxation and trade policies: co-ordination of anti-fraud legislation, administrative and financial follow-up - Joaquin Geraldes PINTO
4 Agriculture and structural operations: anti-fraud legislation, administrative and financial monitoring - Joaquin Geraldes PINTO
5 Direct expenditure: anti-fraud legislation, administrative and financial follow-up, recovery - Joaquin GERALDES PINTO

Directorate B
Investigations and operations
Acting Director - Paul Lachal ROBERTS
1 External investigations and operations: team of advisers - (agriculture) Elisabeth SPERBER, (customs) Thierry CRETIN, (cigarettes) Ian WALTON-GEORGE
2 Internal investigations, direct expenditure and structural actions: team of advisers - Paul Lachal ROBERTS, Johan VLOGAERT, Maria Rosa SA
3 Pool and support functions - Caroline DE GRAEF

Directorate C
Intelligence, operational strategy and information technology
Director - Nicholas ILETT
1 Intelligence: strategic assessment and analysis - Nicholas ILETT
2 Information technology - Harald SONNBERGER
3 Operational Intelligence: information and technical support - Mika MÄKELÄ

Rue de la Loi 200, B-1049 Brussels • Tel +32 22 99 11 11

EUROSTAT

E-mail: eurostat-infodesk@cec.eu.int
Website: http://europa.eu.int/comm/dgs/eurostat/index_en.htm

Commissioner Pedro SOLBES MIRA
Director-General Yves FRANCHET
Assistant to the Director-General Maria Hélena FIGUEIRA
Adviser (responsible for relations with the European Institutions in Brussels) James WHITWORTH
Internal Audit
Head of Unit Christine DUREN-JUNKER

Directorate R
Resources
Director - Marian O'LEARY
1 Administration and staff - Ovidio CROCICCHI
2 Work programme, planning - Giles DECAND
3 Budget policy and management - Roland LANE
4 Legal affairs, statistical confidentiality - Efstratios CHATZIDOUKAKIS

Directorate A
Statistical information system; research and data analysis; technical co-operation with Phare and Tacis countries
Director - Photis NANOPOULOS
1 Computerised management of information systems - Daniel DEFAYS
2 Information and communication technologies for the Community statistical system - Wolfgang KNÜPPEL
3 Reference databases - Jean HELLER
4 Research and development, methods and data analyses - Jean-Louis MERCY
5 Technical co-operation with Phare and Tacis countries - Nikolaus WURM
6 Statistical indicators for short-term analysis of the euro zone - Klaus REEH

Directorate B
Economic statistics and economic and monetary convergence
Director - Bart MEGANCK
1 National accounts methodology, statistics for own resources - Brian NEWSON
2 Economic accounts and international markets: production and analyses - Marco DE MARCH
3 Price comparisons, correction coefficients - John ASTIN
4 Accounts and financial indicators, statistics for the excessive deficits procedure - Jörg Dieter GLÄTZEL
5 International trade in services, direct investments, balance of payments - Jean-Claude ROMAN

Directorate C
Information and dissemination; transport; technical co-operation with non-member countries (except Phare and Tacis countries); external and intra-Community trade statistics
Director - Daniel BYK

Adviser - Marco LANCETTI
1 Information and dissemination - Amador RODRÍGUEZ PRIETO
2 Transport - John ALLEN
3 Technical co-operation with non-member countries (except Phare and Tacis countries) - Gilles RAMBAUD-CHANOZ
4 Methodology, nomenclature and statistics of external and intra-Community trade - Marguerite Christine COIN

Directorate D
Business statistics
Director - Pedro DÍAZ MUÑOZ
Adviser (Phare/Tacis co-ordination; budgetary aspects) - Francisco SOBRINO VÁZQUEZ
1 Methodological co-ordination, structural indicators, classifications and registers - François DE GEUSER
2 Structural business statistics - Inger NILSSON-ÖHMAN
3 Production and short-term business statistics - Adrien LHOMME
4 Energy statistics - Peter TAVOULARIDIS
5 Information society and tourism statistiscs - Douglas KOSZEREK

Directorate E
Social statistics
Director - Gabrielle CLOTUCHE
1 Labour market - Antonio BAIGORRI MATAMALA
2 Living conditions - Anne CLEMENCEAU
3 Health, education and culture - Marleen DE SMEDT
4 Population, social protection - Aarno LAIHONEN

Directorate F
Agricultural, environmental food and regional statistics
Director - Giuseppe CALÒ
Adviser (development and review of Directorate statistics) - Charles PEARE
1 Economic and structural statistics for agriculture - Hubert CHARLIER
2 Land-use, agricultural products and fisheries - Marcel ERNENS
3 Environment and sustainable development - Rainer MUTHMANN
4 Regional accounts and indicators, geographical information systems - Roger CUBITT
5 Food safety, rural development and forestry - Sylvie RIBAILLE

PRESS AND COMMUNICATION

Fax: +32 22 95 01 43

Website: http://europa.eu.int/comm/dgs/press_communication /index_en.htm

Commissioner Romano PRODI
Director-General and Spokesperson Jonathan FAULL
Assistants (responsible for general affairs) Ernesto BIANCHI, (Deputy Spokesperson) Jean Christophe FILORI

Audit
Acting Head of Unit Luis MORENO SERENO

Inspection
Head of Unit Jean-Jacques CHAMLA

Group of spokespersons and support staff
Head of Unit Vacant
Spokespersons
1 Administrative reform - Eric MAMER
2 Agriculture, rural development and fisheries - Gregor KREUZHUBER
3 Budget, fraud prevention - Joachim GROSS
4 Competition - Michael TSCHERNY, Amelia TORRES
5 Development and humanitarian aid - Michael CURTIS
6 Economic and monetary affairs - Gerassimos THOMAS
7 Education and culture - Christophe FORAX
8 Employment and social affairs - Andrew FIELDING
9 Enlargement - Jean-Christophe FILORI
10 Entreprise and the information society - Per HAUGAARD
11 Environment - Pia AHRENKILDE HANSEN
12 External relations - Gunnar WIEGAND
13 Health and consumer protection - Beate GMINDER
14 Health, consumer protection & agriculture - Thorsten MÜNCH
15 General affairs - Emma UDWIN
16 Internal market, taxation and customs - Jonathan TODD, Niamh CARMODY
17 Justice and home affairs - Leonello GABRICI
18 Regional policy - Vacant
19 Research - Andrea DAHMEN
20 Trade - Anthony GOOCH
21 Transport and energy - Gilles GANTELET

Directorate A
Interinstitutional relations, information policy, Representations
Acting Director - Panayotis CARVOUNIS
1 Relations with the European Parliament and other institutions and information policy - Benoît WORINGER
2 Representations: information campaigns, relays and networks - Fabrizia DE ROSA
3 Representations: co-ordination and analysis - Linda CORUGEDO STENEBERG

Directorate B
Communication, media and services
Director - Niels Jorgen THØGERSEN
1 Opinion polls, press reviews, Europe Direct - Antonis PAPACOSTAS
2 Europa, SCAD+ and publications - Lindsay ARMSTRONG
3 TV, radio services and studios - Nicole CAUCHIE

Directorate C
Resources
Director - Panayotis CARVOUNIS
1 Personnel and administration - Alberto HASSON
2 Budget and finances - Giuseppe MENCHI
3 Information technology - José TORCATO

Rue de la Loi 200, B-1049 Brussels • Tel +32 22 99 11 11

PUBLICATIONS OFFICE

Fax: +352 2 92 94 46 19

Website: http://eur-op.eu.int/general/en/index.htm

Commissioner Viviane REDING
Director-General Thomas L CRANFIELD
Adviser (Brussels) Albrecht BERGER
Assistant to Director-General Lucia CECCARELLI

Resources
Head of Unit Jacobus DOGGEN

Infrastructure
Head of Unit Friedrich DÖLL

Author services
Head of Unit Serge BRACK

Directorate A
Production
Reporting directly to the Director of Production
Director - Jacques RAYBAUT
1 Official Journal - Yves STEINITZ
2 Publications - Richard GOLINVAUX
3 Access to law - Pascale BERTE LOOT
4 Multimedia - Philippe LEBAUBE
5 Dissemination - Michel LANGLAIS
6 Support group - Vacant

SECRETARIAT-GENERAL

Fax: +32 22 96 05 54

Website: http://europa.eu.int/comm/dgs/secretariat_general /index_en.htm

Commissioner Romano PRODI
Secretary-General David O'SULLIVAN
Deputy Secretary-General (responsible for Directorates D and E) Echart GUTH
Deputy Secretary-General (responsible for Directorates A, B, C and G) Enzo MOAVERO MILANESI
Advisers hors classe (responsible for preparing the position of the Commission as regards the Convention) Vacant
Chief adviser on European governance Jérôme VIGNON
Adviser on Audit Capability Christian DEWALEYNE
Assistant to the Secretary-General Stephen QUEST
Data protection officer Dieter KOENIG

Protocol service
Director Jacques DE BAENST

Mediation service
Mediator Hedwig EBERT

Directorate A
Registry
Director - Sylvain BISARRE
1 Meetings of the Commission and Heads of Cabinet; oral procedures; follow-up of Commission decisions; dissemination of documents - Patrice BROCHART
2 Written procedures, delegation of powers, application of Community law - Bernard MICHEL

3 Secretariat of the ECSC Consultative Committee* - Paul LAFILI
4 Electronic transmission of documents - Richard JOELS

* Bâtiment Jean Monnet, Rue Alcide de Gasperi, L 2920 LUXEMBOURG

Rue de la Loi 200, B-1049 Brussels • Tel +32 22 99 11 11

Directorate B
Simplification of procedures and working methods, openness
Director - Patricia BUGNOT
Adviser (relations with Agencies) - Niels AHRENDT
1 Simplification of procedures, working methods; monitoring of reform - Mary PRESTON
2 Openness, access to documents, relations with civil society - María Ángeles BENÍTEZ SALAS
3 Simplification and modernisation of archiving systems and historical archives - Frank BRADY

Directorate C
Programme and policy co-ordination
Director - Walter DEFFAA
1 Strategic planning and programming - Michel SERVOZ
2 Policy co-ordination - Jordi AYET PUIGARNAU
3 Publications, annual report and databases - Denise DE RIPAINSEL
4 IRMS - Maurice MAXWELL

Directorate D
Relations with the Council
Director - Jorge DE OLIVEIRA E SOUSA
1 Relations with the Council I - Philippe BURGHELLE-VERNET
2 Relations with the Council II - François GENISSON
3 Co-ordination of institutional matters and co-decision procedure - Una O'DWYER

Directorate E
Relations with the European Parliament, the European Ombudsman, Economic and Social Committee and with the Committee of the Regions
Director - Giuseppe MASSANGIOLI
Adviser (with special responsibility for horizontal and strategic aspects of relations with the European Parliament) - John FITZMAURICE
1 Relations with the European Parliament I - Vacant
2 Relations with the European Parliament II - Rainer LAU
3 Relations with the Economic and Social Committee, the Committee of the Regions and the European Ombudsman, monitoring of Parliamentary committees - Andrea PIERUCCI

Task-Force – Future of the Union and institutional matters
Director - Paolo POZNANO
Adviser - Hartmut ÖFFELE
1 The future of Europe - Pieter VAN NUFFEL
2 Institutional questions and governance - Lars MITEK PEDERSEN
3 Public debate and forum on the future of Europe - Gérard LEGRIS

Directorate G
Resources and general matters
Director - Sarah EVANS
1 Human and financial resources - Marleen HARFORD
2 Commission mail, President's mail, internal information and grant management - Arthur POOLEY
3 Information technology - François KODECK

council of the european union

european council

court of justice

european court of auditors

council of the european union

Rue de la Loi 175, B-1048 Brussels
Phone: +32 22 85 61 11
Fax: +32 22 85 73 97/81
Telex: 21711 Consil B
Telegrammes: Consilium Bruxelles

E-mail format: firstname.surname@consilium.eu.int
General e-mail: public.info@consilium.eu.int
Internet: http://ue.eu.int/en/Info/index.htm

composition

The Council of the European Union, usually known as the Council of Ministers, consists of one representative of each Member State at ministerial level. They are empowered to act on behalf of their government and are also politically accountable to their national parliament. The Foreign Ministers form the 'General Affairs' Council, while other ministers attend meetings of the Council dealing with their specific areas of responsibility (agriculture, environment, health, budget, and so on). Meetings are held in Brussels or Luxembourg. The frequency of Council meetings varies according to the urgency of the subjects dealt with: the General Affairs, Economic and Financial Affairs and Agriculture Councils meet once a month, while the Transport, Environment or Industry and Energy Councils meet two to four times a year. The presidency of the Council of Ministers changes on a fixed rotational basis every six months (January-June and July-December). Sweden held the Presidency for the first half of 2001 with Belgium taking over in July followed by Spain and Denmark in 2002 and Greece in the first half and Italy in the second half of 2003.

role

Under the terms of the Treaty establishing the European Community the Council:

• is the Community's legislative body; for a wide range of Community issues, it exercises that legislative power in co-decision with the European Parliament;

• co-ordinates the general economic policies of the Member States;

• concludes, on behalf of the Community, international agreements between the community and one or more States or international organisations;

• together with the European Parliament constitutes the budgetary authority that adopts the Community's budget.

Under the 1992 Maastricht Treaty on European Union further areas of responsibility were added. The Council:

• takes the decisions necessary for defining and implementing the Common Foreign and Security Policy, on the basis of general guidelines established by the European Council;

• co-ordinates the activities of Member States and adopts measures in the field of police and judicial co-operation in criminal matters.

common foreign and security policy

The Amsterdam Treaty introduced new provisions on the Common Foreign and Security Policy (CFSP). Since October 1999 the Secretary-General of the Council has fulfilled the new function of High Representative for CFSP. The High Representative assists the Council in matters falling within the scope of CFSP, in particular by helping to formulate, prepare and implement policy decisions and when appropriate conduct political dialogue with third parties on behalf of the Council and at the request of the Presidency. The High Representative is nominated unanimously by the Council and is assisted by a Deputy Secretary-General.

At the same time a Policy Planning and Early Warning Unit (PPEWU) was established within the Council Secretariat and under the responsibility of the Council Secretary General/High Representative. Its role is to co-operate, as appropriate, with the Commission in order to ensure full coherence with EU trade and development policies. Its mandate includes monitoring, analysis and assessment of international developments and events and early warning on potential crises.

decision-making in the council

The Treaties specify whether the Council is to take its decisions by unanimous agreement of all members, by qualified majority or by simple majority.

A unanimous decision, which follows from the agreement (or abstention) of all Member States, is required in several areas of importance to the development of the Union. These include the Common Foreign and Security Policy, police and judicial co-operation in criminal matters, asylum and immigration policy, economic and social cohesion policy, environment, social affairs and taxation.

council of the european union

In the case of qualified-majority voting (QMV), which has become the rule for decision-making on many important EU policies, each Member State has a number of votes, weighted to reflect the fact that the Member States are equal as members of the Union but different in terms of population. Under the current system, there is a total of 87 votes (the four most heavily populated countries having 10 votes each, whilst the least populated has two). Qualified majority is obtained if at least 62 votes are cast for a decision (i.e. 71.26 % of the total).

changes introduced by the treaty of nice

It will be very difficult to obtain unanimous agreement in a Union that may one day have as many as 30 Member States. In order to prepare the Union for enlargement the Treaty of Nice proposes changes in the way the Council takes its decisions:

• The scope of decision-making by QMV has been widened. Some 30 provisions changed over completely or partly from unanimity to qualified-majority, including for example, decisions in the field of judicial co-operation in civil matters, industrial policy and some aspects of the common commercial policy.

• The new Treaty provides for a change in the weighting of votes from 1 January 2005. The number of votes assigned to each Member State has been altered and the number to be assigned to the candidate countries when they enter the European Union has also been set (see table below).

weighting of votes for member states and candidate countries after 2005

Member States		Candidate Countries	
Belgium	12	Bulgaria	10
Denmark	7	Cyprus	4
Germany	29	Czech Republic	12
Greece	12	Estonia	4
Spain	27	Hungary	12
France	29	Latvia	4
Ireland	7	Lithuania	7
Italy	29	Malta	3
Luxembourg	4	Poland	27
Netherlands	13	Romania	14
Austria	10	Slovakia	7
Portugal	12	Slovenia	4
Finland	7		
Sweden	10		
United Kingdom	29		

In future, qualified majority will be obtained if a decision receives a predetermined number of votes (this threshold will be reviewed in the light of successive accessions) and a simple majority of Member States.

In addition, a Member State may ask for confirmation that the qualified majority represents at least 62% of the total population of the Union. If this is found not to be the case, the decision will not be adopted.

The Treaty of Nice was signed by the member governments in Nice on 26th February 2001. It entered into force on 1st February 2003 following ratification by all the Member States.

committee of permanent representatives

The Council's work is prepared by the Committee of Permanent Representatives (Coreper), consisting of the Brussels-based ambassadors of the Member States. The ambassadors (permanent representatives) meet as Coreper II and their deputies as Coreper I. The two committees meet each week. Coreper also oversees and co-ordinates the work of some 185 committees and working parties made up of civil servants from the Member States who prepare at the technical level the matters to be discussed by Coreper and the Council.

council of the european union

general secretariat

Secretary-General/High Representative Javier SOLANA
Deputy Secretary-General Pierre DE BOISSIEU

Private office
Head of Cabinet of the Secretary-General/High Representative Director Alberto NAVARRO GONZÁLEZ
Deputy Head of Cabinet of the Secretary-General/High Representative Leonardo SCHIAVO
Head of Cabinet of the Deputy Secretary-General David GALLOWAY
Advisers Paul REIDERMAN, Veronica CODY, Ralph KAESSNER

departments attached to the secretary-general / high representative

Policy Planning and Early Warning Unit (PPEWU)
Director - Christoph HEUSGEN

Task Forces
European Security and Defence Policy (ESDP)
Head of Division Marc OTTE
Western Balkans/central Europe
Head of Division Stefan LEHNE
Situation centre/crisis cell
Head of Division Michael MATTHIESSEN
Horizontal questions; Latin America
Head of Division José GÓMEZ-LLERA
Russia/Ukraine; Transatlantic/Baltics/Asia
Head of Division Cornelis VAN RIJ
Mediterranean/Barcelona; Middle East/Africa
Pascal CHARLAT, Fernando GENTILINI, Andreas STRUB
PU administration/Security
François VAN HÖVELL

Co-ordination Unit for Special Representatives
Head of Division Vacant

departments attached to the secretary-general / high representative and to the deputy secretary-general

directorate for general political questions

Director Max J KELLER-NOËLLET

Meetings
Antici Group Georges ZBYSZEWSKI
Mertens Group Nikolaos FRILINGOS
General political questions David GALLOWAY, Luís TEXEIRA DA COSTA

Military Staff
General Director-General of the EU Military Staff Rainer SCHWIRTH
General Deputy Director-General of the EU Military Staff Graham MESSERVY-WHITING

Press
Head of Press Office Dominique-Georges MARRO
Matters for Coreper II Nicholas KERLEROUX
Matters for Coreper I François HEAD
Press Adviser to Mr Solana Christina GALLACH

Security Office
Alexandro LEGEIN

Financial control
José Antonio MARIGUESA

Data protection
Pierre VERNHES

INFOSEC (Information systems security)
Bartolomeo MANENTI

Unit for the Analysis of Resources, Methods and Organisation (URMO)
Dominique ANGLARET
Johnny ENGELL-HANSEN

council of the european union

legal service

Director-General and Legal Adviser to the Council Jean-Claude PIRIS
Deputy Director-General Vacant
Assistant to the Director-General Thérèse BLANCHET

legal service teams

Team I

Internal market, industry, telecommunications, tourism, energy, civil protection, research, trans-European networks, transport, social affairs, culture, education, youth, regional policy, environment, harmonisation of food legislation, consumer protection, health, competition rules/public procurement
Directors - Jean-Paul JACQUÉ, Jürgen HUBER

Team II

Agriculture, fisheries, Economic and Monetary Union/EMU, taxation, free movement of capital, structural funds and generally all matters for the Ecofin Council prepared by Coreper
Director - Giorgio MAGANZA

Research and documentation unit

Legal adviser - Christos MAVRAKOS

Team III

External relations (including CFSP, development co-operation, ACP, all questions relating to international agreements and relations with international organisations) and enlargement
Director - Ricardo GOSALBO BONO

Team IV

Institutional/budgetary questions
Director - Jill AUSSANT

Team V

Justice and home affairs
Director - Julian SCHUTTE

Legal/Linguistic experts

Head of Lawyer/Linguists Group - Tito GALLAS

directorates-general of the secretariat

Directorate-General A

Personnel and administration
Director-General - Vittorio GRIFFO
Assistant to the Director-General - Dirk HELLWIG

Staff Regulations
Laurent TRUQUET

Directorate I
Personnel and administration
Director - Percival E TARLING
Deputy to the Director - Lieve VAN DEN BOSSCHE
1 Welfare Office, privileges and immunities - Lieve VAN DEN BOSSCHE
2 Directorate advisers; studies; organisation; disputes and other questions concerning administrative matters and the staff regulations; interinstitutional relations; Joint Bodies; relations to staff representation - Jean-Frédéric FAURE
3 Data processing - Philippe DEMONCEAU
4 Sickness insurance, accident insurance, inter-institutional relations concerning the staff regulations - Daniel DULBECCO
5 Medical Service - Dr Manuel GARCÍA PÉREZ
6 Personnel; staff office; recruitment service; human resources; annual leave - Yves CRETIEN
7 Salaries/pensions/missions - Maarten BOGAARDT
8 Staff training - Serenella MORELLI

Directorate II
Conferences, organisation, infrastructures, information technology
Director - Stephen ELLIS
1 Conferences - Walpurga SPECKBACHER
2 Information technology - Hans-Werner GRENZHÄUSER
3 Logistics services - Vacant
4 Restaurant - Graziella SCEBBA
5 Buildings - Johan BURGERS

Directorate III
Translation and document production
Director - Margarida LACERDA
1 Translation Department - Hendrik BAES
2 Secretarial Department - Gertrud QUERTON
3 Reproduction, document circulation, imaging, registry, photocopying, central office, telex, special reprography - Jennifer WADLEY

4 Central co-ordination - Margarida LACERDA
5 Language co-ordination - Andrew UNWIN
6 Agreements Office - Philip EVANS
7 Classified Information Office (C.I.O.) - Gabriel OLIVER

Directorate IV
Internal finances
Director - José Antonio MARIGUESA
Deputy to the Director - Alan PIOTROWSKI
Financial Counsellor - Jacob VRIES
1 Budget management - Johannes GILBERS
2 Horizontal matters - Michel KOLTZ
3 Procurement co-ordination unit - Sergio ZANGAGLIA
4 Accounting - Ingrid RULLKOETTER

Directorate-General B

Agriculture; fisheries
Director-General - Angel BOIXAREU CARRERA

Directorate I
Agricultural policy (including international aspects); organisation of the markets in agricultural products; harmonisation of veterinary and zootechnical legislation
Director - Luigi MAZZASCHI
1 Co-ordination of international aspects of agricultural policy, particularly WTO, OECD and FAO; enlargement, fresh and processed fruit and vegetables, potatoes; bananas; floriculture; wine, spirits, aromatised wines, alcohol, vinegar; olive oil and table olives; international aspects relating to these sectors - David SWIFT
2 Food safety: veterinary and zootechnical harmonisation; animal welfare; beef, veal and sheepmeat; milk and milk products; pigmeat; eggs and poultry; international aspects relating to these sectors - Georges ADELBRECHT
3 Horizontal problems of agricultural policy; arable crops (cereals, oilseeds, protein crops, rice and fodder); sugar, cotton and other textile fibres, silkworms; tobacco; other products (seeds, hops, and products not listed in Annex I); international aspects relating to these sectors - Johannes TEN HAVE

Directorate II
Agricultural structures policy; agri-monetary and agri-financial questions; harmonisation of plant health legislation; organic products
Director - Francisco Javier MATUT ARCHANCO
1 Financial questions; agri-monetary questions; strengthening of controls; national aid; forestry agricultural structures; agricultural statistics; rural development; agri-environment; genetic resources - Claudia D'ALOYA
2 Food safety: horizontal questions concerning agriculture; harmonisation of legislation on plant health, animal feeding stuffs and seeds and plants; precautionary principle; Codex alimentarius (FAO and WHO); foodstuff quality; pesticide residues; plant protection; organic products - Marc SCHOBER

Directorate III
Fisheries policy (including external relations)
Director - Svend KRISTENSEN
1 Structural policy; market organisation; Mediterranean; relations with countries in Africa, the Indian Ocean and Latin America; Antarctica - Aldo SIRAGUSA
2 Resource management and conservation policy; monitoring of fishery activities; relations with countries in northern and eastern Europe and North America; North Atlantic and Baltic Sea international organisations; research - Luis TEIXERA DA COSTA, Christian FRØIK

Directorate-General C

Internal market; customs union; industrial policy; telecommunications; information society; research; energy; transport
Director-General - Klaus GRETSCHMANN

Directorate I
Industrial policy; SMEs; Competition rules; iron and steel; tourism; telecommunications; HDTV/Post; data protection
Director - Vacant
1 Industrial policy; iron and steel/SMEs; tourism; competition rules - Gérard GROSJEAN
2 Post and telecommunications; information society; multimedia; HDTV; data protection - Emilio GONZÁLEZ-SANCHO

Directorate II
Internal market; customs union technical barriers, including motor vehicles; chemical and pharmaceutical products and medical devices; intellectual property; right of establishment and freedom to provide services, including insurance; public procurement; company law
Director - Anders OLANDER
1 Internal market; intellectual property; technical barriers, including motor vehicles; chemical products - Keith MELLOR
2 Technical barriers; chemical and pharmaceutical products and medical devices - Pia SELLERUP
3 Customs union - Danielle LAVEAU
4 Right of establishment and freedom to provide services, including insurance; public contracts; company law - Lauri RAILAS

Directorate III
Research and energy policies
Director - Barbara HUMPHREYS ZWART
1 Research policy: European co-operation on scientific and technical research (COST); Scientific and Technical Research Committee (CREST) - Donald ELLIS
2 Energy policy: coal; hydrocarbons; nuclear energy; new forms of energy; electricity; rational use of energy; measures to be taken in the event of crisis; external relations in the field of energy; European Energy Charter - Jean-Paul DECAESTECKER

Directorate IV
Transport policy
Director - Gaetano TESTA
1 Surface transport (roads, railways, inland waterways); relations with the European Conference of Ministers for Transport - Luc LAPERE
2 Sea transport - Carine CLAEYS
3 Air transport - Joaquim MARINHO DE BASTOS

Directorate-General E

External economic relations, common foreign and security policy

Director-General - Robert COOPER
Director-General (Enlargement, development and multilateral economic affairs) - Vacant
Deputy Director-General - Anastassios VIKAS
Deputy Director-General (ESDP) - Pieter Cornelis FEITH
Deputy Director-General (New York: United Nations liaison office) - Elda STIVANI

Directorate I
Enlargement
Director - Antti KUOSMANEN
1 Enlargement - Christos KATHARIOS
2 Pecos agreements - Gabriele SCARAMUCCI

Directorate II
Development
Director - Jacques BEL
1 Development co-operation; CDI/CTA; food aid; United Nations Conferences on Development, including UNCTAD - Charles MURDOCK
2 ACP/OCT; generalised system of preferences; commodities - Karl BUCK

Directorate III
Division for multilateral economic affairs
Director - André DONNADOU
1 WTO; Commercial policy - Massimo PARNISARI
2 Commercial policy instruments; national co-operation agreements; ECSC Agreements; shipbuilding; reports from commercial counsellors; fairs and Exhibitions; OECD - Josef BREULS
3 EEA/EFTA; Switzerland; Faroe Islands; Andorra; San Marino; OECD; textile agreements - Wolfgang BÄRWONKEL

Directorate IV
Transatlantic relations, United Nations and human rights
Director - Jim CLOOS
1 Transatlantic relations - Noel PURCELL O'BYRNE
2 United Nations; human rights; public international law - Maryem VAN DEN HEUVEL

Directorate V
Mediterranean Basin, Middle East, Africa, Asia
Director - Franz EICHINGER

1 Barcelona Process, Common Strategy on the Mediterranean region, Turkey, Malta, Cyprus, Mashreq/Maghreb, Persian Gulf, Iran, Iraq, Yemen - Dominique SARAT
2 Middle East Peace Process - Nessa DELANEY
3 Asia/Oceania - James BANEHAM
4 Africa - Peter CLAUSEN
5 Analysis and previews - Paul CLAIRET

Directorate VI
Eastern Europe, Western Balkans Region
Director - Leopold RADAUER
1 Western Balkans: RFY, Kosovo, Montenegro, FYRM, Croatia, Albania, Bosnia-Herzegovina - Alessandro CORTESE, Jean-Claude MEYER, Lene HOVE, Patrice BERGAMINI
2 Eastern Europe, Eastern Balkans region - Jukka LESKELÄ
3 Regional co-operation; Stability pact - Leopold RADAUER

Directorate VII
European Security and Defence Policy
Director - Annalisa GIANNELLA

Directorate VIII
Defence issues
Director - Claude-France ARNAUD
Head of Division - Patrick NAMER

Directorate IX
Instruments for Civilian Crisis Management; Administrative Co-ordination
Director - Michael MATTHIESSEN

Geneva: Office for Liaison with the European Office of the United Nations
Director - Jacques BRODIN

New York: United Nations Liaison Office
Director - Elda STIVANI

Directorate-General F

Press; communication; protocol

Director-General - Hans BRUNMAYR

Directorate I
Press
Director - Dominique-Georges MARRO
1 Matters for Coreper II - Nicholas KERLEROUX, Jesús CARMONA NÚÑEZ
2 Matters for Coreper I - Luis AMORIM, Georg BIERKÖTTER, Laurent BENHAMON
3 Press and audiovidisual centre - Margarete GILOT-KÖHLER

Directorate II
Spokesperson to the Secretary-General / High Representative for Common Foreign and Security Policy
Spokesperson - Christina GALLACH

Directorate III
Communication, information policy, interinstitutional relations
Director - Ramón JIMÉNEZ FRAILE
1 The Internet, media, monitoring - Johan SLOTBOOM
2 Transparency, access to documents, information to the public - Jacob VISSCHER
3 Publications, documentation, relations with the Publications Office - Jorge TAVARES DA SILVA
4 Visits, public events - Charis XIROUCHAKIS
5 Libraries - Anne OSTRY
6 Budget - Gerda DAIDONE

Directorate IV
Protocol
Director - Maria Cristina BERTACCA

Directorate V
Archives
Director - Willem STOLS

Directorate-General G

Economic and social affairs; EMU

Director-General - Sixten KORKMAN

Directorate I
Economic affairs
1 EMU, economic policies, EIB, own resources - Arthur BRAUTIGAM
2 Tax policy - Michael GRAF
3 Financial legislation - Bodil NIELSEN, Tomás BRÄNNSTRÖM
4 Export credits - Liam O'LUANAIGH, Monique DERELOU

Directorate II
Social and regional affairs
1 Employment and social policy - Andrew GEORGE
2 Regional policy and economic and social cohesion - Vacant

Directorate III
Budget and financial regulations
Director - Merrick BRYAN-KINNS
1 Budget/Finance - José Lus GÓMEZ-LASAGA

Directorate-General H

Justice and home affairs

Director-General - Charles ELSEN

Directorate I
Director - Stephen ELLIS
Section I: Asylum immigration (+CIREA + Cirefi + Eurodac) - Guillermo TRONCOSO GONZÁLEZ

Directorate II
Director - Gilles DE KERCHOVE D'OUSSELGHEM
1 Section II: Police and customs co-operation - Johannes VOS
2 Section III: Judicial co-operation - Hans NILSSON
3 Sector IV: SIS - Luc VANDAMME
4 Horizontal questions (relations with the Parliament, Title VI financing, Commission on Racism and Xenophobia) - Johannes VOS
5 Former Schengen affairs - Wouter VAN DE RIJT
6 Secretariat for Data Protection - Peter MICHAEL

Directorate-General I
Protection of the environment and of consumers; civil protection; health; foodstuffs legislation; drug addiction; AIDS; education and youth; culture; audiovisual media
Director-General - Kerstin NIBLAEUS
Director - Sabine EHMKE GENDRON
1 Environment/consumer affairs/civil protection - Wolfgang GAEDEA
2 Health, foodstuffs legislation - Adele AIROLDI
3 Education and youth, culture, audiovisual arts - Carlo FREDANI

NB: Directorate-General D no longer exists

175

european council

General: http://ue.eu.int/en/info/eurocouncil/index.htm
Greek presidency: http://www.ue2003.gr

The European Council brings together the Heads of State or Government of the Member States of the Union and the President of the European Commission at least twice a year. They are assisted by their Ministers for Foreign Affairs and by a member of the Commission. These meetings are also referred to as European Summits. The European Council is not one of the five Community institutions, and originally had no formal Treaty status. Its existence was formally recognised in the Single European Act of 1986.

The European Council sets out the broad policy guidelines of the Union and, as part of European political co-operation, discusses topical international issues. It has a major role to play in providing impetus for the development of the Union and policy guidance in every area of the Union's activity.

The European Council primarily makes political decisions, not legislative ones, although since the Treaties of Maastricht (1993) and Amsterdam (1999) came into force it has been able to adopt legislative decisions as well. In addition to the task of providing impetus and defining general political guidelines, the Treaty on European Union assigns the European Council other tasks in the specific fields of Common Foreign and Security Policy (CFSP), police and judicial co-operation in criminal matters, economic and monetary policy and employment.

location

At present the European Council's meetings take place in the country holding the presidency of the Council of Ministers or in Brussels, and they are presided over by the Head of State or Government of the Member State holding the Presidency of the Council. The stipulation that one European Council meeting per presidency be held in Brussels from 2002 was annexed to the Treaty of Nice. When the Union comprises 18 members, all formal European Council meetings will be held in Brussels. Presidencies will be free to organise informal European Council meetings wherever they wish.

decision-making

The European Council does not make decisions in the same way as the Council of the European Union. It does not take votes, nor does it apply the rules of unanimity or qualified majority, unlike the Council composed of the Ministers of the Fifteen. The Treaties do not in general dictate rules for decision-making in the European Council, and it is rare that they enable it to adopt formal acts. The members of the European Council reach political agreement by consensus. With certain exceptions, it is for the European institutions to give legal status to those political decisions by following the procedures set down in the Treaty. The guidelines issued by the European Council are included in the Presidency conclusions. Declarations or resolutions are often adopted in the area of Common Foreign and Security Policy, to show the wishes, analyses and intentions of the European Council.

european council meetings

Belgian Presidency

• Informal extraordinary European Council, Brussels, on 21 September 2001 following the terrorist attacks in the United States

• Informal European Council, Ghent, on 19 October 2001

• European Council, Brussels-Laeken, on 14-15 December 2001

Spanish Presidency

• European Council, Barcelona, on 15-16 March 2002

Danish Presidency

• European Council, Brussels, on 24-25 October 2002

• European Council, Copenhagen, on 12-12 December 2002

Greek Presidency

• European Council, Brussels, on 21 March 2003

• Informal European Council, Athens, on 16 April 2003 for the signing of the Accession Treaty by the new member states

• European Council, Thessaloniki, on 20 June 2003

court of justice of the european communities and court of first instance

L-2925 Luxembourg
Tel: +352 4303-1
Fax (administration): +352 43 03 26 00
Fax (press and information): +352 43 03 25 00
E-mail: info@curia.eu.int
Website: http://www.curia.eu.int/en/index.htm

The Court of Justice ensures compliance with the law in the application and interpretation of the Treaties. Based in Luxembourg, it is the European Union's supreme judicial authority. It should not be confused with the International Court of Justice in The Hague which is a United Nations body or with the European Court of Human Rights in Strasbourg which comes under the Council of Europe.

The Court of Justice worked alone until September 1989 when the Council attached to it a Court of First Instance in order to reduce its heavy workload. The Court of First Instance now has jurisdiction to deal with all actions brought by individuals and companies against decisions of the Community institutions and agencies. It can rule in 'technical' areas such as competition or anti-dumping, and also on staff disputes.

composition and organisation

The Court of Justice comprises 15 judges and 8 advocates general. They are appointed by common accord of the governments of the Member States and hold office for a renewable term of six years with half of them being replaced or re-appointed every three years. The most recent appointment of half the members of the Court was made in October 2000 and the next appointments will take place in October 2003. The judges select one of their number to be President of the Court for a renewable term of three years. The President directs the work of the Court and presides at hearings and deliberations. The Advocates General assist the Court in its task. They deliver, in open court and with complete impartiality and independence, opinions on the cases brought before the Court.

The Court of First Instance is composed of 15 judges, appointed by common accord of the governments of the Member States to hold office for a renewable term of six years. The Members of the Court of First Instance select one of their number as President. There are no permanent Advocates General. The duties of Advocate General are performed, in a limited number of cases, by one of the judges.

plenary sessions and chambers

The Court of Justice may sit in plenary session or in chambers of three or five judges. It sits in plenary session when a Member State or a Community institution that is a party to the proceedings so requests, or in particularly complex or important cases. Other cases are heard by a chamber.

The Court of First Instance sits in chambers of three or five judges. It too may sit in plenary session in certain particularly important cases.

the registries and the administration

The Registrar is appointed by the Court of Justice to hold office for a term of six years. He has the same court duties as the registrar or clerk of a national court, but he also acts as secretary-general of the institution.

The Court of Justice, as an independent and autonomous institution, possesses, in addition to the registry, its own administrative infrastructure, which includes a large translations and interpreting service since the Court has to use all the official languages of the Community in the course of its work.

The Court of First Instance appoints its own Registrar. For its administrative needs it relies on the services of the Court of Justice.

procedure

Procedure before the Court of Justice is based on that followed before national courts. Whatever the type of case, there is always a written stage and almost always an oral stage, which takes place in open court. There are two types of cases that may be brought before the Court of Justice - direct actions and requests for preliminary rulings.

Direct actions may be brought directly before the Court by the Commission, by other Community institutions or by a Member State. Cases brought by individuals or companies challenging the legality of a Community act are brought directly before the Court of First Instance.

Preliminary rulings may be requested by courts or tribunals in the Member States when they need a decision on a question of Community law in order to be able to give a judgement. The Court of Justice is not a court of appeal from the decisions of national courts and can only rule on matters of community law. Once the Court of Justice has given its decision, the national court is bound to apply the principles of Community law as laid down by the Court in that decision.

court of justice

Judgments of the Court of Justice are reached by a majority vote. There are no dissenting opinions, and all the judges who took part in the deliberations sign the judgments. The judgments of the Court and the opinions of the Advocates General are published in reports of cases before the Court of Justice and the Court of First Instance in all the official languages of the Community.

the treaty of nice

The Court of Justice and the Court of First Instance are already facing a substantial increase in their caseload - a problem that can only increase with the accession of new Member States. In order to relieve the workload of the Court, the Treaty of Nice seeks to share tasks between the Court of Justice and the Court of First Instance more effectively and allows for the creation of specialised chambers for particular areas (such as disputes involving EU officials). The Treaty also stipulates that the Court of Justice, which in an enlarged Union will continue to consist of one judge for each Member State, may sit in a Grand Chamber of 13 judges instead of always meeting in a plenary session attended by all judges. The Treaty of Nice was signed by member governments on 26 February 2001 and entered into force on 1 February 2003 once ratified by all the Member States.

court of justice

Order of precedence (from 7 October 2002)

Gil Carlos RODRIGUEZ IGLESIAS, President
Jean-Pierre PUISSOCHET, President of the Third and Sixth chambers
Melchior WATHELET, President of the First and Fifth chambers
Romain SCHINTGEN, President of the Second Chamber
Jean MISCHO, First Advocate General
Christiaan TIMMERMANS, President of the Fourth Chamber
Francis JACOBS, Advocate General
Claus GULMANN, Judge
David EDWARD, Judge
Antonio LA PERGOLA, Judge
Pierre LEGER, Advocate General
Peter JANN, Judge
Damaso RUIZ-JARABO COLOMER, Advocate General
Siegbert ALBER, Advocate General
Vassilios SKOURIS, Judge
Fidelma MACKEN, Judge
Ninon COLNERIC, Judge
Stig VON BAHR, Judge
Antonio TIZZANO, Advocate General
José Narcisco CUNHA RODRIGUES, Judge
Leendert GEELHOED, Advocate General
Christine STIX-HACKL, Advocate General
Allan ROSAS, Judge

Roger GRASS, Registrar

Composition of the Chambers

First Chamber
President Melchior WATHELET
Judges Peter JANN, Allan ROSAS

Second chamber
President Romain SCHINTGEN
Judges Ninon COLNERIC, Vassilios SKOURIS

Third chamber
President Jean-Pierre PUISSOCHET
Judges Claus GULMANN, Fidelma MACKEN, José Narcisco CUNHA RODRIGUES

Fourth chamber
President Christiaan TIMMERMANS
Judges David EDWARD, Antonio LA PERGOLA, Stig VON BAHR

Fifth chamber
President Melchior WATHELET
Judges Stig von BAHR, David EDWARD, Antonio LA PERGOLA, Peter JANN, Christiaan TIMMERMANS, Allan ROSAS

Sixth Chamber
President Jean-Pierre PUISSOCHET
Judges Ninon COLNERIC, Claus GULMANN, Fidelma MACKEN, Romain SCHINTGEN, Vassilios SKOURIS, José Narcisco CUNHA RODRIGUES

court of first instance

Order of precedence (1 April 2003 to 30 September 2003)

Bo VESTERDORF, President
Rafael GARCIA VALDECASAS Y FERNÁNDEZ, President of
Chamber
Koenraad LENAERTS, President of Chamber
Virpi TIILI, President of Chamber
Nicholas FORWOOD, President of Chamber
Pernilla LINDH, Judge
Joséf AZIZI, Judge
John COOKE, Judge
Marc JAEGER, Judge
Jörg PIRRUNG, Judge
Paolo MENGOZZI, Judge
Arjen MEIJ, Judge
Mihalis VILARAS, Judge
Hubert LEGAL, Judge
Maria Eugénia MARTINS de Nazaré RIBEIRO, Judge

Hans JUNG, Registrar

Composition of the chambers (2 April 2003 to 30 September
2003)

First Chamber
President Bo VESTERDORF
Judges Maria MARTINS RIBEIRO, Hubert LEGAL

First Chamber, Extended Composition
President Bo VESTERDORF
Judges Marc JAEGER, Joséf AZIZI, Maria MARTINS RIBEIRO,
Hubert LEGAL

Second Chamber
President Nicholas FORWOOD
Judges Jörg PIRRUNG, Arjen MEIJ

Second Chamber, Extended Composition
President Nicholas FORWOOD
Judges Mihalis VILARAS, Jörg PIRRUNG, Paolo MENGOZZI,
Arjen MEIJ

Third Chamber
President Konraad LENAERTS
Judges Marc JAEGER, Joséf AZIZI

Third Chamber, Extended Composition
President Konraad LENAERTS
Judges John COOKE, Marc JAEGER, Pernilla LINDH, Joséf AZIZI

Fourth Chamber
President Virpi TIILI
Judges Mihalis VILARAS, Paolo MENGOZZI

Fourth Chamber, Extended Composition
President Virpi TIILI
Judges Mihalis VILARAS, Jörg PIRRUNG, Paolo MENGOZZI,
Arjen MEIJ

Fifth Chamber
President Rafael GARCIA VALDECASAS Y FERNÁNDEZ
Judges John COOKE, Pernilla LINDH

Fifth Chamber, Extended Composition
President Rafael GARCIA VALDECASAS Y FERNÁNDEZ
Judges John COOKE, Pernilla LINDH, Maria MARTINS RIBEIRO,
Hubert LEGAL

european court of auditors

Rue Alcide De Gasperi 12, L-1615 Luxembourg
Tel: +352 43 98-1
Fax: +352 43 93 42
Brussels Office: Bâtiment Eastman, 135 rue Belliard, B-1040 Brussels
Tel: +32 22 30 50 90
Fax: +32 22 30 64 83
E-mail format: firstname.surname@eca.eu.int
General e-mail: euraud@eca.eu.int
Internet: http://www.eca.eu.int/EN/menu.htm

The European Court of Auditors is responsible for checking that the European Union spends its money according to its budgetary rules and regulations, and for the purposes for which it is intended.

It consists of 15 Members originating from the 15 Member States and appointed for a term of six years. They are independent and have specific experience in the audit of public finances. The Court Members elect their President for a renewable term of three years. With the prospect of enlargement of the Union, the Treaty of Nice states that the Court will consist of a national of each Member State. It will also be able to set up chambers to adopt certain types of report or opinion. The Court of Auditors has approximately 550 qualified staff of whom about 250 are auditors.

The Court of Auditors publishes:

• an annual report concerning the implementation of the European Union budget for each financial year

• a statement of assurance on the reliability of the accounts and the legality and regularity of the underlying transactions for each financial year

• specific annual reports concerning certain Community bodies

• special reports on subjects of particular interest.

These reports are, as a rule, published in the *Official Journal of the European Communities* and are accessible on the Internet at the Court's website.

The Court of Auditors must be consulted for its opinion prior to the adoption of certain Community regulations of a financial nature. The other Community institutions may also ask the Court for an opinion.

discharge on the implementation of the budget

Audit reports issued by the Court of Auditors form an important part of the discharge procedure. They are addressed to the discharge authority (composed of the European Parliament and the Council of the European Union), which takes them into account when deciding whether discharge may be granted to the Commission in respect of budgetary management for the financial year in question.

sanctions

The Court of Auditors has no juridical powers. When auditors discover cases of irregularities, including suspected fraud, the information obtained is communicated as quickly as possible to the Community bodies responsible in order that they may take the appropriate action.

fraud and irregularities

It is the responsibility of the European Community and the Member States to prevent fraud and all other illegal activities which are detrimental to the financial interests of the Community. The Court of Auditors contributes to this fight against fraud and irregularities, both through recommendations for prevention and through detection by the effectiveness, range and nature of its audits.

secretariat-general

Secretary-General Michel HERVÉ
Assistant to the Secretary-General Vital SCHMITT
Financial Controller Marceliano CUESTA DE LA FUENTE
Secretariat of the Court
Pilar CALVO FUENTES
Personnel and Administration Division
Jean-Jack BEUROTTE
Informatics and Telecommunications Division
Raija PELTONEN
Budget
Neil USHER
Accounting
Patrick WELDON
Translation Service
Ulla GUBIAN

court of auditors

members of the court and their resonsibilities

President of the Court Juan Manuel FABRA VALLÉS
Supervision of the Court's activities, legal matters, institutional external relations and information policy

Giorgio CLEMENTE
Regional sector, Cohesion Fund

Hubert WEBER
Co-operation with developing and third countries (General budget of the EU)

Aunus SALMI
Own resources (revenue)

François COLLING
Internal policies including research

Maarten B. ENGWIRDA
Expenditure relating to Central and East European Countries and the Commonwealth of newly independent states

Jean-François BERNICOT
Agricultural policy, animal and plant product markets, rural development, fisheries and the sea

Robert REYNDERS
European development funds (ACP States)

Máire GEOGHEGAN-QUINN
ADAR Sector, audit and training methodology, relations with European Anti-Fraud Office (OLAF)

Vitor Manuel DA SILVA CALDEIRA
DAS Sector: co-ordination regarding statement of assurance

Lars TOBISSON
Social and Employment policies

Hedda VON WEDEL
EAGGF-Guarantee: arable crops, milk and milk products, beef and veal

David BOSTOCK
EAGGF- Guarantee: financial audit, export refunds, clearance of accounts

Morten Louis LEVYSOHN
Administrative expenditure of the institutions, office for official publications of the European Communities, external offices and delegations of the Communities, subsidies

Ioannis SARMAS
Borrowing and lending, banking sectors and community agencies including ECSC, European schools, decentralised bodies, Euratom Supply Agency

other eu bodies:

committee of the regions

economic and social committee

european central bank

european investment bank

european investment fund

european ombudsman

committee of the regions

Rue Montoyer 92-102, B-1040 Brussels
Tel: +32 22 82 22 11
Fax: +32 22 82 23 25
E-mail format: firstname.surname@cdr.be
Website: http://www.cor.eu.int

Secretariat to UK delegation
Local Government Information Bureau
Local Government House, Smith Square, London SW1P 3HZ
Tel: 0207 664 3100
Fax: 0207 664 3128
Website: http://www.lgib.gov.uk/ukint/ukint_e1.htm

The Committee of the Regions is an advisory body of the European Union set up in 1993 by the Maastricht Treaty. It aims to ensure that locally elected representatives are consulted on EU policy and legislative proposals where local citizens are directly affected. The Committee upholds the principle of subsidiarity, which says that decisions should be taken at the lowest level of authority that can act effectively. Under the Maastricht Treaty the Committee must be consulted by the European Commission or the Council in five areas:

- economic and social cohesion (including the Structural Funds)
- trans-European networks in the fields of transport, telecommunications and energy
- public health
- education and youth
- culture

In 1999 these areas were extended by the Amsterdam Treaty to include:

- employment
- social policy
- environment
- vocational training
- transport

The Committee of the Regions also has the right to issue own-initiative opinions and it may be consulted by the other institutions on additional issues. The Committee of the Regions meets in plenary sessions five times a year and adopts some 50 opinions a year.

Members are drawn from local and regional bodies, including mayors of large cities and heads of local authorities. The 222 members and 222 alternates are nominated by the Member States and appointed for a four-year term by the Council. The current term runs from 2002-2006.

The members are drawn from the EU member states as follows:

Austria	12	Italy	24
Belgium	12	Luxembourg	6
Denmark	9	Netherlands	12
Finland	9	Portugal	12
France	24	Spain	21
Germany	24	Sweden	12
Greece	12	United Kingdom	24
Ireland	9	TOTAL	222

With the prospect of enlargement of the Union, it was decided under the Treaty of Nice that there would be a ceiling of 350 members for the Committee of the Regions. This means that the number of seats currently allocated to each Member State can be retained and the new Member States can be allocated a corresponding number of seats. The Treaty of Nice was signed by member governments in February 2001 and entered into force on 1 February 2003 once ratified by all Member States.

commissions

Since 2002 most of the work of the Committee is carried out in six commissions specialising in various fields:

- Commission for Territorial Cohesion Policy
- Commission for Economic and Social Policy
- Commission for Sustainable Development
- Commission for Culture and Education
- Commission for Constitutional Affairs and European Governance
- Commission for External Relations

uk full members (24)

Labour

Cllr Muriel BARKER CBE
Tel: 0147 232 4185
Fax: 0147 232 4132
Humber Regional Assembly

Cllr Derek BODEN
Tel: 0161 253 5103
Fax: 0161 253 5108
D.Boden@bury.gov.uk
North West Regional Assembly

Cllr Ken BODFISH OBE
Tel: 0127 329 1005
Fax: 0127 329 1003
ken.bodfish@brighton-hove.gov.uk
Brighton and Hove City Council

Cllr Sir Albert BORE
Tel: 0121 303 2030
Fax: 0121 303 3242
Mail@euroteam.bham.demon.co.uk
Birmingham City Council

Rosemary BUTLER
Tel: 0292 089 8470
Fax: 0292 089 8527
rosemary.butler@wales.gov.uk
National Assembly for Wales

Cllr Michael DAVEY
Tel: 0167 053 3052
Fax: 0167 053 3072
mdavey@northumberland.gov.uk
Northumberland County Council

Cllr Christine MAY
Tel: 0159 241 6181
Fax: 0159 241 3219
christinemay@cableinet.co.uk
Fife Council

Irene OLDFATHER MSP
Tel: 0129 431 3078
Fax: 0129 431 3605
irene.oldfather.msp@scottish.parliament.uk
Scottish Parliament

Cllr Dame Sally POWELL
Tel: 0207 940 1542
Fax: 0207 403 1742
alg-euro-london@geo2.poptel.org.uk
London Borough of Hammersmith and Fulham

Cllr Brian SMITH
Tel: 0163 348 2757
Fax: 0149 575 5513
Torfaen County Borough Council

Cllr The Hon Joan TAYLOR
Tel: 0177 381 2655
Fax: 0177 381 1770
joantaylor@selab.globalnet.co.uk
Nottinghamshire County Council

Conservative

Sir Simon DAY
Tel: 0139 238 2000
Fax: 0139 238 2286
SDAY@mf.Devpm-cc.gov.uk
Devon County Council

Cllr Margaret EATON
Tel: 0127 475 2086
Fax: 0127 473 5150
sally.tomlinson@bradford.gov.uk
Bradford Metropolitan Borough Council

Cllr Baroness Joan HANHAM
Tel: 0207 937 8692
Fax: 0207 361 3105
cgsbl@rbkc.gov.uk
Royal Borough of Kensington and Chelsea

Cllr The Lord HANNINGFIELD OF CHELMSFORD
Tel: 0124 549 2211
Fax: 0124 543 0741
robert.colmer@lga.gov.uk
Essex County Council

Cllr Gordon KEYMER
Tel: 0188 371 7363
Fax: 0188 371 7363
gordon@gckeymer.freeserve.co.uk
Tandridge District Council

Liberal Democrat
Cllr Ruth COLEMAN
Tel: 0124 972 0080
Fax: 0124 972 0103
rcoleman@northwilts.gov.uk
North Wiltshire County Council

Cllr Peter MOORE
Tel: 0144 272 6444
Fax: 0144 273 5003
sangimoore@aol.com
Sheffield Metropolitan Borough Council

Nicol STEPHEN MSP
Tel: 0131 556 8400
Fax: 0131 244 1469
roddy.maclean@scotland.gov.uk
Scottish Executive

Cllr The Lord Graham TOPE CBE
Tel: 0207 983 4413/0208 770 7269
Fax: 0207 983 4057/0208 642 8595
Graham.Tope@London.gov.uk
Greater London Authority (GLA)

UUP (Northern Ireland)
Dermot NESBITT
Tel: 0284 483 1561
Fax: 0284 483 1722
dermotnesbitt@hotmail.com
Northern Ireland Executive

SDLP (Northern Ireland)
Alban MAGINNESS MLA
Tel: 0289 022 0520
Fax: 0289 022 0522
a.maginness@sdlp.ie
Northern Ireland Assembly

SNP
Cllr Keith BROWN
Tel: 0125 974 3005
Fax: 0125 974 3768
kbrown@clacks.gov.uk
Clackmannanshire Council

Independent
Cllr Milner WHITEMAN
Tel: 0195 272 7340
Fax: 0195 272 7340
milner.whiteman@virgin.net
Bridgnorth District Council

uk alternate members (24)
Members are substituted on the basis of political party rather than region.

Labour
Cllr Jennette ARNOLD
Tel: 0207 983 4000
Fax: 0207 983 5879
jennette.arnold@london.gov.uk
Greater London Authority

Cllr Ruth BAGNALL
Tel: 0122 345 7022
Fax: 0122 345 7029
ruth.bagnall@dial.pipex.com
Cambridge City Council

Cllr Olive BROWN
Tel: 0138 876 6555
Fax: 0138 876 6660
o.brown@wearvalley.gov.uk
Wear Valley District Council

Cllr Diane BUNYAN
Tel: 0117 922 2000
Fax: 0117 922 2024
diane-bunyan@bristol-city.gov.uk
Bristol City Council

Cllr Dr Ruth HENIG JP OBE
Tel: 0152 422 1280
Fax: 0152 422 1280
r.henig@lancaster.ac.uk
Lancashire County Council

Cllr The Lord Tarsem KING JP
Tel: 0121 569 3041
Fax: 0121 569 3050
ann_oneill@sandwell.gov.uk
Sandwell Metropolitan Borough Council

Cllr Corrie McCHORD OBE
Tel: 0178 644 3378
Fax: 0178 644 2962
mcchord@stirling.gov.uk
Stirling Council

Jack McCONNELL
Tel: 0131 244 5218
Fax: 0131 244 6915
firstminister@scotland.gsi.gov.uk
Scottish Executive

committee of the regions

Conservative
Cllr Susie KEMP
Tel: 0118 971 2777
Fax: 0118 971 4398
susie.kemp@btinternet.com
Newbury Council

Cllr David SHAKESPEARE OBE
Tel: 0129 639 5000
Fax: 0129 638 3441
dshakespeare@buckscc.gov.uk
Buckinghamshire County Council

Cllr Sue SIDA-LOCKETT
Tel: 0144 978 1327
Fax: 0144 978 0280
sue.sida-lockett@members.suffolkcc.gov.uk
Suffolk County Council

Cllr Jim SPEECHLEY CBE
Tel: 0152 255 2089
Fax: 0152 255 2072
rose.dobbs@lincolnshire.gov.uk
Lincolnshire County Council

Cllr Sir Ronald WATSON CBE
Tel: 0151 934 2061
Fax: 0151 934 2060
conservatives@sefton.gov.uk
Sefton Metropolitan Borough Council

Liberal Democrat
Cllr Flo CLUCAS
Tel: 0151 428 6957
Fax: 0151 225 2983
flo.clucas@liverpool.gov.uk
Liverpool City Council

Bob NEILL
Tel: 0207 983 4354
Fax: 0207 983 4419
robert.neill@london.gov.uk
Greater London Authority

Cllr Shirley SMART
Tel: 0198 382 3690
Fax: 0198 382 3678
shirley.smart@iow.gov.uk
Isle of Wight Council

Cllr Elizabeth TUCKER
Tel: 0190 579 6639
Fax: 0190 576 6664
Worcester County Council

SDLP (Northern Ireland)
Cllr Margaret RITCHIE
Tel: 0284 461 2882
Fax: 0284 461 9574
Down District Council

SNP
Irene McGUGAN MSP
Tel: 0131 348 5711
Fax: 0131 348 5944
irene.mcgugan.msp@scottish.parliament.uk
Scottish Parliament

UUP (Northern Ireland)
Cllr George SAVAGE MLA
Tel: 0129 639 5000
Fax: 0129 638 3441
g.k.savage@dial.pipex.com
Northern Ireland Assembly and Craigavon Borough
Council

Plaid Cymru
Cllr Jonathan HUISH
Tel: 0144 342 4005
Fax: 0144 342 4006
jonathan.huish@rhondda-cynon-taff.gov.uk
Rhondda Cynon Taff County Borough Council

Margaret Elin JONES
Tel: 0154 557 1688
Fax: 0154 557 1567
elin.jones@wales.gov.uk
National Assembly for Wales

Independent
Cllr Joan ASHTON
Tel: 0120 535 5994
Fax: 0120 536 4604
joan.ashton@boston.gov.uk
Boston Borough Council

Cllr Hugh HALCRO-JOHNSTON
Tel: 0185 687 3535
Fax: 0185 687 7292
hugh.halcro-johnston@orkney.gov.uk
Orkney Islands Council

economic and social committee

Rue Ravenstein 2, B-1000 Brussels
Tel: +32 25 46 90 11
Fax: +32 25 13 48 93
E-mail: info@esc.eu.int
Website: http://www.esc.eu.int/pages/en/home.htm

President Roger BRIESCH (France)
Vice-Presidents Göke FRERICHS (Germany), Lief NIELSEN (Denmark)
Secretary-General Patrick VENTURINI

The Economic and Social Committee was founded by the Treaty of Rome in 1958. Its 222 members are drawn from organisations representing employers, workers, farmers, small and medium-sized enterprises, commerce, crafts, co-operatives, mutual benefit societies, the professions, consumers, environmentalists, families, "social" non-governmental organisations etc. The Committee is consulted before the adoption of most Community decisions and may also issue opinions on its own initiative. Its opinions are adopted by a straight majority vote and are published in the *Official Journal of the European Communities*.

The 222 members are drawn from the EU member states as follows:

Austria	12	Italy	24
Belgium	12	Luxembourg	6
Denmark	9	Netherlands	12
Finland	9	Portugal	12
France	24	Spain	21
Germany	24	Sweden	12
Greece	12	United Kingdom	24
Ireland	9	TOTAL	222

Members are nominated by national governments and appointed by the Council of the European Union for a renewable four-year term of office. The current term of office runs from October 1998 until September 2002.

With the prospect of enlargement of the Union, it was decided under the Treaty of Nice that there would be a ceiling of 350 members for the Economic and Social Committee. This means that the number of seats currently allocated to each Member State can be retained and the new Member States can be allocated a corresponding number of seats. The Treaty of Nice was signed by member governments in February 2001 and entered into force on 1 February 2003 once ratified by all the Member States.

economic and social committee

groups

Members belong to one of three groups:

- Employers (Group I)
- Workers (Group II)
- Various interests (such as agriculture, transport, trade, small business, the professions and consumers) (Group III)

sections

The Committee conducts its advisory work by means of six sections:

- Agriculture, Rural Development and the Environment (NAT)
- Economic and Monetary Union and Economic and Social Cohesion (ECO)
- Employment, Social Affairs and Citizenship (SOC)
- External Relations (REX)
- The Single Market, Production and Consumption (INT)
- Transport, Energy, Infrastructure and the Information Society (TEN)

uk members

Richard ADAMS Group III
Director of Contraflow
Director of Warm Zones Ltd
18, Northumberland Avenue,
Newcastle-upon-Tyne NE3 4XE
Tel: 0191 246 1463
Fax: 0191 284 0052
richarda@contraflow.com

Robert BAIRD Group I
Banker/Economist
126 High Street, Edinburgh, EH1 1QS
Tel: 0131 225 5489
Fax: 0131 225 5489
roddy.maclean@scotland.gsi.gov.uk

Sandy BOYLE Group II
Deputy Secretary General UNIFI (Finance sector union)
9 Learmouth Street, Falkirk, FK1 5AG
Tel: 0132 462 6708
Fax: 0132 462 4910
sandy.boyle@unifi.org.uk

Ben BUTTERS Group I
Director of smallbusiness europe
Rue du Luxembourg 23, B-1000 Brussels
Tel: 0032 25 03 10 62
Fax: 0032 25 03 15 86

Brian CASSIDY Group I
EU Affairs Consultant, MEP (1984-1999)
Cassidy and Associates International
11, Esmond Court, Thackery Street, London, W8 5HB
Tel: 0207 937 3558
Fax: 0207 937 3789
bmdcassidy@aol.com

Brian CURTIS Group II
RMT (National Union of Rail, Maritime and Transport Workers) Regional Organiser Wales and the West of England
22 Hawthorn Road, Barry, Wales CF26 6LE
Tel: 0144 674 9272
Fax: 0144 674 9272

Ann DAVISON Group III
Executive Director of European Research into
Consumer Affairs, (ERICA) - Advisor to Consumers in
Europe Group (UK)
Drivers, Elgin Road, Weybridge, Surrey KT13 8SN
Tel: 0193 284 4273
Fax: 0193 285 6252
anndavison@net-consumers.org

Rose D'SA Group III
Consultant in European Union, Commonwealth and
International Law - Consultant in Legal Education/
Distance Learning
64, Blossom Close, Langstone, Newport NP18 2LT
Tel: 0163 341 3291
Fax: 0163 341 3291

David FEICKERT Group II
European Officer - Trades Union Congress (UK)
TUC Office, ITUH
Boulevard du Roi Albert II 5, B-1210 Brussels
Tel: +32 2 224 0477
Fax: +32 2 224 0479
dfeicker@tuc.etuc.org

Derek HUNTER Group II
Regional Secretary GMB (Britain's Modern Union)
102 Westwood Park, Forest Hill, London SE23 3QH
Tel: 0208 699 0308
Fax: 0208 699 0308
derek.hunter@lycos.co.uk

Ken JACKSON Group II
General Secretary - Amalgamated Engineering and
Electrical Union (AEEU)
Hayes Court, West Common Road, Bromley,
Kent BR2 7AU
Tel: 0208 325 8457
Fax: 0208 315 8203
jacksonkenaeeu@compaq40.freeserve.co.uk

Brenda KING Group I
Consultant Royal Mail Group
Royal Mail Group, 148 Old Street, London EC1V 9PP
Tel: 0207 012 3064
Fax: 0207 012 3131
brenda.king@consignia.com

Judy McKNIGHT Group II
General Secretary, National Association of Probation
Officers (NAPO)
3-4 Chivalry Road, London SW11 1HT
Tel: 0207 223 4887
Fax: 0207 223 3503

Maureen O'NEILL Group III
Director of Age Concern Scotland
Age Concern, Leonard Small House, 113 Rose Street,
Edinburgh EH2 3DT
Tel: 0131 220 3345
Fax: 0131 220 2779
maureen.o'neill@acscot.org.uk

Sheila RITCHIE Group I
Solicitor The Grant Smith Law Practice
Kinghorn Cottage, Newmachar AB21 0QH
Tel: 0122 462 1620
Fax: 0122 462 1620
sheilaritchie@cix.co.uk

David SEARS Group I
Former Deputy Director General British Chambers of
Commerce
3 Albany Villas, Howe, East Sussex BN3 2RS
Tel: 0127 373 7135
Fax: 0127 320 7433
searsdj@tiscali.co.uk

Madi SHARMA Group I
Madi Group
40 Ridge Hill, Lowdham, Nottinghamshire NG14 7EL
Tel: 0115 966 5188
Fax: 0115 966 5188
original.madi@tiscali.co.uk

economic and social committee

Sukhdev SHARMA Group III
Chairman Board of the Migration and Policy Group
Member Board of the Runnymede Trust
17, Heath Mount, Free School Lane,
Halifax HX1 2YR
Tel: 0142 236 6238
Fax: 0142 236 6359
ssh7766@cs.com

Alison SHEPHERD Group II
Vice-President UNISON
Middlesex University, Bounds Green Road,
London N11 2NQ
Tel: 0208 362 5117
Fax: 0208 362 6311
a.shepherd@mdx.ac.uk

John SIMPSON Group III
Economics Consultant/Adviser
3, Glenmachan Drive, Belmont, Belfast BT4 2RE
Tel: 0289 076 9399
Fax: 0289 076 9399
johnvsimpson@cs.com

Donna ST HILL Group I
Employment Equity, Gender Analysis - Independent
Advisor National Employment Panel, Department of
Work and Pensions
60 Thorndon Hall, Ingrave, Brentwood, Essex CM13 3RJ
Tel: 0127 781 2898
Dsthill@getfreeinternet.co.uk

Monica TAYLOR Group II
Executive Council Member Transport and General
Workers' Union (TGWU)
Denso Ltd, Shaftmoor Lane, Hall Green,
Birmingham B28 8SW
mtaylor@denso-midlands.co.uk

Claire WHITTEN Group III
Executive Director Northern Ireland Centre in Europe
Northern Ireland Centre in Europe, Regus House,
33 Clarendon Dock, Belfast BT1 3BW
Tel: 0289 051 1231
Fax: 0289 051 1201
cw@ni-centre-in-europe.com

Clive WILKINSON Group I
Consultant to the Gin and Vodka Association
Strangford, Amport, Andover, Hants SP11 8AX
Tel: 0126 477 2596
Fax: 0126 477 3085
106530.3221@compuserve.com

european central bank

Address: Kaiserstrasse 29, D-60311 Frankfurt am Main, Germany
Postal address: Postfach 16 03 19, D-60066 Frankfurt am Main, Germany
Tel (switchboard): +49 69 13 44-0
Fax: +49 69 13 44 60 00
Telex: 411 144 ecb d
E-mail: info@ecb.int
Website: http://www.ecb.int

The European Central Bank (ECB) is responsible for the monetary policy of the euro zone, i.e. the 12 Member States that have opted for the single currency. The ECB and the national central banks of the Member States form the European System of Central Banks (ESCB), whose main objective is to maintain price stability.

The ESCB's basic tasks are to:

- define and implement the single monetary policy of the Community;
- conduct foreign exchange operations;
- hold and manage the official foreign reserves of the Member States;
- promote the smooth operation of payment systems and;
- contribute to the smooth operation of policies pursued by the competent authorities relating to the prudential supervision of credit institutions and the stability of the financial system.

The ECB ensures that the tasks conferred upon the ESCB are implemented either by its own activities or through the national central banks.

Assisted by the national central banks, the ECB also collects any necessary statistical information and contributes to the harmonisation of the rules and practices governing the collection, compilation and distribution of statistics in the areas within its fields of competence. It draws up and publishes reports on the activities of the ESCB at least quarterly and a consolidated financial statement is published each week.

european central bank

the euro

European Central Bank: http://www.euro.ecb.int/en.html
HM Treasury euro business: http://www.euro.gov.uk
European Commission: http://europa.eu.int/euro

The following countries have adopted the euro:

Austria, Belgium, Finland, France, Germany, Greece, Ireland, Italy, Luxembourg, Netherlands, Portugal and Spain. The participating countries also share a single interest rate set by the European Central Bank.

Denmark and the United Kingdom exercised their right under the Maastricht Treaty not to participate in economic and monetary union from January 1999. Sweden did not meet the necessary conditions. As long as the UK remains outside the euro area, the exchange rate between the euro and sterling will fluctuate, just like the exchange rate between sterling and other currencies.

Euro notes were introduced on 1 January 2002. The notes are in different colours and sizes to enable easy identification. There are eight denominations of coin ranging from 1 cent to 2 euro.

decision-making bodies

The Governing Council comprises the 12 governors of the central banks of the euro zone and the six members of the Executive Board. The Governing Council formulates the monetary policy of the Community including decisions relating to intermediate monetary objectives, key interest rates and the supply of reserves in the European System of Central Banks (ESCB), and establishes the necessary guidelines for their implementation. The Executive Board implements monetary policy in accordance with these guidelines and decisions. In doing so the Executive Board gives the necessary instructions to national central banks.

executive board

Appointed 1998, terms of office in brackets
Willem F DUISENBERG, President of the ECB (8 years)
Lucas PAPADEMOS, Vice-President of the ECB (4 years appointed 1 June 2002)
Eugenio Domingo SOLANS (6 years)
Sirkka HÄMÄLÄINEN (5 years)
Otmar ISSING (8 years)
Tommaso PADOA-SCHIOPPA (7 years)

Governors of the national central banks
Guy QUADEN, Governor, Nationale Bank van België

Ernst WELTEKE, President, Deutsche Bundesbank
Nicholas GARGANAS, Governor, Bank of Greece
Jaime CARUANA, Governor, Banco de España
Jean-Claude TRICHET, Governor, Banque de France
John HURLEY, Governor, Central Bank of Ireland
Antonio FAZIO, Governor, Banca d'Italia
Yves MERSCH, Governor, Banque centrale du Luxembourg
Nout WELLINK, President, De Nederlandsche Bank
Klaus LIEBSCHER, Governor, Oesterreichische Nationalbank
Vítor Manuel RIBEIRO CONSTÂNCIO, Governor, Banco de Portugal
Matti VANHALA, Governor, Suomen Pankki

european investment bank

Boulevard Konrad Adenauer 100, L-2950 Luxembourg
Tel: +352 43 79-1
Fax: +352 43 79 31 89
E-mail: info@eib.org
Website: http://www.eib.org

London office
68 Pall Mall, London SW1Y 5ES
Tel: 0207 343 1200
Fax: 0207 930 9929

President Philippe MAYSTADT

The European Investment Bank (EIB) is the European Union's long-term lending institution. It was created in 1958 as an autonomous body set up to finance capital investment furthering European integration by promoting EU economic policies through borrowing and lending activity.

Its main task is to provide long-term loans in support of capital investment projects, contributing towards one or more the following EU policy objectives: developing less-advanced regions, establishing trans-European transport, telecommunications and energy transfer networks, fostering industrial modernisation, strengthening the activities of small and medium sized enterprises, protecting the environment and ensuring efficient management and use of energy resources.

Outside the Union the EIB implements the financial components of agreements concluded under European development aid and co-operation policies in favour of some 150 non-member countries. In the regions bordering Europe to the south and east it is preparing for enlargement and supporting economic modernisation with a view to the future free trade area with the Mediterranean countries.

Its shareholders are the 15 Member States of the European Union, who have all subscribed to its capital. The Bank raises the resources needed to finance its lending by borrowing on capital markets, chiefly through its public bond issues. Promoters in both the public and private sectors, including banks, can borrow individual loans in euro and other currencies.

The EIB is managed by a Board of Governors, a Board of Directors and a Management Committee.

The **Board of Governors** consists of Ministers of the EU Member States - generally the Finance Ministers.

The **Board of Directors** consists of 25 directors and 13 alternates appointed by the Board of Governors for five years. The appointments of the directors and alternates are renewable.

european investment bank

The **Management Committee** consists of the President and seven Vice-Presidents who together conduct the day-to-day business of the Bank. Members of the Management Committee are appointed by the Board of Governors on a proposal from the Board of Directors for renewable six-year terms.

management committee

President Philippe MAYSTADT

Vice-Presidents Wolfgang ROTH, Massimo PONZELLINI, Ewald NOWOTNY, Francis MAYER, Peter SEDGWICK, Isabel MARTÍN CASTELLÁ, Michael G. TUTTY

general secretariat

Secretary-General Francis CARPENTER

General administration
Director Rémy JACOB

directorates

Directorate for lending operations - Europe
Director-General Terence BROWN

Directorate for lending operations - other countries
Director-General Jean-Louis BIANCARELLI

Finance Directorate
Director-General René KARSENTI

Projects Directorate
Director-General Michel DELEAU

Legal Affairs Directorate
Director-General Eberhard UHLMANN

other

Credit Risk
General Counsel Pierluigi GILIBERT

Human resources
Director Andreas VERYKIOS

Operation Evaluation
Director Horst FEUERSTEIN

Financial Control
Director Patrick KLAEDTKE

Information technology
Director Luciano DI MATTIA

Internal Audit
Peter MAERTENS

european investment fund

Avenue J.F. Kennedy 43, L-2968 Luxembourg
Tel: +352 4 26 68 81
Fax: +352 4 26 68 82 00
E-mail: info@eif.org
Website: http://www.eif.org

The European Investment Fund (EIF) is a European Union financial institution established in 1994 as a joint venture between the European Investment Bank (EIB), the European Union (represented by the European Commission) and European banks and financial institutions. Following the EIF's recent reform, the European Investment Bank has become the majority shareholder and has confirmed the role of the EIF as the venture capital and small and medium-sized enterprise (SME) guarantees arm of the EIB group. The authorised capital of the EIF amounts to euro 2 billion. The EIF does not finance SMEs directly, but always acts through financial intermediaries and venture capital funds. The EIF conducts its activities in the 15 Member States of the European Union and in the accession countries.

Chief executive Walter CERNOIA

Secretary and Head of Services Robert WAGENER

Head of Operations John HOLLOWAY

201

european ombudsman

European Ombudsman
Avenue du Président Robert Schuman 1, B.P. 403, 67001 Strasbourg Cedex, France
Tel: +33 3 88 17 40 01
Fax: +33 3 88 17 90 62
E-mail: euro-ombudsman@europarl.eu.int
Website: http://www.euro-ombudsman.eu.int

Ombudsman Nikiforos DIAMANDOUROS

The European Ombudsman investigates complaints about maladministration by institutions and bodies of the European Community. The Ombudsman cannot deal with complaints concerning national, regional or local administrations of the Member States.

Anyone who is a citizen of a Member State of the European Union, or living in a Member State, may make a complaint to the European Ombudsman. Businesses, associations or other bodies with a registered office in the Union may also complain to the Ombudsman.

The last Ombudsman elections took place on 1 April 2003. The next are due at the end of the parliamentary term in 2004. The current term of office is shorter than the usual 5 years owing to the mid-term retirement of the previous ombudsman.

community agencies:

community plant variety office

european agency for the evaluation of medical products

european agency for reconstruction

european agency for safetyand health at work

european centre for the development of vocational training

european environment agency

european foundation for the improvement of living and working conditions

european monitoring centre for drugs and drug addiction

european monitoring centre on racism and xenophobia

european training foundation

europol - european police office

office for harmonisation in the internal market

translation centre for the bodies of the european union

community plant variety office (CPVO)

Boulevard Maréchal Foch 3, F-49100 Angers
Postal address: PO Box 2141, 49021, Cedex 02, F-49021 Angers
Tel: +33 2 41 25 64 00
Fax: +33 2 41 25 64 10
E-mail: cpvo@cpvo.eu.int
Website: http://www.cpvo.eu.int

President Barteld P. KIEWIET
Deputy Chairman José ELENA

The Community Plant Variety Office, set up in 1995, implements and applies a system for the protection of plant variety rights established by Community legislation. This system allows intellectual property rights, valid throughout the Community, to be granted for plant varieties.

european agency for the evaluation of medicinal products (EMEA)

7 Westferry Circus, Canary Wharf, London E14 4HB
Tel: 0207 418 8400
Fax: 0207 418 8416
E-mail: mail@emea.eu.int
Website: http://www.emea.eu.int

Executive Director Thomas LÖNNGREN

The Agency is in charge of co-ordinating scientific resources existing in the Member States with a view to evaluating and supervising medicinal products for both human and veterinary use. On the basis of the Agency's opinion the European Commission authorises the marketing of innovative products and arbitrates between Member States for other medicinal products in case of disagreement.

european agency for reconstruction (EAR)

Egnatia 4, GR-546 26 Thessaloniki
Tel: +30 23 10 50 51 00
Fax: +30 23 10 50 51 72
Website: http://www.ear.eu.int
Operational centres: Kosovo (Tel: +381 38 51 31 00, Fax: +381 38 54 99 63); Serbia (Tel: +381 1 13 02 34 00, Fax: +381 1 13 02 34 55); Montenegro (Tel: +381 81 23 17 40, Fax: +381 81 23 17 41)
Back-up office: FYRM (Tel: +389 2 29 03 66, Fax: +389 2 22 53 50)

Director Richard ZINK

The European Agency for Reconstruction was set up in January 2000. It is responsible for the management of the main EU assistance programmes in Kosovo, Serbia and Montenegro. The Agency has its headquarters in Thessaloniki and its operational centre in Pristina, and the Republics of Serbia and Montenegro.

european agency for safety and health at work

Gran Vía 33, E-48009 Bilbao
Tel: +34 9 44 79 43 60
Fax: +34 9 44 79 43 83
E-mail: information@osha.eu.int
Website: http://europe.osha.eu.int

Director Hans-Horst KONKOLEWSKY

The Agency was set up by the European Union in 1974 to serve the information needs in the field of safety and health at work. The Agency has three key areas of activity: collecting information (through Europe-wide networks of designated experts); communicating information, in particular through the website, and developing knowledge through major pan-European Information projects on important occupational safety and health themes.

european centre for the development of vocational training (Cedefop)

PO Box 22427 - Thessaloniki, GR-55102
Tel: +30 31 49 01 11
Fax: +30 31 49 01
E-mail: info@cedefop.eu.int
Website: http://www.cedefop.eu.int
Interactive website: http://www.trainingvillage.gr

Director Johan VAN RENS
Deputy Director Stavros STAVROU

The Centre was set up in 1975. It is the European agency that helps policy-makers and practitioners of the European Commission, the Member States and social partner organisations across Europe make informed choices about vocational training policy. It is able to provide the latest information on the present state of, and future trends in, vocational education and training in the European Union.

european monitoring centre for drugs and drug addiction (EMCDDA)

Palacete Mascarenhas, Rua da Cruz de Santa Apolónia, 23-25, P-1149-045 Lisbon
Tel: +351 2 18 11 30 00
Fax: +351 2 18 13 17 11
E-mail: info@emcdda.org
Website: http://www.emcdda.org

Executive Director Georges ESTIEVENART

The EMCDDA became operational in 1994. Its main task is to provide the Member States and the Community as a whole with objective, reliable and comparable information at European level on drugs, drug addiction and their consequences.

european environment agency (EEA)

Kongens Nytorv 6, DK-1050 Copenhagen
Tel: +45 33 36 71 00
Fax: +45 33 36 71 99
E-mail: eea@eea.eu.int
Website: http://www.eea.eu.int

Interim Executive Director Gordon MCINNES

The aim of the European Environment Agency is to establish an environmental information system to assist the Community in its attempts to improve the environment and move towards sustainability, including the EU's efforts to integrate environmental aspects into economic policies. Information is gathered by around 500 European institutions participating in the European Environment Information and Observation Network (EIONET). In January 2001 the European Commission adopted a series of proposals which will enable the 13 candidate countries to join the European Environment Agency, making the EEA the first European body open to the candidate countries before their accession.

european foundation for the improvement of living and working conditions

Loughlinstown, Ireland
Tel: +353 12 04 31 00
Fax: +353 12 82 64 56
E-mail: postmaster@eurofound.ie
Website: http://www.eurofound.ie

Director Raymond-Pierre BODIN

The task of the Foundation, which was set up in 1975, is to gather and disseminate information on living and working conditions, promote and co-ordinate research and to provide technical support to the European Commission in these areas.

european monitoring centre on racism and xenophobia

Rahlgasse 3, A-1060 Vienna
Tel: +43 15 8 03 00
Fax: +43 15 80 30 99
E-mail: information@eumc.eu.int
Website: http://www.eumc.at

Director Beate WINKLER

The Centre was established in 1997 to provide the Community and the Member States with objective, reliable and comparable data at European level on the phenomena of racism, xenophobia and anti-Semitism. It has set up a European Racism and Xenophobia Information Network (RAXEN) to be an instrument for collecting and collating data and statistics from the national level to a central unit of the EUMC.

european training foundation

Villa Gualino, Viale Settimio Severo 65, I-10133 Turin
Tel: +39 01 16 30 22 22
Fax: +39 01 16 30 22 00
E-mail: info@etf.eu.int
Website: http://www.etf.eu.int

Director Peter DE ROOIJ
Deputy Directors Ulrich HILLENKAMP, Livio PESCIA

The Foundation was established in 1995. Its mission is to contribute to the process of vocational education and training reform that is currently taking place within its partner countries and territories. It also provides technical assistance to the Tempus Programme. The Foundation's partner countries and territories are those that are eligible to participate in the EU's various assistance programmes for Central and Eastern Europe, the New Independent States and Mongolia and the Mediterranean regions - namely the Phare, Tacis and MEDA Programmes.

europol

Raamweg 47, The Hague, The Netherlands
Postal address: PO Box 90850, NL-2509 LW The Hague
Tel: +31 7 03 02 50 00
Fax: +31 7 03 45 58 96
E-mail: info@europol.eu.int
Website: http://www.europol.eu.int

Director Jürgen STORBECK

Europol is the EU law enforcement organisation and it handles criminal intelligence. It started limited operations in January 1994 and took up its full range of activities in July 1999. Its aim is to improve the effectiveness and co-operation between the competent authorities of the Member States in preventing and combating terrorism, unlawful drug-trafficking and other forms of serious international organised crime.

office for harmonisation in the internal market (trade marks and designs) (OHIM)

Avenida de Aguilera 20, E-03080 Alicante
Tel: +34 9 65 13 91 00
Fax: +34 9 65 13 91 73
E-mail: information@oami.eu.int
Website: http://www.oami.eu.int

President Wubbo DE BOER

The Office's task is to promote and manage trademarks and designs within the European Union. It carries out registration procedures for titles to Community industrial property and keeps public registers of these titles. It shares with the courts in Member States of the EU the task of pronouncing judgement on requests for invalidation of registered titles. The Office is a public establishment which enjoys legal, administrative and financial independence.

translation centre for bodies of the european union

Bâtiment Nouvel Hémicycle 1, rue du Fort Thüngen, L-1499 Luxembourg
Tel: +352 4 21 71 11
Fax: +352 4 21 71 12 20
E-mail: cdt@cdt.eu.int
Website: http://www.cdt.eu.int

Director Francisco DE VICENTE

The Centre provides the necessary translation services for the operation of the agencies and bodies of the EU.

other institutions:

council of europe

european bank for reconstruction and development

nato

council of europe

Council of Europe, 67075 Strasbourg Cedex, France
Tel: +33 3 88 41 20 33
Fax: +33 3 88 41 27 81/82/83
Email: infopoint_i@coe.int
Website: http://www.coe.int

Secretary-General Walter SCHWIMMER (Austria)

member states (45)

Albania
Andorra
Armenia
Austria
Azerbaijan
Belgium
Bosnia-Herzegovina
Bulgaria
Croatia
Cyprus
Czech Republic
Denmark
Estonia
Finland
France
Georgia
Germany
Greece
Hungary
Iceland
Ireland
Italy
Latvia
Liechtenstein
Lithuania
Luxembourg
Malta
Moldova
Netherlands
Norway

Poland
Portugal
Romania
Russian Federation
San Marino
Serbia and Montenegro
Slovakia
Slovenia
Spain
Sweden
Switzerland
The former Yugoslav Republic of Macedonia
Turkey
Ukraine
United Kingdom

Applicant members
Monaco

Observers to the Committee of Ministers
Canada
Holy See
Japan
Mexico
United States of America

Observers to the Parliamentary Assembly
Canada
Israel
Mexico

council of europe

The Council of Europe is an intergovernmental organisation which has met in Strasbourg since 1949. It aims to:

- protect human rights, pluralist democracy and the rule of law
- promote awareness and encourage the development of Europe's cultural identity and diversity
- seek solutions to problems facing European society (discrimination against minorities, xenophobia, intolerance, environmental protection, human cloning, AIDS, drugs, organised crime, etc.)
- help consolidate democratic stability in Europe by backing political, legislative and constitutional reform

The Council of Europe covers all major issues facing European society other than defence. Its work programme includes the following fields of activity: human rights, media, legal co-operation, social and economic questions, health, education, culture, heritage, sport, youth, local democracy and transfrontier co-operation, the environment and regional planning.

The **Committee of Ministers** is the Council of Europe's decision-making body, and is composed of the Foreign Ministers of the 45 member states (or their Permanent Representatives).

The **Parliamentary Assembly** is the Organisation's deliberative body, the members of which are appointed by national parliaments. They meet in plenary session four times a year, usually in Paris.

Website: http://assembly.coe.int

The **Congress of Local and Regional Authorities of Europe** (CLRAE) is a consultative body representing local and regional authorities. There are two chambers, one representing local authorities and the second regional authorities.

Website: http://www.coe.fr/cplre/indexe.htm

The Council of Europe's work leads to European conventions and agreements, in the light of which member states may subsequently harmonise and amend their own legislation to comply with them. One of the earliest conventions drawn up by the Council of Europe in 1950 was the **European Convention on Human Rights.** This Convention guarantees such civil and political rights as the right to a fair trial, freedom of expression, free elections and respect of property. All the Member States of the EU have signed the convention. The website http://www.echr.coe.int contains a section on 'Information for persons wishing to apply to the European Court of Human Rights' which includes an application form. The database of the case law of the ECHR is available at http://www.echr.coe.int/Hudoc.htm.

european bank for reconstruction and development

One Exchange Square, London EC2A 2JN
Tel: 0207 338 6000
Fax: 0207 338 6100
Telex: 8812161 EBRD L G

Requests for publications:
Tel: 0207 338 7553
Fax: 0207 338 6102
E-mail: pubsdesk@ebrd.com

General enquiries:
Tel: 0207 338 6372
Fax: 0207 338 6690

Project enquiries/proposals:
Tel: 0207 338 6282
Fax: 0207 338 6102
E-mail: projectenquiries@ebrd.com

Website: http://www.ebrd.com

The European Bank for Reconstruction and Development (EBRD) was established in 1991. It exists to foster the transition towards open market-oriented economies and to promote private and entrepreneurial initiative in those countries of central and eastern Europe and the Commonwealth of Independent States (CIS) that are committed to and are applying the principles of multiparty democracy, pluralism and market economics.

The EBRD seeks to help its 27 countries of operations to implement structural and sectoral economic reforms, promoting competition, privatisation and entrepreneurship. Through its investments it promotes private sector activity, the strengthening of financial institutions and legal systems, and the development of the infrastructure needed to support the private sector. The Bank encourages co-financing and foreign direct investment from the private and public sectors, helps to mobilise domestic capital, and provides technical co-operation in relevant areas. It works in close co-operation with international financial institutions and other international and national organisations.

219

european bank for reconstruction and development

organisation and management

President Jean LEMIERRE
Director of President's Office Arnaud PRUDHOMME

Banking
First Vice President Noreen DOYLE
Deputy Vice President David HEXTER

Finance
Vice President Steven KAEMPFER
Deputy Vice President Vacant

Personnel and Administration
Vice President Hanna GRONKIEWICZ-WALTZ

Evaluation, Operational and Environmental Support
Vice President Joachim JAHNKE
Deputy Vice President Jean-François MAQUET

Office of the Secretary General
Acting Secretary General Nigel CARTER

Office of the General Counsel
General Counsel Emmanuel MAURICE
Deputy General Counsel Norbert SEILER

Office of the Chief Economist
Chief Economist Willem BUITER
Deputy Chief Economist Steven FRIES

Internal Audit
Head Tarek ROUCHDY
Deputy Head Ray PORTELLI

Office of the Chief Compliance Officer
Chief Compliance Officer Jean Pierre MÉAN

Communications
Director Brigid JANSSEN
Deputy Director Laurence SHERWIN

north atlantic treaty organisation

Blvd Leopold III, B-1110 Brussels
Tel: +32 27 07 41 11
Fax: +32 27 07 41 17
E-mail: natodoc@hq.nato.int
Website: http://www.nato.int/home.htm

Secretary-General Lord ROBERTSON
Deputy Secretary-General Ambassador Minuto RIZZO

member countries of the north atlantic alliance (19):

Belgium	Luxembourg
Canada	Netherlands
Czech Republic	Norway
Denmark	Poland
France	Portugal
Germany	Spain
Greece	Turkey
Hungary	United Kingdom
Iceland	United States
Italy	

The fundamental role of NATO is to safeguard the freedom and security of its member countries.

history

The North Atlantic Treaty was signed in Washington in April 1949, creating an alliance of 12 independent nations committed to each other's defence. Four more European nations later acceded to the Treaty between 1952 and 1982. On 12 March 1999, the Czech Republic, Hungary and Poland were welcomed into the Alliance. Ten countries are currently participating in NATO's Membership Action Plan. Participation does not guarantee future membership; countries are expected to meet certain political, economic and military goals. Participants are: Albania, Bulgaria, Croatia, Estonia, Latvia, Lithuania, Romania, Slovakia, Slovenia and the Former Yugoslav Republic of Macedonia.

Today, following the end of the Cold War and division of Europe, the Alliance has been restructured to enable it to contribute more effectively to the development of co-operative security structures for the whole of Europe. It has also transformed its political and military structures in order to adapt them to peacekeeping and crisis management tasks undertaken in co-operation with countries that are not members of the Alliance and with other international organisations.

New forms of partnership and co-operation with other countries within the framework of the Alliance have been created through initiatives such as the creation of the North Atlantic Co-operation Council (NACC), Partnership for Peace (PfP) and the establishment of a new Euro-Atlantic Partnership Council (EAPC). In May 1997, in Paris, NATO and Russia signed an agreement on their future relations. A few days later a NATO-Ukraine Charter was initialled in Portugal. A dialogue with the Mediterranean countries, initiated in December 1995, is also under development.

relationship with the eu

The EU has resolved to develop a common European policy on security and defence (ESDP) which would militarily underpin its Common Foreign and Security Policy. It aims to be able to deploy military forces able to undertake a range of tasks including humanitarian and rescue tasks; peacekeeping tasks; and tasks of combat forces in crisis management, including peacemaking. These forces would be used by the EU in response to international crisis, in circumstances where NATO as a whole is not engaged militarily. The ESDP will avoid unnecessary duplication with NATO structures and does not imply the creation of a European army. EU-NATO ties are being developed through joint meetings of the EU's Political and Security Committee and the North Atlantic Council, the setting up of joint EU/NATO Committees and joint meetings of the NATO Parliamentary Assembly and the European Parliament.

committees and institutions of the alliance

The **North Atlantic Council** (NAC) has effective political authority and powers of decision and consists of Permanent Representatives of all member countries meeting together at least once a week. The Council also meets at higher levels involving Foreign Ministers, Defence Ministers or Heads of Government but it has the same authority and powers of decision-making, and its decisions have the same status and validity, at whatever level it meets.

Chairman (Secretary-General of NATO) Lord Robertson

The **Defence Planning Committee** (DPC) is normally composed of Permanent Representatives but meets at the level of Defence Ministers at least twice a year. It deals with defence matters and subjects related to collective defence planning. All member countries are represented in this forum, with the exception of France. The Defence Planning Committee provides guidance to NATO's military authorities.

The **Euro-Atlantic Partnership Council** (EAPC) was established in 1997 as a multilateral forum where NATO member and Partner countries meet on a regular basis to discuss political and security-related issues and develop co-operation in a wide range of areas. At present, there are 46 members: 19 NATO member countries and 27 partner countries. All EAPC members are members of the Partnership for Peace programme, except for Tajikistan.

Partnership for Peace (PfP) has been since 1994 the basis for practical security co-operation between NATO and individual Partner countries in central and eastern Europe. Activities include defence planning and budgeting, military exercises and civil emergency operations. There are now 26 members of PfP, which are all members of the EAPC.

The establishment of the **North Atlantic Co-operation Council** (NACC) in December 1991 brought together the member countries of NATO and nine Central and Eastern European countries in a new consultative forum. In March 1992, participation in the NACC was expanded to include all members of the Commonwealth of Independent States and by June 1992, Georgia and Albania had also become members.

The **NATO Parliamentary Assembly** is the inter-parliamentary organisation of legislators from the 19 member countries of the NATO Alliance as well as 17 associate members.

NATO Parliamentary Assembly
3 Place du Petit Sablon, B-1000 Brussels
Tel: +32 25 13 28 65
Fax: +32 25 14 18 47
E-mail: secretariat@nato-pa.int
Website: http://www.naa.be

indexes:

glossary

name index

country index

glossary of acronyms and abbreviations

ACP	77 African, Caribbean and Pacific countries associated with the EU by the Lomé Convention
ADAR	Audit Development and Reports (Court of Auditors)
ADMIN	Personnel and Administration DG (Commission)
AFCO	Committee on Constitutional Affairs (EP)
AFET	Committee on Foreign Affairs, Human Rights, Common Security and Defence Policy (EP)
AGRI	Committee on Agriculture and Rural Development (EP)
AGRI	Agriculture DG (Commission)
AM	Assembly Member (Welsh)
AOCTS	Associated Overseas Countries and Territories
ASEAN	6 South-East Asian countries associated with the EU (Brunei, Indonesia, Malaysia, Philippines, Singapore and Thailand)
AUDIT	Financial Control DG (Commission)
BUDG	Committee on Budgets (EP)
BUDG	Budget DG (Commission)
CAP	Common Agricultural Policy
CCT	Common Customs Tariff
CEDEFOP	European Centre for the Development of Vocational Training
CESDP	Common European Security and Defence Policy
CFI	Court of First Instance
CFSP	Common Foreign and Security Policy
CLRAE	Congress of Regional and Local Authorities in Europe (Council of Europe)
CoE	Council of Europe
COMP	Competition DG (Commission)
CONT	Committee on Budgetary Control (EP)
CoR	Committee of the Regions
COREPER	Committee of Permanent Representatives
COST	European Co-operation on Scientific and Technical Research
CPVO	Community Plant Variety Office

glossary

CREST	Scientific and Technical Research Committee
CULT	Committee on Culture, Youth, Education, the Media and Sport (EP)
DAS	Court of Auditors (Déclaration d'Assurance)
DEV	Development DG (Commission)
DEVE	Committee on Development and Co-operation (EP)
DG	Director-General; Directorate-General
EAC	Education and Culture DG (Commission)
EAEC	European Atomic Energy Community
EAGGF	European Agricultural Guidance and Guarantee Fund
EAR	European Agency for Reconstruction
EBRD	European Bank for Reconstruction and Development
ECB	European Central Bank
ECE	Economic Commission for Europe (United Nations)
ECFIN	Economic and Financial Affairs DG (Commission)
ECHO	European Community Humanitarian Aid Office (Commission)
ECHR	European Court/Commission of Human Rights (Council of Europe)
ECJ	European Court of Justice
ECOFIN	Economic and Finance Council of Ministers
ECON	Committee on Economic and Monetary Affairs (EP)
ECR	European Court Report
ECSC	European Coal and Steel Community
EDC	European Documentation Centre
EDD	Group for a Europe of Democracies and Diversities (EP)
EDF	European Development Fund
EEA	European Economic Area
EEA	European Environment Agency
EEC	European Economic Community
EFA	European Free Alliance (EP Group)
EI	Environment Institute (JRC)
EIA	European Information Association
EIB	European Investment Bank
EIC	European Information Centre
EIC	European Information Centre
EIF	European Investment Fund
ELARG	Enlargement DG (Commission)
ELDR	Group of the European Liberal, Democrat and Reform Party (EP)

EMCDDA	European Monitoring Centre for Drugs and Drug Addiction
EMEA	European Agency for the Evaluation of Medicinal Products
EMPL	Committee on Employment and Social Affairs (EP)
EMPL	Employment and Social Affairs DG (Commission)
EMS	European Monetary System
EMU	Economic and Monetary Union
ENTR	Enterprise DG (Commission)
ENV	Environment DG (Commission)
ENVI	Committee on Environment, Public Health and Consumer Protection (EP)
EP	European Parliament
EPIC	European Public Information Centre
EPLP	European Parliamentary Labour Party
EPP-ED	European People's Party (Christian Democrats and European Democrats Group) (EP)
ERC	European Reference Centre
ERDF	European Regional Development Fund
ESC	Economic and Social Committee
ESCB	European System of Central Banks
ESDP	European Security and Defence Policy
ESF	European Social Fund
ETF	European Training Foundation
EU	European Union
EUL-NGL	Confederal Group of the European United Left/Nordic Green Left (EP)
EUMC	European Monitoring Centre on Racism and Xenophobia
EUMC	European Union Military Committee
EUMS	European Union Military Staff
Euratom	European Atomic Energy Community
EUR-OP	European Communities' Publications Office
EUROPOL	European Police Office
EUROSTAT	Statistical Office of the Commission
FEMM	Committee on Women's Rights and Equal Opportunities (EP)
FISH	Fisheries DG (Commission)
FYROM	Former Yugoslav Republic of Macedonia
HUDOC	Case-law database of the ECHR
IAM	Institute for Advanced Materials (JRC)
IDEA	European Union's on-line staff directory

glossary

IHCP	Institute for Health and Consumer Protection (JRC)
IMAC	Internal Market Advisory Committee
INFSO	Information Society DG (Commission)
IPTS	Institute for Prospective Technological Studies (JRC)
IRMM	Institute for Reference Materials and Measurements (JRC)
ISIS	Institute for Systems, Informatics and Safety (JRC)
IST	Information Society technologies
ITRE	Committee on Industry, External Trade, Research and Energy (EP)
ITU	Institute for Transuranium Elements (JRC)
JAI	Justice and Home Affairs DG (Commission)
JHA	Justice and Home Affairs
JICS	Joint Interpreting and Conference Service (Commission)
JRC	Joint Research Centre (Commission)
JURI	Committee on Legal Affairs and the Internal Market (EP)
LAM	Member of the Greater London Assembly
LIBE	Committee on Citizens' Freedoms and Rights, Justice and Home Affairs (EP)
MAGHREB	Algeria, Morocco and Tunisia
MARKT	Internal Market DG (Commission)
MASHREQ	Egypt, Lebanon, Jordan and Syria
MEP	Member of the European Parliament
MSP	Member of the Scottish Parliament
NATO	North Atlantic Treaty Organisation
NGO	Non-governmental organisation
NI	Non-attached MEPs
OHIM	Office for Harmonisation in the Internal Market (Trade Marks and Designs)
OJ	Official Journal of the European Communities
OLAF	European Anti-Fraud Office (Commission)
OPOCE	Publications Office (Commission)
OSHA	European Agency for Safety and Health at Work
PECH	Committee on Fisheries (EP)
PES	Party of European Socialists (EP)
PETI	Committee on Petitions (EP)
PHARE	Programme of Community Aid for East and Central Europe
PPE-DE	European People's Party (Christian Democrats and European Democrats Group) (EP)

PPEWU	Policy Planning and Early Warning Unit (Council)
PRESS	Press and Communication DG (Commission)
PSC	Political and Security Committee
PSE	Party of European Socialists (EP)
QMV	Qualified majority voting
RAXEN	European Racism and Xenophobia Information Network
REGI	Committee on Regional Policy, Transport and Tourism (EP)
REGIO	Regional Policy DG (Commission)
RELEX	External Relations DG (Commission)
RETT	Committee on Regional Policy, Transport and Tourism (EP)
RTD	Research DG (Commission)
SAARC	South Asia Association for Regional Co-operation
SAI	Institute for Space Applications (JRC)
SANCO	Health and Consumer Protection DG (Commission)
SAPARD	Special Accession Programme for Agriculture and Rural Development
SCIC	Joint Interpreting and Conference Service (Commission)
SDLP	Social Democratic and Labour Party
SDT	Translation Service (Commission)
SEA	Single European Act
SG	Secretariat General (Commission)
SJ	Legal Service (Commission)
SME	Small and medium-sized enterprise
TACIS	Technical assistance programme to the independent states of the former Soviet Union and Mongolia
TAXUD	Taxation and Customs Union DG (Commission)
TEU	Treaty on European Union (Maastricht)
TGI	Technical Group of Independent Members (EP)
TRADE	Trade DG (Commission)
TREN	Transport and Energy DG (Commission)
Troika	The current President of the Council of Ministers together with his/ her immediate successor and predecessor
UEN	Union for Europe of the Nations Group (EP)
UKIP	United Kingdom Independence Party
UKREP	Permanent UK Representative to the EU

name index

A

index

235

index

index

index

G

index

H

index

index

index

index

index

index

index

W

index

country index

A

B

C

D

E

F

index